AUTOBIOGRAPHICAL ACTS

ELIZABETH W. BRUSS

Autobiographical Acts

THE CHANGING SITUATION
OF A LITERARY GENRE

The Johns Hopkins University Press

BALTIMORE AND LONDON

Manufactured in the United States of America

The Johns Hopkins University Press, Baltimore, Maryland 21218
The Johns Hopkins Press Ltd., London

Library of Congress Catalog Card Number 76–13460
ISBN 0-8018-1821-4

Library of Congress Cataloging in Publication data
will be found on the last printed page of this book.

To my father and mother,
in appreciation

====================================

ACKNOWLEDGMENTS

====================================

Two separate interests converged to produce this study: first, a concern to explain the mode of existence of a literary genre, how it changes while remaining the same; second, a desire to make more flexible and relevant use of linguistics in literary criticism. Professors Marvin Felheim and Richard W. Bailey provoked my curiosity and prodded me to refine my questions when I was their student at the University of Michigan. I am also indebted to Professor Jean Starobinski of the University of Geneva for his generous response to the letter of an unknown graduate student, to Professor John Searle of the University of California—Berkeley for his stimulating remarks at the summer institute of the Linguistic Society of America (SUNY—Buffalo, 1971), to Professor William Heath of Amherst College for reading and encouraging my revised work, and finally to the trustees of Amherst College for their financial support. There is no adequate way for me to acknowledge here the patience, advice, and persistent attention of my chief critic, Neal Bruss.

CONTENTS

INTRODUCTION

=======================================

LITERARY ACTS

=======================================

> ... all one can do is to herd books into groups ... and thus we
> get English literature into A B C; one, two, three; and lose all
> sense of what it's about.
> Virginia Woolf, Letter to Julian Bell, 1 December 1935

Anyone who studies literature at some point deserves the fine impatience of Virginia Woolf, but especially those of us who undertake to study a genre. How can one justify this rage to classify, this Linnean lust to define and categorize? It is easy enough to impose a definition on autobiography, but, as Woolf reminds us, a definition which obscures "all sense of what it's about" is not merely useless but potentially pernicious. The only valuable definition would be one that reflects a literary category that actually "exists," in the sense that it can be experienced as something that constrains or directs the acts of reading and writing, or at least provides readers and writers with an interpretation of their actions. Obviously, genre studies are justifiable if we follow Alastair Fowler in believing that: "Traditional genres and modes, far from being mere classificatory devices, serve primarily to enable the reader to share types of meaning economically . . . understanding is genre bound."[1] But to capture this requires that we learn more precisely how a genre exists—how we are able to recognize it and respond to the types of meaning it conveys to us.

Faulty or naive assumptions about the nature of a genre impair the criticism of autobiographical writing, since the critical statements which result are either too broad to be explanatory or too rigid to cope with change and development. Such statements as, for example, "autobiography is confessional" or "the autobiographer must trace the teleology of his life," or even "autobiography is an act of artistic memory," all of which have some currency and plausibility, are still only too easy to refute. Neither Lillian Hellman's *An Unfinished Woman* nor the diary cycles of Anaïs Nin reach a teleological resolution, and Bishop Hall and Henry Adams have written autobiographies more notable for reticence than intimacy. The *Confessions* of Saint Augustine do possess both of these qualities, but Augustine does not limit himself to what he actually remembers, opening his narrative with: "this period of my life, which I cannot remember having lived, which I take on the word of others, and which, no matter how reliable the evidence may be, is still a matter of conjecture from the behavior of other infants."[2]

Of course, one could simply reject whatever does not conform with the definition of autobiography one has accepted, or use that definition prescriptively to reflect what autobiographical writing ought to be if not what it is. This has been the practice of critics like Roy Pascal, when he directs his attention to the twentieth century in *Design and Truth in Autobiography*.

Its success in representing the whole man is relatively meager. I do not think this is due to the technical difficulty of combining many threads in a story; it arises above all from a certain falling short in respect of the whole personality. With the greatest number of autobiographies, this is simply an inadequacy in the persons writing, a lack of moral responsibility towards their task, a lack of awareness and insight. . . . I do not think one can evade the conclusion that the supreme task of autobiography is not fulfilled in modern autobiography.[3]

Leaving aside the justice of a moral attack upon a failure to accomplish what might not have even been attempted, there is still the question of what underwrites Pascal's or any other critic's prescriptive definition. What power or principle can be invoked to determine the nature of autobiography's supreme task, or even to stipulate that there must be one and only one such task? Thus both prescriptive and naive classification lead equally to claim and counterclaim, and possibly to the sense that no useful generalizations can be made at all—that genres are nominalistic fictions, mere idols of the critical marketplace.

We can avoid this impasse, and at the same time remain responsible critics, if we can explain how there can be both change and continuity in autobiographical writing, and frame our explanation in a way that will not distort individual autobiographies. We can achieve this, but only after first distinguishing between "form," the immanent material properties of a text, and the "functions" assigned to that text. Form and function are not isomorphic; several functions can be and usually are allotted to the same structure, and most functions are capable of being realized through more than one form. That this is a live distinction becomes clear in the following example. An interview, as an exchange of questions and responses between two participants, is obviously different from an autobiography, in which the direction of inquiry is controlled by one man alone. Yet Vladimir Nabokov can use language which is literally and syntactically identical to fulfill these divergent functions. Responding to an interviewer's question about his travel habits, Nabokov mentions:

As a youth of seventeen, on the eve of the Russian Revolution, I was seriously planning (being the independent possessor of an inherited fortune) a lepidopterological expedition to Central Asia that would have involved a great deal of camping. Earlier, when I was, say, eight or nine, I seldom roamed further than the fields and woods of our country estate near St. Petersburg. At twelve, when aiming at a particular spot half-a-dozen miles or more distant, I would use a bicycle to get there with my net fastened to the frame; but not many forest paths were passable on wheels. It was possible to ride there on horseback, of course; but, because of our ferocious Russian tabanids, one could not leave a horse haltered in a wood for any length of time. My spirited bay almost climbed up the tree it was tied to one day trying to elude them: big fellows with watered-silk eyes and tiger bodies. [4]

As a response to the question, "How did you usually travel?" Nabokov's words function as a description of all that worked to confine the mobility of an eight-year-old boy and to inconvenience, with impassable roads and horseflies, a traveler in the Russian countryside at the turn of the century. But what appear merely to be hindrances in this context become precious bits of memory in Nabokov's autobiography.

When, nowadays, I attempt to follow in memory the winding paths from one given point to another, I notice with alarm that there are many gaps, due to oblivion or ignorance, akin to the terra-incognita blanks map makers of old used to call "sleeping-beauties." Beyond the park, there were fields, with a continuous shimmer of butterfly wings over a shimmer of flowers. . . . At first—when I was, say, eight or nine—I seldom roamed farther than the fields and woods between Byra and Batovo. Later, when aiming at a particular spot half-a-dozen miles or more distant, I would use a bicycle to get there with my net strapped to the frame; but not many forest paths were passable on wheels; it was possible to ride there on horseback, of course, but, because of our ferocious Russian tabanids, one could not leave a horse haltered in a wood for any length of time: my spirited bay almost climbed a tree it was tied to one day trying to elude them: big fellows with watered-silk eyes and tiger bodies.[5]

The impassable roads, the microscopically delicate picture of the horseflies, are valued as points which yet remain intact in Nabokov's metaphorical mapping of his own distant past.

Of course, literal identity of this sort is very rare, but it is not at all unusual to find incidents, motifs, even styles, which are shared by texts which otherwise have markedly different functions. Again, consider the way Nabokov has used much the same information, performed the same "mimetic function," in both an early novel, *Glory*, and in *Speak, Memory*.

The kind of Russian family to which I belonged—a kind now extinct—had, among other virtues, a traditional leaning toward the comfortable products of Anglo-Saxon civilization. Pears' Soap, tar-black when dry, topaz-like when held to the light between wet fingers, took care of one's morning bath. Pleasant was the decreasing weight of the English collapsible tub when it was made to protrude a rubber underlip and disgorge its frothy contents into the slop pail. . . . All sorts of snug, mellow things came in a steady procession from the English Shop on Nevski Avenue: fruitcakes, smelling salts, playing cards, picture puzzles, striped blazers, talcum-white tennis balls. I learned to read English before I could read Russian.[6]

In St. Petersburg she was known as an Anglo-maniac, and relished this fame—she would discuss eloquently such topics as Boy Scouts or Kipling, and found a quite special delight in frequent visits to Drew's English Shop, where, still on the stairs, before a large poster (a woman thickly lathering a boy's head) you were greeted by a wonderful smell of soap and lavender, with something more mixed in, something that suggested collapsible rubber tubs, soccer balls, and round, heavy, tightly swaddled Christmas puddings. It follows that Martin's first books were in English.[7]

The similarity is only between two passages in this case, but a novel as a whole could have roughly the same information and the same arrangement of that information into a plot as an autobiography. The scenic arrangement of Cellini's *Life*, for example, has much in common with the Florentine novelle,[8] while "intrigue" is as important to the development of Rousseau's *Confessions* as it is in either his *Julie* or his *Emile*. Despite formal differences, we are able to recognize instances of the same style or plot, and it is this very ability, I suggest, which allows us to recognize when two texts have the same generic function.

In any particular work, of course, different functions are inextricably combined. The same sentences which advance the story also serve as manifestations of style.[9] We can separate these functions only in the abstract, following implicit "rules" which tell us where and how to look at a text, what criteria to apply in counting or discounting some portion of the material before us as evidence of one of the various functions. We are, in fact, so successful at this kind of activity that it is often difficult to recognize that we are abstracting when we talk about the plot or the genre of a text, and abstracting in different ways, according to distinct sets of criteria. The generic value of a text is not determined in the same way that one determines its style or its structure, its mimetic or thematic value. Indeed, it could not be the same, for a total integration of the generic function with each of the other functions of a text would make all pieces of literature sui generis, with any alteration in subject matter or structure, however slight, creating a new generic category. It is easy to see, then, why naive attempts to define autobiography according to compositional or stylistic criteria fail, despite the fact that there is a correlation, yet to be explained, between genre and these other functions.

All reading (or writing) involves us in choice: we choose to pursue a style or a subject matter, to struggle with or against a design. We also choose, as passive as it all may seem, to take part in an interaction, and it is here that generic labels have their use. The genre does not tell us the style or construction of a text as much as how we should expect to "take" that style or mode of construction—what force it should have for us. And this force is derived from the kind of action that text is taken to be. Surrounding any text are implicit contextual conditions, participants involved in transmitting and receiving it, and the nature of these implicit conditions and the roles of the participants affects the status of the information contained in the text. Literature as well as "ordinary language" (if that spurious distinction may be allowed to stand for the moment) has its "illocutionary" dimension.

The notion of illocutionary action was developed by philosophers of language, particularly Austin, Strawson, and Searle, in order to discuss the phenomena of asserting and commanding, promising and questioning, which are as important in constituting language as grammar or propositions.[10] Just as speaking is made up of different types of action carried out by means of language, the system of actions carried out through literature consists of its various genres.[11] An illocutionary act is an association between a piece of language and certain contexts, conditions, and intentions; a question, for example, "counts as an attempt (on the part of a Speaker) to elicit information from a Hearer."[12] The syntax of a question does not explain its illocutionary value, in the same way that the style or structure of autobiography cannot explain what is at the heart of its generic value: the roles played by an author and a reader, the uses to which the text is being put.

But to become a genre, a literary act must also be recognizable; the roles and purposes composing it must be relatively stable within a particular community of readers and writers. We could not locate a genre, even to describe its changes, unless it were what Merleau-Ponty describes as an institution. "What we understand by the concept of institution are those events in experience which endow it with durable dimensions, in relation to which a whole series of other experiences will acquire meaning, will form an intelligible series or a history."[13] Why some acts become institutionalized while other do not, and why some institutions are more durable than others, is one of the deepest questions that confronts a student of any aspect of culture. A literary institution must reflect and give focus to some consistent need and sense of possibility in the community it serves, but at the same time, a genre helps to define what is possible and to specify the appropriate means for meeting an expressive need. We can speculate on what cultural conditions promote an emphasis upon individual identity, but conceptions of individual identity are articulated, extended, and developed through an institution like autobiography. I cannot hope to explain why autobiography exists, but I can at least begin to describe how the process of originating and sustaining it and other genres works.

Because autobiography is an "institutional" rather than a "brute" fact, its existence depends upon the organized efforts of human intelligence. The mere physical endurance of the writen text is not enough, since the association between form and function is conventional rather than natural. John Searle's analogy between the speech act of promising and the value of currency applies equally to literary acts: "it is only given the institution of money that I now have a five dollar bill in my hand. Take away the institution and all I have is a piece of paper with various gray and green markings. These "institutions" are systems of constitutive rules. Every institutional fact is underlain by a (system of) rule(s) of the form 'X counts as Y in context C.' "[14] Although ordinarily there are elements within a text which help us to recognize what generic force it should have, we cannot state a priori what these features will be. It is only by virtue of the constitutive rules of literature that the features of a given text "count as" signals of autobiography. Outside of the social and literary conventions that create and maintain it, autobiography has no features—has in fact no being at all.

Living as we do at a time and in a literary community which recognizes autobiography as a distinct and deliberate undertaking, it is difficult for us to realize that it has not always existed. We read older texts, or texts of other cultures, and find in them autobiographical intentions, but it is often our own conventions which inform this reading and give the text this force. The classical historians of Greece and Rome, for example, could temporarily adopt a rhetorical first person for the sake of a more vivid commentary, but the author in no way claimed to have been actually present, an autobiographic participant, in the events he described in this way.[15] The Psalms collected in the Old Testament appear in our eyes to imply a personal history, but the distinction between an idealized individual narrator and a particular, identifiable speaker is alien to the psalmist. The Psalms formed a body of liturgical poetry to be used by any speaker, on any appropriate occasion—the emotions and experiences attributed to the "I" were purely potential.[16] What is autobiography for us may have originally been only the by-product of another act, an apology undertaken in self-defense or a self-exhibition for the sake of selling the man himself, as an instructor in the rhetorical skills exemplified in the text.[17] None of these constitute true cases of autobiography as an autonomous act with its own peculiar responsibilities.

Autobiography could not be said to exist until it was distinguished from other illocutionary acts. Contingent or occasional properties of other acts had to coalesce into something that was experienced as a departure from previous acts, something significantly different, with its own sanctions and boundaries, to be violated only at the price of ambiguity or unintelligibility. Autobiography thus acquires its meaning by participating in symbolic systems making up literature and culture. Like other genres, it is defined only within and by means of these systems, in terms of the way it resembles or departs from other potential acts. The value of autobiography is "diacritical," to use Saussure's famous term for the workings of symbolic systems (here interpreted by Merleau-Ponty): "We have always to do only with sign structures whose meaning, being nothing other than the way in which the signs behave toward one another and are distinguished from one another, cannot be set forth independently of them."[18] If not a reason for anxiety, this is at least a reason for critical caution in setting up isolated definitions of autobiography. What autobiography is in part depends on what it is not—on how it is related to and distinct from other kinds of activity available in its original context.

Even if the autobiographical act is recognized, however, it may not be recognized as literature, that is, as a form of belles-lettres. Pretensions to aesthetic worth were alien to English autobiography throughout the sixteenth and seventeenth centuries and rare even into the eighteenth. The term most frequently applied to it, "memoir," had the connotation of informality, a casually constructed affair and not a serious literary effort.[19] Although the term "biography" became current after 1680, it was not until 1809, when Robert Southey coined or translated the word for the *Quarterly Review*, that "autobiography" became a familiar designation in England.[20] We see reflected in this brief terminological history the change in status and literary reputability which English autobiography has undergone since the Renaissance. As formalist critic Jurij Tynjanov put it: "The very existence of a fact *as literary* depends on its differential quality, that is, on its interrelationship with both literary and extra-literary orders. . . . What in one epoch would be a literary fact would in another be a common matter of social communication. . . . Thus one has the literariness of memoirs and diaries in one system and their extra-literariness in another."[21]

A complicated business indeed. But there is no reason to expect that the dimensions of autobiography should be any easier to fix than those of any other human action. But lest it appear that I have gratuitously multiplied distinctions in the foregoing account, recall that what we seek is a theory capable of explaining how autobiography can be at once one and many, different and the same. This paradoxical "sameness," the continuity of autobiography despite historical change, for example, cannot be explained without reference to symbolic systems which preserve autobiography as a distinct category of action, no matter how the features which distinguish it may change. Tynjanov cited the "variable nature" of genres several decades ago in his work "On Literary Evolution": "The novel, which seems to be an integral genre that has developed in and of itself over the centuries, turns out to be not an integral whole but a variable. Its material changes from one literary system to another . . . we cannot . . . define the genre of a work if it is isolated from the system. For example, what was called an ode in the 1820's or by Fet was so labeled on the basis of features different from those used to define an ode in Lomonsov's time."[22]

From what I have said, then, about the functional nature of the genre, the constitutive rules which are required to make a text of a particular form "count as" an instance of a literary act, and the way such rules are in turn defined by the symbolic systems to which they belong, it should be evident that autobiography might be expected to vary in at least four ways while retaining its generic identity. These potential variations include:

1. Variability in the kind of textual features which signal the generic function of a text.
2. Variability in the degree of integration between the generic function and other functional aspects of the text.
3. Variability in the literary value attached to the genre.

And, since, the dimensions of the act itself may be altered or ultimately obliterated as significant distinctions within the various symbolic systems making up a culture:

4. Variability in the illocutionary value of the genre.

All four of these potential sources of variation must be taken into account by any definition of autobiography, since it has changed and can continue to change in any or even all of these respects. While it may be impossible, for reasons I shall discuss later on, to predict the nature of the changes which occur, such distinctions at least make it possible to discuss developments in autobiography with some subtlety and without panicking over the differences we observe. For example, since a genre is defined differentially, with implicit boundaries which distinguish it from other recognized acts, if anything happens to alter or obscure these boundaries, the nature and the scope of autobiography will be changed. Autobiography as we know it is dependent on distinctions between fiction and nonfiction, between rhetorical and empirical first-person narration. But these distinctions are cultural artifacts and might be differently drawn, as they indeed once were and might become again, leading to the obsolescence of autobiography or at least its radical reformulation.

Less drastic and more common are the changes in autobiography resulting from developments in other literary acts or in the literary system as a whole. The emergence and extinction of other genres, the exploitation of new materials, and the vernacularization of literature itself necessarily affect autobiography as well.[23] Thus the obsolescence of the literary epistle makes it possible for autobiography to take on some of the functions it once performed as a mode for intimacy and spontaneity. On the other hand, changes in the scope of the lyric, and its increasing prominence in the nineteenth century, made it a competitor for the subject matter and the self-expression once associated solely with autobiography. The same process of mutual adjustment affects autobiographical form. Textual features, whole narrative structures, once exclusively associated with one genre may be appropriated by another, with the result that these formal features will no longer be sufficient to signal the illocutionary force of a text and other devices will be discovered or promoted to prevent ambiguity. When the first-person experiencer, narrator and hero, was appropriated from autobiography for the sake of "realism" in the new, bourgeois novel, the presence of such a narrator was no longer enough to distinguish autobiography from fiction. Although autobiographers continued to use this device, it was no longer dominant in either the formal or the functional definition of the genre—in fact, one could argue that the autobiographical "I" took on a new, less empirical and more subjective value as a result of this. When the formal delights of direct observation, eyewitness testimony, and density of domestic detail became more general literary phenomena, they no longer appeared distinctively autobiographical. These features continued, for the most part, to be present in autobiographical texts, but they were less visible—functionally "effaced" as Tynjanov might have put it. "Its function simply changes and becomes auxiliary. If the meter of a poem is 'effaced,' then the other signs of verse, the other elements of the work become more important in its place."[24]

Of course, autobiography has also appropriated forms and techniques from other types of discourse. The "apology," for example, is a form now almost exclusively associated with autobiography, its original literary and nonliterary functions all but forgotten. It is possible to trace the medieval dream vision in later autobiographical permutations, with fascinating changes in the psychological ambience of the technique. Consider also the development of new formal possibilities, such as those offered by film, for example. Fellini's *8 1/2* is purportedly an autobiographical account, yet the autobiographer controls only the form of the script and the direction. Independent contributions, no matter how well supervised, are necessarily made by those who edit and those who operate the cameras and, even more interestingly, perhaps, by those who portray remembered friends and antagonists—even the autobiographer himself. Will the formal possibilities, the distinction between various aspects of creation and the absolute division of the autobiographical "self" revealed in such a film have an effect on autobiographical prose? One could imagine, for example, an autobiographer who explicitly stipulates that his only contribution to his text has been to assemble what others have written about him or that the physical features, gestures, and postures he attributes to himself have been copied from another man. (The figure thus selected to "play" himself could be as revealing as the self-imaging which occurs in traditional autobiography, so the possibility is less far-fetched than it may at first seem.)

In citing as a second kind of variation the "degree of integration between genre and other function," I was alluding to a process which can be easily discerned in the history of English autobiography. It seems to be the case that as a genre becomes more familiar to the reading public, there is less need for the author to provide internal signals to assure that his text will be read with the proper force. In early stages, it is often difficult to isolate generic values from such other values as style level or plot. The elements of the text are "synthetic," performing several functions simultaneously, with one result being the great similarity found between works written in the same genre.[25] Many critics have, for example, mentioned that John Bunyan's autobiography (written in the seventeenth century, when the genre was still relatively new to England) appears highly derivative, differing only in a few details from the conversion narratives of his sectarian contemporaries.[26] At later stages in its history, when the genre becomes a clearly differentiated type of literary activity, the elements of a text can become more "analytic," since fewer and more isolated signals are needed to identify the act being performed. The title page or mode of publication alone may be enough to suggest its illocutionary force. For example, we may know that a text is to be taken as autobiography simply because it appears in a magazine devoted to "True Confessions." By the twentieth century, an autobiographer like Gertrude Stein could simultaneously invoke and frustrate a whole set of conventional expectations by her title pages alone: *"The Autobiography of Alice B. Toklas*, by Gertrude Stein" and *"Everybody's Autobiography*, by Gertrude Stein."

A more probing and fine-grained discussion of the flexibility and range of English autobiography during the past four centuries, as exemplified in the work of John Bunyan, James Boswell, Thomas De Quincey, and Vladimir Nabokov, will be the business of the chapters to follow. The diversity of these works alone should be enough to demonstrate that there is no intrinsically autobiographical form. But there are limited generalizations to be made about the dimensions of action which are common to these autobiographies, and which seem to form the core of our notion of the functions an autobiographical text must perform. One may put these generalizations in the form of rules to be satisfied by the text and the surrounding context of any work which is to "count as" autobiography.[27] In fact, we must have something on the order of rules which accounts for our ability to recognize that there is something wrong, paradoxical in a title like *Everybody's Autobiography*.

> *Rule 1.* An autobiographer undertakes a dual role. He is the source of the subject matter and the source for the structure to be found in his text. (*a*) The author claims individual responsibility for the creation and arrangement of his text. (*b*) The

individual who is exemplified in the organization of the text is purported to share the identity of an individual to whom reference is made via the subject matter of the text. (*c*) The existence of this individual, independent of the text itself, is assumed to be susceptible to appropriate public verification procedures.

Rule 2. Information and events reported in connection with the autobiographer are asserted to have been, to be, or to have potential for being the case. (*a*) Under existing conventions, a claim is made for the truth-value of what the autobiography reports—no matter how difficult that truth-value might be to ascertain, whether the report treats of private experiences or publicly observable occasions. (*b*) The audience is expected to accept these reports as true, and is free to "check up" on them or attempt to discredit them.

Rule 3. Whether or not what is reported can be discredited, whether or not it can be reformulated in some more generally acceptable way from another point of view, the autobiographer purports to believe in what he asserts.

Any and all of these rules may be and occasionally are broken. But what is vital for creating the illocutionary force of the text is that the author purport to have met these requirements, and that the audience understand him to be responsible for meeting or failing to meet them. We are able to locate these rules in part because we can observe the consequences entailed by their violation. An autobiographer can be convicted of "insincerity" or worse if he is caught in a premeditated distortion. On the other hand, when Clifford Irving claimed to be only the editor of an autobiography of Howard Hughes, having in fact written the manuscript himself without contact with or authorization by Hughes, he was sentenced to prison for literary fraud.[28]

Although centered largely on the responsibilities of the author, these rules also create the rights of the readers of autobiography and stipulate the legitimate extent of the expectations allowed them. (Of course, in another sense, readers understand the act as something they might also perform, and this is part of its power over the apparently passive imagination of the audience.) A reader of autobiography has the right to try to fit the text to his expectations or to complain when he finds something that seems pragmatically unintelligible—which is not to say that one may not modify expectations by the act of reading or discover new ways to intelligibility. But "discovery" and "modification" occur only when attention is already engaged and responsible for what it finds; without our tacit knowledge of the role(s) we are assigned in the act, there could be no such engagement or responsibility.[29]

It may seem that I have been too timid in the rules I have

proposed—and I admit that I have indeed been cautious, both for the reasons I have cited above and for some yet to be set forth. But though few in number, and even self-evident on their surface, these rules have dramatic consequences for both the readers and the writers of the genre. Rule 1, for example, necessitates that some shared identity bind author, narrator, and character together; no matter how vague, no matter how great the tension or disparity, the relationship itself is inescapable. The nature of the man or woman writing, the stance and voice adopted within the text, and the features of the emerging characterization must converge, to qualify or even contradict each other, since all are within the specified scope of the autobiographical act. Moreover, the shape into which these various aspects of the act finally coalesce is by definition that of a personality, a self, an identity; it must have, as Blake might say, a "human face," whether the author or the reader is ultimately responsible for imposing it. There are many strategies for coping with this implication of the act, and they may move or chill us, enrich or impoverish our sense of the human condition.[30] If the results are not always equally admirable, they are nonetheless autobiographical—something which prescriptive critics are at times loath to admit. Because all of the autobiographer's extratextual life and identity is potentially relevant to the act, omissions are inevitable. Not that all omissions are felt absences for either the writer or his audience; some aspects of identity may seem totally unremarkable. Depending upon his purposes and the nature of the audience he envisions, the autobiographer will find different aspects of himself receding into a background of what can be taken for granted. (A new or unexpected audience may, of course, experience these "typified" elements as deliberate or psychologically revealing gaps.)[31]

There are differences not only in what is included in or excluded from the autobiographical act—either from the subject matter or from the narrational posture—but also in how the act is related to whatever else the author or the readers may know about the life. For some autobiographers, for example, the act may be experienced as a willing simplification of himself, imposing a more personally satisfying or more rhetorically effective coherence. Other autobiographers might achieve a simplification without intending it, in which case the simplicity lies in he eyes of the reader. An autobiographer may act to rebut his public character in the form of an apology or to sustain it in the form of (what is now called) a memoir. Some autobiographies have even been written to attain a publicly recognized identity or notoriety (with attendant new responsibilities and complications arising from living one's life thereafter eternally and only "in character"). These strategies, like those used for coping with the multiple threads of identity involved in the autobiographical act, are many, and each is equally legitimate.

All that the rules for the act provide is a field within which the task of self-imaging and self-evaluation is understood to take place, making whatever does take place recognizable as a form of self-evaluation. As readers we are aware of this, and thus the amount and kind of revelation, the shaping, and the expressions of intention that we meet become focal to our reading of an autobiographical text.

Another point of focus for readers of autobiography is the arrangement and the process of narration in the text. Of course, any sophisticated act of reading will involve some attention to these aspects of the work, but in autobiography the structural display of the text is stipulated to be a demonstration of certain of the capacities and habits of the man about whom we are reading. The way the autobiographer has arranged his text is therefore experienced as a "sample" of his epistemology and his personal skill.[32] Because of the rules, there is no way the autobiographer can evade personal responsibility for the shape of his work—even conventional choices reflect his individual identity, perhaps as a man with little need or talent for originality. An even more complicated implication of these rules is the fact that the assumptions the autobiographer makes about the nature of his audience also come under the scrutiny of that audience. From the way an autobiographer imagines and manipulates his readers, we are allowed to draw inferences about his habitual mode of interaction with others. And identity, as psychiatrist R. D. Laing has pointed out, is composed not only by acts of self-perception but by "other-perception" as well:

self-identity ("I" looking at "me") is constituted not only by our looking at ourselves, but also by our looking at others looking at us and our reconstitution of and alteration of these views of others about us. . . . even if a view of me is rejected it still becomes incorporated in its rejected form as a part of my self-identity. My self-identity becomes my view of me which I recognize as the negation of the other person's view of me. Thus "I" become a "me" who is being misperceived by another person. This can become a vital aspect of my view of myself. (E.g., "I am a person whom no one really understands.")[33]

In reading the *Confessions* of Jean Jacques Rousseau, for example, we are acutely aware of how much of the autobiographer's identity is bound up with the notion of "being misunderstood," both by former friends and by his immediate audience. (The things he ascribes to the latter, in fact, throw into a paradoxical light whatever he may say about the former.) But an autobiographer need not be as explicit as Rousseau in his treatment of his audience for us to recognize the assumptions he cannot help but make about them. Just as portions of the author's identity may be treated as irrelevant or undistinguished, aspects of the audience's individual or collective identity may be more or less cavalierly neglected. This may be reflected in the interests or the attitudes the text attempts to satisfy, and even in what the author

expects his readers to find familiar. These assumptions become especially visible, of course, when the audience envisioned by the author is
not the one that reads him; but we may resist the identity thrust upon
us even by one who knows us all too well. Indeed, we may become
particularly sensitive to the way we are treated when this is the case.
There is a moral or at least social symbolism in all this of which the
rules for the autobiographical act make us aware, however tacitly.

But the rules, as I have stated above, deliberately leave much
unspecified. Aside from stating that some portions of the subject
matter must concern the identity of the author, I have placed no
further restriction on the subject matter, not even to stipulate whether
autobiography must concern the "inner" or the "outer" man or devote
more time to the delineation of self than to others. These very general
rules, meant to reflect the implications shared by autobiographies from
distinct literary communities and widely separated points in time, do
not and cannot specify such further issues as how much of a lifetime an
autobiography must represent or to what degree the subject matter
must concern the autobiographer's past, rather than his present or his
future. I have avoided giving any general rule for the nature of the
relationship the autobiographer must establish with his represented
self—elegaic, ironic, clear, or confused—both because limiting or sub-
classifying the act in this way seems to me artificial and because I
believe that more delicate distinctions cannot be made without reference to far less broad literary contexts. If our task is to capture living
generic distinctions, and not simply to "herd books into groups," then
we must seek for any further specifications—on the relationship between autobiographer and audience, for example—in the context where
they emerge and within the literary community which animates them.
Definitions of what is appropriate to the autobiographical act are never
absolute: they must be created and sustained. The rules I have sketched
simply reflect major distinctions which have survived and which continue to be observed.

In the chapters to follow, I will be seeking for a language to cover
the subtler and more transitory aspects of autobiography as well as
these areas of agreement. One can begin this search profitably, I believe,
from the remarks made by John Searle on the dimensions which
customarily enter into illocutionary action.

First and most important, there is the point or purpose of the act (the difference,
for example, between a statement and a question); second, the relative positions of
S (the speaker) and H (the hearer) (the difference between a request and an order);
third, the degree of commitment undertaken (the difference between a mere
expression of intention and a promise); fourth, the difference in propositional
content (the difference between predictions and reports); fifth, the difference in
the way the proposition is related to the interests of S and H (the difference

between boasts and laments, between warnings and predictions); sixth, the different possible expressed psychological states (the difference between a promise, which is an expression of an intention, and a statement, which is an expression of belief); seventh, the different ways in which an utterance relates to the rest of the conversation (the difference between simply replying to what someone has said and objecting to what he has said).[34]

For a particular community of writers and readers, the conventional meaning of the autobiographical act could include additional implications in any one or even in several of these directions. Thus while all autobiography is potentially "exemplary," it could become necessarily so, in which case the "purpose," the "relative position of Speaker and Hearer," and the "way the proposition relates to the interests of Speaker and Hearer" would be fixed, and didacticism, an authoritative voice, and hortatory guidance to the perplexed would be values automatically associated with the autobiographical act. I have already remarked on the way apologists define their act with respect to another of Searle's dimensions—"the different ways an utterance relates to the rest of the conversation" (or, in this case, antecedent publicity). One can imagine autobiographical plaints, autobiographies of intention, autobiographies with conventional degrees of uncertainty: whatever contexts or purposes, interests or capacities a culture cares to associate with its literary institutions. Even the seven "continua of illocutionary force" suggested by Searle far from exhaust all the dimensions which are anthropologically possible. And, as one act among all those that human beings might want to undertake through their language and their literature, autobiography could simply become obsolete if its defining features, such as individual identity, cease to be important for a particular culture. As Wittgenstein said in one of the first accounts of what later became known as illocutionary action: "But how many kinds of sentences are there? Say assertion question, and command?— There are *countless* kinds: countless different kinds of use of what we call 'symbols', 'words', 'sentences'. And this multiplicity is not something fixed, given once for all; but new types of language, new language-games, as we may say, come into existence, and others become obsolete and get forgotten."[35]

The evolution of any literary act is, to borrow Freud's term for it, "overdetermined." The pressures on autobiography come from the culture at large and at the same time from more restricted literary domains. Because of the place it holds within a literary system, formal modifications and changes in the status or vitality of other genres will eventually affect it as well; a change in any part of a system alters the shape of the whole. Because the various symbolic and nonsymbolic institutions of a culture are also related to each other systematically, changes in any of the occupations and preoccupations that constitute a social order will affect autobiography as necessarily (if not quite as dramatically) as social cataclysms. But to recognize the existence of such pressures is not to claim a neat and mechanical determinism. Like all human action, autobiography is at least partly self-determining. The dimensions of the act must be reconstituted each time it is performed, and without these performances one can speak of the autobiographical act only in potential or historical terms. As Robert Weimann states in his critique of the overly zealous schemata of some literary structuralism: "the history of literature, if considered as a changing system of creative possibilities, is permanently reconstituted from within by the social and aesthetic activity of its creators and recipients: the whole system of the literary *langue* (its available conventions and perspectives, its stock of thematic or verbal devices, etc.) is constantly changed and renewed through the Praxis of the creation and the reception of new literary works."[36]

Actually, not only new literary works but also new ways of reading old works must be considered. Either reader or writer can use his performance to modify the rules of the autobiographical act to meet his own needs, although few modifications will be taken up or even perceived by the community at large. When one is perceived, and when other members of the community use it as a pattern for modifying their own performances—audience demanding new works and new works demanding an audience—we arrive at literary evolution in its most immanent form. Certainly, some cultures and some literatures will be less tolerant of this kind of experiment, and often the most profound experiments will be conducted without any revolutionary intent. Of the experiments which did not take hold, we shall probably never know; the paradox of historical invention is, according to Merleau-Ponty, that "it touches in things only what they have in them that belongs to the future." "All symbolic systems—perception, language, history—only become what they were, although in order to do so they need to be taken up into human initiative."[37]

But Merleau-Ponty reminds us that the relationship is not merely between any particular creative or critical performance and what has preceded it; performances initiate history, give definition to the possibilities of a future, "open up a field of investigation." "In man the past is able not only to orient the future or to furnish the frame of reference for the problems of an adult person, but beyond that to give rise to a *search*, . . . or to an indefinite elaboration."[38] Thus, each autobiographer not only attempts to resolve problems about his own nature and the nature of the act of self-analysis and self-exhibition in which he is engaged, he also provokes new questions about the subject, new ambitions to test or extend the scope of his observations and the depth of his expression and aesthetic control.

It would be not only perverse but impossible to avoid talking about the changes in autobiography between John Bunyan's *Grace Abounding* and Vladimir Nabokov's *Speak, Memory*, but it would be equally perverse and impossible to speak of change as something occurring outside and beyond the contributions these and other individual autobiographers have made. It is for this reason that I am devoting an entire chapter to the work of each man, as well as to the work of Boswell and De Quincey. I hope that it is by now evident that a close critical analysis of four individual autobiographies is not an evasion of larger issues of history and generic definition but that it is, instead, the only way of facing these issues while remaining responsible to Woolf's principle of not losing "all sense of what it's all about." According to Robert Weimann, "At the level of his most elementary decisions, the literary historian does not even have a choice: were he to view only the individual work (or a succession of works) as *parole*, no historical-systematic generalizations, such as about genre and society, would be possible. Similarly, a preoccupation with *langue* would tend to neglect the great works themselves and to reduce the constitutive quality of their contributions to the growth of literature."[39]

Each of the four autobiographers I have elected to study represents a moment in the history and the progressive articulation of the autobiographical act, although it would be silly to claim that any single work is only and adequately "representative"—that there are not other equally important works one might have chosen, even some with superior aesthetic claims. But *Grace Abounding*, the *London Journal*, the *Autobiographical Sketches*, and *Speak, Memory* are all significant works in the way they demonstrate the varying attitudes and expectations surrounding the autobiographical act in four epochs of English and American literature separated from each other by intervals of almost a century. In each writer one can observe changes in the familiarity, the conscious ability to foresee and control the ends of the act in which he is engaged. But these four writers have also been selected because of the insight they allow us into the literary and cultural systems within which they work and in terms of which their autobiographical acts are defined. Each is an author of a contrasting work, a literary act which for that particular writer and his community competes with and gives rise to important distinctions with respect to autobiography. "The philological question of how the text is 'properly' to be understood . . . can be best answered if the text is considered in contrast to the background of works which the author could expect his contemporary public to know either explicitly or implicitly."[40] I obviously have neither world enough nor time to produce what Jauss has called the "best answer," but if I cannot fully environ the autobiographical act I can at least make the most of the oppositions, the choices, the subtle alterations which these four authors use to distinguish autobiography from a competitor. For Bunyan, the distinguishing feature of autobiography is facticity. Although all of his writing is concerned with the same "spiritual truth," only his autobiography is empirical as well as exemplary. But writing a century later, Boswell no longer finds the distinction between "fact" and "fiction" sufficient; a new opposition must be made between competing kinds of fact—between the objective fact and affective psychology of observation associated with biography and the more arbitrary and capricious realm of subjective fact and private sensibility that is the domain of autobiography. This subjective realm was itself subdivided by the nineteenth century, becoming the "transcendental subject" on the one hand and the mundane, individual subject on the other. Thus, Thomas De Quincey reserves his deepest and most universal subjective truths for the "impassioned prose" of his lyrics and allows his *Autobiographical Sketches* to record the amusing accidents of history and society which superficially distinguish him from other men. In the work of Vladimir Nabokov, there is the opportunity of seeing one of the most delicate of all distinctions, the difference between autobiography and its parody. Unlike his predecessors, Nabokov does not limit autobiography to the conveying or even the uncovering of truth. For Nabokov, autobiography is viable only when one recognizes that it creates truth as much as expresses it; thus his burlesque of autobiography in *Lolita* exposes the delusions of sincerity and the narcissistic indulgence of the confessional tradition. Not only does his own autobiography flaunt its artificiality, but achieves an almost Olympian impersonality as well, suggesting that no autobiographer ought to depict himself without first becoming aware of how much fiction is implicit in the idea of a "self."

Changes in form, and particularly in the felt adequacy and legitimacy of available forms, can also be observed as one moves from author to author. But despite the fact that autobiography emerges now in the borrowed guise of hagiography, now in the indeterminate shape of a journal, despite even more fundamental changes in its function and its purpose, the autobiographical endeavor has endured, and variety, human variety, may be the secret of its endurance.

CHAPTER ONE

= =

FROM ACT TO TEXT

= =

> I always say something that is what I am doing . . . there is no
> content but there is the form of question and answer.
>
> Gertrude Stein

To say autobiography is an act rather than a form solves some critical
questions, but it raises others. Given only a text or even a contrasting
set of texts, how can one hope to seize its dimensions as an action? The
rules that make form dynamic, that ascribe intention and direction to a
textual design, are tacit even for members of the same literary community—how much more silent they must be for readers looking on a
century or more away. Fortunately, there does remain one partial
ingress into contexts that are lost to us, if we are able to follow certain
clues embedded in the language of the text.

Language is itself positional, a vivid reflector and also a shaper of
pragmatic situations. In every language there are elements that respond
to features in the context in which they are used, features not only of
the physical setting, but including whole ranges of cultural distinctions
regarding interests and capacities, appropriate social relations, and possible relationships to the world. The particular elements that are sensitive to context and the features in the context to which they must
respond differ from language to language, but dimensions of action that
are important for a community are included among them. In fact,
certain linguistic distinctions seem to survive principally because they
help to define and communicate the nature of an action. According to
sociologist and linguist John Gumperz, "Just as intelligibility presupposes underlying grammatical rules, the communication of social information presupposes the existence of regular relationships between language usage and social structure."[1]

One can ask of any piece of discourse, then, what are the centers of
its orientation and also what is the nature of that orientation—whether
this is measured in terms of proximity or any of various other positional scales a language may provide. One can also ask, particularly of a
piece of literature, what kind of coherence, consistency, and pattern
there is to this process of orientation. Does the language of the text
suggest ambivalence, indecisiveness perhaps, or ambiguity of focus? Is
there a name, implicit or explicit, for the controlling force behind the

perspectives that are chosen? Attitudes and roles may gradually emerge with the unfolding of the text, or there may be sporadic achievements, points of clarity and obscurity, which nonetheless form a compelling autobiographical design. (The rules of autobiography are after all such that we can read any text symptomatically, and even delight in our ability to see what an author busily engaged in his task cannot.)

We already know a great deal about how to situate ourselves in and through our listening and speaking, and from this knowledge, once its linguistic sources are made articulate, we can proceed to grope our way into the situations surrounding various autobiographical acts. I cannot provide more than a rudimentary analysis of the elements of English which mirror and create our sense of context. But even this could be a serviceable beginning. A few elements can form a matrix on which such values as the "self-consciousness," the earnestness or playfulness of the autobiographical act can begin to be measured. From the distribution and frequency of these linguistic indexes one can erect judgments of the angle and the apparent strength of an autobiographer's attention, as well as of what draws or deflects his attention.

We must start with some notion of the contextual features our linguistic map is capable of reflecting.[2] Both spatial and temporal geography are registered, as well as the social meanings—"Christmas," for example, or "home"—they have acquired. Then there are the participants, those who actively and passively take part, whether as a source or spokesman, addressee or only witness to the proceedings, in the communication. There is also the instrument or channel of communication, a feature especially important in the case of literary texts, which often take on an autonomous life of their own. Any of these physical presences may serve as a center of orientation, but speakers may also establish a perspective from a point in memory, allusion, or imagination. But equally as important as these brute features are the relationships which hold between them, the relative positions ascribed to the participants, the way they in turn relate to their instruments and settings, and the way they perceive the roles they must play, their purposes, and the likelihood of their success in a particular act of communication. Linguistically relevant relations include degrees of power, solidarity, commitment, proximity, novelty, certainty, centrality, continuity, and autonomy. Of course, any individual speaker may further analyze his situation and discuss it in subtler terms than these. I have merely suggested those features and relations which are automatically encoded in the language, affecting any speaker whether or not he consciously chooses to reflect on his situation.

One of the more obvious contextually motivated choices in our speech is that between first, second, and third "person." "I," "we," and "you" are all terms reserved for the participants in an act of communication. To speak in the first person is to identify oneself as the immediate source of the communication, and to make of this a focal issue of that communication. A speaker or writer may also choose to focus upon the intended receiver of his communication, invoking "your" presence and explicit participation. The use of the third person denies or at least treats as irrelevant the connection between participation and the subject matter of a discussion; "he," "she," "it," and "they" are removed from the immediate field of "our" action. There are further discriminations to be made between those who participate, however. One may specify not only whether there are one or many senders or receivers, but also less tangible qualities such as the degree of impersonality or idiosyncrasy in "one's" position as speaker. An author may elect to include or exclude his audience from his domain, joining with them in a communal "we" or making his individual role so indefinite, through the use of "one" or its informal varient, "you," that it applies to any person who may share the circumstances described. Autobiographical identity varies considerably with respect to all of these dimensions. "It may well be my posterity should be informed that to this little artifice, with the blessing of God, their ancestor owed the constant felicity of his life, down to his 79th year, in which this is written" (Benjamin Franklin, *Autobiography*).[3] By adopting a point in the future and a position among his own posterity as a temporary point of vantage, Franklin can view himself as a historical personality. Even more artful are the evasions of the first person in *The Education of Henry Adams*: "He had expected it; on Hay's account, he was even satisfied to have his friend die, as we would all die if we could, in full fame, at home and abroad, universally regretted, and wielding his power to the last. One had seen scores of emperors and heroes fade into cheap obscurity even when alive; and now at least, one had not that to fear for one's friend."[4] Such language is hardly surprising from one who found the chief lesson of Rousseau's *Confessions* to be a "warning against the Ego."

The pronoun system of English once included a distinction between "thou" and "you," which distinguished more than simply number of addressees, also registering the relative status and familiarity of speaker and addressee. The right to address someone as "thou" came only with intimacy or power, whereas "you" was extended to equals lacking any special claims to intimacy. The distinctions themselves continue to be important in modern English, but they are marked in other ways, through the use of titles such as "Mr." or "Professor" in pertinent combinations with first and last names and diminutives.[5] For autobiography this means that audiences may be treated with disdain or with respect, as well as given degrees of recognition for their participation in the act, with resulting inferences to be drawn about the character of the author. Nor need the author treat his audience as an undifferentiated whole; he may divide them into peers and nonpeers, into hostile and sympathetic camps. Consider the strategies adopted in Sir Thomas Browne's preface to *Religio Medici*: "I have at present represented unto the world a full and intended copy of that piece which was most imperfectly and surreptitiously published before. . . . He that shall peruse that work and shall take notice of sundry particularities and personal expressions therein will easily discern [that] the intention was not public; and, being a private exercise directed to myself, what is delivered therein was rather a memorial unto me than an example unto any other."[6] Here, the audience is at once distant, indefinite, and yet individualized—a collection of potential "others" which together make up the "world." Browne does not directly address any one of these unspecified individuals, remaining circumspect and discreet under what he takes to be the impersonal and ultimately intrusive scrutiny of his "public."

One can easily see from the Browne excerpt that grammatical person is not the only resource for qualifying the respective roles of writer and reader. There are myriad possibilities for reference and invocation through the use of what Bertrand Russell was wont to call "definite descriptions"—titles with a unique application to one of the participants in the communicative context. Of course, by choosing such titles, the author has already elected against a less oblique form of reference, and this also enters into the meaning of the descriptive title he does elect. "*Nota Bene*—The Poet within a point and a half of being damnably in love" (Robert Burns, *Journal of the Border Tour*).[7] In the way he labels himself, Burns reveals not only a playful irony with regard to his posture as an author, but also something of the function of his journal, which is the diary of a poet and not primarily a piece of travel literature. The selection of titles, then, reflects a great deal about the autobiographical situation, its purpose, and its implied audience as well as about the author's role and his relation to his material. All of these features of the situation become criteria for choosing titles that are relevant and recognizable.

What we mean by "recognizability" is that the hearer can perform operations on the name—categorize it, find as a member of which class it is being used, bring knowledge to bear on it, detect which of its attributes are relevant in context, etc. . . . The selection of the "right" term, and the hearing of a term as adequate, appears to involve sensitivity to the respective locations of the participants and referent (which can change over the course of the interaction); to the membership composition of the interaction, and the knowledge of the world seen by members to be organized by membership categories . . . and to the topic or activity being done in the conversation at that point in its course.[8]

One could, in principle, look at every choice of wording as sensitive in this way to assumptions that are made about the communicative situation, but the assumptions are much more clear when an author is overtly striving to make a thing identifiable in the eyes of his audience. When, for example, he expects them to be able to respond to his calling them "by name": "Can it be that the public takes for granted that anything written by a professional writer is *eo ipso* untrue? The professional writer is looked on perhaps as a 'storyteller' like a child who has fallen into that habit and is mechanically chidden by his parents even when he protests that *this time* he is telling the truth" (Mary McCarthy, *Memories of a Catholic Girlhood*).[9] Although Mc-Carthy derides the xenophobia and condescension of this mass reading public, she continues to assume that there are fundamental distinctions between herself and her own reading audience. It appears that there are no fellow writers among her public and that their collective beliefs are as alien to her as are her mimetic practices to them. "I was born in Tuckahoe, near Hillsborough, and about twelve miles from Easton, in Talbot county, Maryland. I have no accurate knowledge of my age, never having seen any authentic record containing it" (*Narrative of the Life of Frederick Douglass, An American Slave, Written by Himself*). [10] The precision of Douglass's hierarchy of location could, in part, be credited to a desire to guide his audience to a place outside their ordinary range, requiring that he cite for them a list of more familiar names. But no sensitive reader could fail to feel the pride that Douglass takes in his precision; for a man denied the knowledge of his birth date and his parentage, a birthplace becomes a spiritual as well as a physical location, and the knowledge of it a source of self-control.

In addition to the use of labels and landmarks, we have also various categories of "deictic" adverbs and verbs through which we manipulate and reflect spatial relations. Depending on the chosen reference point, we can locate ourselves as "here" or "there," in terms of our proximity to that point, and also locate "this" or "that" object in terms of its relative proximity. Prepositions as well as adverbs may have an implicit reference point situated in the communicative context, as when one says "it is behind the tree"—the direction being a function of a given point of view and not of the tree itself.[11] The point of view may also determine whether there are two or three dimensions, whether one is "at" or "in" a house. Finally, there are sets of verbs which also reflect an implicit orientation, pairs such as "go" and "come," or "depart" and "arrive," for example.[12]

Speakers and writers of English may choose to position themselves in space, but they are obliged to give their temporal position. Tense inflection is required of every completed sentence, measuring the proximity of an event or state to what is "now" occurring in the actual or projected context of communication. The scale is actually quite limited, since all that tense can measure is absolute distinctions between the "past" or "nonpast" quality of events. According to John Lyons,

"The reason is that, whereas the past tense does typically refer to "before-now," the non-past is not restricted to what is contemporaneous with time of utterance: it is used for "timeless" or "eternal" statements (*The sun rises in the east*, etc.) and in many statements that refer to the future ('after-now')."[13]

Supplementing this basic temporal dichotomy are adverbs and prepositional phrases which may be used to specify the open-ended present tense, giving it, for example, habitual or future readings, as in "she leaves tomorrow."[14] Sets of temporal adverbs—such as "tomorrow," "today," and "yesterday," or "now" and "then"—are organized around contextual points of orientation and thus are similar to tense and spatial adverbs in their operation. Yet other dimensions are added to the measurement of time through the English aspect system. The "perfective" aspect is characteristically used for something begun in the past but not completed then, a state which still continues or which still retains its relevance.[15] (Past perfective therefore marks an action initiated before but continuing beyond a reference point that is already past, as in "she had gone when I arrived.") The "progressive" aspect, which also may be either past or present, indicates an ongoing activity— "she was leaving when I arrived"—a process which entirely surrounds and includes within its own surpassing scope what we have chosen for our reference point. The impression we have of density and richness in our temporal system is principally a matter of this ability to choose our reference points, and in any autobiographical use of the grammar of time we must, as Robin Lakoff states, "consider not only the superficially present elements of the sentence and the time of utterance, but the point of view of the speaker of the sentence as well . . . the choice of tense is based in part on the subjective factor of how the speaker feels himself related to the event."[16]

Thus, we can gauge something of how the speaker feels about the event in the lines concluding Bertrand Russell's autobiography. "This has been my life. I have found it worth living, and would gladly live it again if the chance were offered me."[17] Our knowledge of tense and aspect tells us how to read Russell's statement, how to see the epistemic relevance his past experiences continue to have for him. Had Russell chosen another reference point—the printed text rather than the man who writes it—his conclusion might have quite other implications, his life might have been seen as eternally present rather than what "has been."

But in reading Russell we are also only too aware of the contingency and the merely wishful status of the final clause, its proposition reflecting only his desires and not his expectation or belief that he will live again. Here we recognize another sort of measurement embedded in the language, a mapping of what we might loosely call degrees of possibility. The devices triggering our recognition include the complementizer "if," the inflected verb form "were," and the auxiliary "would." All of these are part of the dispersed "modality" system of our language, made up of these devices and the adverbs to which they are functionally related, such as "certainly" and "possibly." The fact that some of the same auxiliaries and adverbs also serve in measurements of time illustrates M. A. K. Halliday's remark that language may "relate what is being said to the "speaker-now," both by allowing options of mood and by giving a reference point in either time or the speaker's judgment."[18]

Modality not only qualifies the probability of an event, but also reflects the degree of certainty and the nature of the commitment expressly undertaken by the speaker. He may, for example, show his reservations with respect to his own capacity: "I cannot tell whether my first memories go back to the eastern or the western bank of the muddy, slow-moving Rio de la Plata—to Montevideo, where we spent long, lazy holidays in the villa of my Uncle Francisco Haedo, or to Buenos Aires." (Jorge Luis Borges, "An Autobiographical Essay").[19] He may indicate that the force of his assertion is to be tempered, that he is only relatively certain or even quite uncertain about his information. "We must have moved out to the suburb of Palermo quite soon" (Borges, p. 135). "On the closing page of that book, I am told of a man who sets out to make a picture of the universe. After many years, he has covered a blank wall with images . . . only to find out at the moment of death that he has drawn a likeness of his own face. This may be the case of all books; it is certainly the case of this particular book" (Borges, p. 180). According to his judgment—or what he imputes to his audience or his culture—the writer can distinguish between a moral or a logical contingency as opposed to a necessity: "At my age, one should be aware of one's limits and this knowledge may make for happiness" (Borges, p. 185).

Modality is thus an important linguistic resource, one which allows an author to mitigate his position and to delimit his responsibilities. Many of his modifications will reflect his anticipations, the responses from his readers that he already hears and attempts to meet through admissions, conciliations, or bold reaffirmations. "Perhaps these pages are more particularly addressed to poor students. As for the rest of my readers, they will accept such portions as apply to them. I trust that none will stretch the seams in putting on the coat for it may do good service to him whom it fits" (Henry David Thoreau, *Walden*).[20] As one can see from this passage, capacities, intentions, and obligations may also be ascribed to an audience. An author may restrict his readers to roles they "must" perform or exhort their efforts by telling them what they "can" perform. Above all, his predictions and the certainty with which he makes them tell us a great deal about his own intentions, his way of handling his relationships, and how and where he cares to place his trust.

While the force of the so-called subjunctive, of conditionals and statements contrary to fact is obvious, even exclamations imply something of the strength with which the speaker holds or dares to proffer his opinion. Emphasis reflects the distance from the normal, "normality" in turn being defined according to the writer's or the reader's expectations. For example, in John Ruskin's *Praeterita*: "The black Forest! The fall of Schaffhausen! The chain of the Alps! Within one's grasp for Sunday! What a Sunday, instead of customary Walworth and the Dulwich fields!"[21]

Ruskin displays the depth and the tendency of his enthusiasms, as well as his assumption that his standards for excitement and boredom will be shared by the reader. But it is in grammatical mood, rather than in modality, that we see the interpersonal dimension of communication most directly captured and manipulated. Both the imperative and the interrogative are signs of a reaching out from author to audience, an active call for aid in solving a need or an uncertainty. Orders and requests also mirror the attributes of the persons involved, insofar as their relative rights and duties are concerned, although power can be claimed and responsibility imposed by invoking other features of the situation. One may, for example, command in the name of a principle when one's own status would not be sufficient. If the interpersonal situation is obvious, and both the speaker's power and the ease and necessity of the desired response are self-evident, there may be substitutions in the mood; one could in this case issue an order by simply stating a need or questioning the actions of one's interlocutor.[22] But even in these derived cases the invitation to respond remains, and the ofttimes hidden engagement of an author with his audience erupts into full view.

Think of it! Was it all to end in a counting-house on top of a cinder-heaps, with Podsnap's drawing-room in the offing, and a Whig committee dealing out champagne to the rich and margarine to the poor in such convenient proportions as would make all men contented together, though the pleasure of the eyes was gone from the world, and the place of Homer was to be taken by Huxley? Yet, believe me, in my heart, when I really forced myself to look towards the future, that is what I saw in it. [William Morris, "How I Became a Socialist"] [23]

Morris commands his audience by the power of his passion rather than by any literal status he may possess—the role he assigns to his readers is the same role he once assigned to himself. They are "forced to look" even as he himself was. This conjoining of audience and at least one aspect, if long past, of the author mitigates against a too-imperious tone. The reader is a sympathetic peer throughout the interchange, a full participant to whose sympathy and belief Morris may appeal.

While we are accustomed to seeing the interpersonal dimension of imperatives and questions, the pragmatic values of the indicative mood are usually far less easily discerned. But this mood, too, reflects relationships between an author and an audience, since, according to philosopher Paul Grice, "it is assumed that one will say as much as one knows to be relevant to the concerns of one's audience."[24] In reporting something to his readership, an author thus delimits the scope of what ostensibly they already know. He makes assumptions about their ignorance and their need, if not actually their desire, to be acquainted with some fact. As a tribute to their sophistication, an author may choose instead to pose a rhetorical question if the information is too basic to report without insulting implications. For autobiographers in particular, the requirement that the substance of a report be both unknown and relevant to the interests of an audience has proved to be a problem. Especially in the early stages of the genre, autobiographers have felt the need to defend themselves against attacks upon the novelty or necessity of their self-exhibition. For example, in the *Life of Benvenuto Cellini:* "All men of whatsoever quality they be, who have done anything of excellence, or which may properly resemble excellence, ought, if they are persons of truth and honesty, to describe their life with their own hand."[25] And from Rousseau's *Confessions:* "I am made unlike any one I have ever met; I will even venture to say that I am like no one in the whole world. I may be no better, but at least I am different."[26] Whereas Rousseau stresses that his is a report that his audience could not have foreseen even from their own acts of introspection, Cellini puts emphasis on the duty which has been imposed on him as a man made exemplary by the "grace" of excellence. Even for contemporary autobiographers, working within an established tradition, vestiges of the same polemical stance can often be found. In Henry Miller's *My Life and Times*, for example, "Everybody thinks he's got to know what I'm doing, what is my life like, what has it been and so on. And I'm utterly disgusted in a way, rehashing everything about my own life or future projects . . . in a sense I sometimes feel I'm a victim of my own creation."[27] Miller, unlike Cellini, is not apotheosized but rather victimized by Fama; his autobiography is written not as homage to the public nature of virtue but in the posture of annoyed submission to public curiosity.

In addition to reflecting interpersonal relations, mood does of course also exert a pressure on how we take a piece of information, particularly its ontological status. Mood establishes conditions on when and how a proposition may be verified, imperatives by definition concerning states of affairs which do not yet exist and questions calling something into doubt.[28] Authors may seem at times to use mood inappropriately, as Morris does when he asks questions (above) about events long after his own doubts have been resolved. In such cases, the author is simply altering his frame of reference and adopting some new vantage point, either that of a former self, the reader, or some other (imaginary) person. "A particularly frequent occurrence in prose is the case in which some such question as "What is to be done now?" introduces the hero's inner deliberations or the recounting of his actions—the question being equally the author's and also one the hero poses to himself in a predicament . . . it is the author who steps forward, but he does so on his hero's behalf, he seems to speak for him."[29]

The context of communication is thus complicated and recursive; a speech act may enclose another act, verbal or mental, which has its own associated context. The relationship between the immediate context and the embedded context may vary, with the current speaker allowing different degrees and different kinds of autonomy to the words he is reporting. By using direct discourse and separating reported speech from his own discourse by quotation marks, a writer purports to transmit the original speech without interference, reproducing both the manner and the matter (within conventional limits) of another speaker's words. " 'Call the fire brigade,' cried Mrs. Prothero as she beat the gong" (Dylan Thomas, "A Child's Christmas in Wales").[30] Indirect discourse allows for greater distortion of reported material. The embedded speech has been fully assimilated, with no quotation marks or shift of tense to set it off as an autonomous act.[31] "Smoke, indeed, was pouring out of the dining-room, and the gong was bombilating and Mrs. Prothero was announcing ruin like a town crier in Pompeii" (Thomas, p. 21).

By using an indirect report, the writer indicates that what he transmits is not the original speech act but his own analysis of that act. His analysis may emphasize either the matter or the manner of the speech he reproduces; he may simply paraphrase the message or, as Thomas does, may portray the mode of its delivery. Between the poles of indirect and direct stands "quasi-direct discourse," a range of reported speech which may lack formal signals of direct discourse such as quotation marks while still preserving some of the diction and grammar of the original material. The ambiguous play between analysis and report facilitates irony and parody. "And mothers loudly warned their proud pink daughters or sons to put that jelly fish down" (Thomas, "Holiday Memory").[32] The author may also use the framework of his quotation to suggest a reading of the material he quotes or to emphasize a particular aspect of it. Thomas would have us hear mothers "warning loudly," and also have us see the humor that the sunburnt families are doubtless missing in their own situation.

But the names given to these reported speech acts—crying and warning, announcing and saying—can just as easily be used for naming the act in which the author himself is engaged. These terms are what Austin has called "performatives," in that one may use them not only to describe but actually to perform an illocutionary act, in the proper circumstances. For literature, these terms include not only "promise" and "apologize," but also "narrate," "create," and "describe." The sorts of terms an author chooses for his act, whether verbs or nouns and adjectives derived from performative verbs, tell us a great deal about the nature of his act—even the frequency with which these terms appear can be important in determining the self-consciousness of the text. Nonliteral terms used to perform and describe an autobiographical act are an equally important literary resource; these may range from single terms such as "paint," "envision," or "remember"—borrowed from another art or discipline—to the most wildly extended metaphors: "Within the groves of Chivalry, I pipe/To shepherd swains" (William Wordsworth, *The Prelude*).[33]

There are implications for the status of the act in the very grammatical categories an autobiographer uses. Rather than stressing his individual responsibility by selecting performative nouns such as "narrator," he may focus all attention on the process of the act itself, using nominalizations and passive sentences in which no agent need be specified. "It seems as if time had not yet been created, for all thoughts connected with emotion and place are without sequence" (William Butler Yeats *Autobiography*).[34]

The choice between performative verbs and other grammatical categories, adjectives, for example, is also a choice about whether to reflect upon the temporal dimensions of the act, to see it as perfective or copresent, as an event or an ongoing process. With respect to any performative verb, there are also associated syntactic cases—agent, instrument, beneficiary, locative, and patient—which may be distributed between an author and his readers in a variety of ways.[35] "To knock at the door of the past was in a word to see it open to me quite wide—to see the world within begin to 'compose' with a grace of its own" (Henry James, *A Small Boy and Others*).[36] In this case, James exchanges the traditional role of author-as-agent for that of an experiencer, relegating himself to the position of one who merely observes the act of composition. Similarly, an autobiographer has the choice of "telling" his readers something, "describing" it "for" them as his beneficiaries, or even making them the location or the goal "to" which he directs the act. Switching his point of view, the author may choose instead to treat the audience as agent of the act of reading and even give an extended commentary on the way his readers are or should be performing their own parts in the autobiographical act.

But all verbs, not simply the performative variety, have associated cases. A great deal of information about the role of any person, entity, or object in an action is communicated through its position in recurring syntactic forms, and this is even more important information when we consider how an autobiographer projects his own sense of himself as an actor. "I am being ground slowly on the grim grindstone of physical pain" (*The Diary of Alice James*).[37] In addition to perceiving herself as a victim, Alice James also makes her victimage the theme and subject of her musings. Positions, the sequential ordering of items in a clause, also have their implications and allow an author to draw attention to the item or deflect attention from it. Here the position at the end of the clause, which is characteristically saved for focal "new" or qualifying information, is occupied by the place of victimization.[38] We see the ambience but not the agent of her pain.

Even so simple a thing as the physical placement of words in clauses can therefore tell us something about the shape and the dynamic of self-evaluation and also reflect intensities of self-preoccupation. The heads of clauses are the points of integration; the elements which appear here link the chain and turn sentences into text. Conjunction, ellipsis, lexical and grammatical parallelisms are additional resources for cohesion and coherence. One may ask of any text how these resources are used—the kind and the extent of textual integration.[39] In autobiography, one would especially like to know how much depends upon the intercession of the author, his own intrusions a posteriori into the substance of events. Does his life, his self, have a continuity, logical or temporal, without his imposed interpretations?[40] Is his autobiography a shadow dependent on his life and self or does it have its own autonomy? Consider the following two paragraphs from Norman Mailer's *Advertisements for Myself*.

The author, taken with an admirable desire to please his readers, has also added a set of advertisements, printed in italics, which surround all of these writings with his present tastes, preferences, apologies, prides, and occasional confessions. Like many another literary fraud, the writer has been known on occasion to read the Preface of a book instead of a book, and bearing this in mind, he tried to make the advertisements more readable than the rest of his pages.

Since such a method is discursive, and this is a time in which many hold a fierce grip on their wandering attention, a Second Table of Contents is offered to satisfy the specialist. Here all short stories, short novels, poems, advertisements, articles, essays, journalism, and miscellany are posted in their formal category.[41]

Both paragraphs are obviously the work of a writer highly conscious of his text; indeed, the litter of textual self-reference makes these paragraphs almost opaque. But there are also differences between the integration of the two. In the first, every sentence seems to hang upon the author, that "literary fraud," that "writer" and that "he" which charges to the front of every clause and serves as the point of every new departure. The second paragraph, however, suppresses any mention of an author. It is the "method" and the seemingly self-propelling organizing energy of the text itself which have become the theme. The final passive sentence, for example, eliminates any need to refer to the man responsible for the "posting."

One could go further, noting how the change is associated with changes in the audience, impersonality arising when Mailer faces not "his readers" but an implacable "specialist." One should also note, however, that in neither case does Mailer leave the refuge of his identity as an author. But these and other refinements of interpretation must await the more exhaustive analyses of the following four chapters. Here I limit myself to sketching possibilities of action and elements of language which trace their trajectory. (A summary display of the linguistic markers I have discussed can be found in Table 1.)

To this point I have concerned myself with potentialities—their actualization must be sought in individual autobiographies, in the work of Bunyan and Boswell, Nabokov and De Quincey, and of course many others. But what I hope I have demonstrated is that the choices which give character to an act and provide for each autobiographer, "caught in the act," his own tenuous immortality are also in some measure universal. An autobiographer may inhabit an apparently private world, but it is a world to which, in writing, he cannot help but give us a key.

TABLE 1
SOME LINGUISTIC MARKERS SENSITIVE TO CONTEXT

Person or Title	1st person: I, We (± Exclusive); 2d person: (Thou), You; 3d person: He, She, It, (One), They; definite descriptive labels: "the author" or "the reader"
Space	Demonstration pronouns: here vs. there, this vs. that; prepositions: to (directional), at (dimensional); directional verbs: go vs. come, arrive vs. depart; locative labels: "London," "home," "the corner drugstore"
Time (tense)	± Present; temporal adverbs: now vs. then; prepositional phrases: "at night"; temporal labels: "Monday," "Labor Day," "the week after next"
(aspect)	Perfective: have; progressive: be + -ing
Modality	Modal auxiliaries: can, may, will, etc.; modal adverbs: certainly, possibly, perhaps, etc. (relating to capacity, certainty, obligation, and permission); exclamation; complementizer constructions: if, would that, etc. (along with verb inflectional adjustments related to contingency, conditionality, contrariety, optionality)

(Continued)

TABLE 1—*Continued*

Mood	Indicative; interrogative; imperative
Reported speech	Direct discourse; quasi-direct discourse; indirect discourse; speech frames: said, declared, etc. (along with associated analyses of the content or the texture of the reported speech)
Performatives	Lexical types: write, narrate, ask, read; grammatical categories: to write, writer, or writing; written or writerly
Case	Agent, patient, object, experiencer, instrument, beneficiary, locative (including source and goal), essive (existential equation)

Focus (theme) (information)	Theme or topic, "To write	rheme or comment is to communicate" new information
	Given information,	

CHAPTER TWO

===================================

JOHN BUNYAN: THE PATRIARCH AND THE WAY

===================================

> I could have enlarged much in this my discourse of my tempta-
> tions and troubles for sin, as also of the merciful kindness and
> working of *God* with my Soul: I could also have stepped into a
> stile much higher then this in which I have here discoursed, and
> could have adorned all things more then here I have seemed to do;
> but I dare not: *God* did not play in convincing of me; the *Devil*
> did not play in tempting of me; neither did I play when I sunk
> into a bottomless pit, when *the pangs of hell caught hold upon
> me*; wherefore I may not play in my relating of them, but be
> plain and simple, and lay down the thing as it was.
>
> John Bunyan

When John Bunyan published *Grace Abounding to the Chief of Sinners*
early in the third quarter of the seventeenth century, he was performing
an act which was still relatively rare in England. There were, to be sure,
journals and commonplace books which were written in ever increasing
numbers during the sixteenth and seventeenth centuries, but these were
essentially private documents. The typical seventeenth-century autobiography, according to Paul Delaney, was "not intended to circulate
widely; it might be drawn up for the good of the author's own soul, or
for a restricted audience of family, friends, or members of a congregation."[1] If the manuscript were published, it was done posthumously or
by someone other than the author himself—a minister, for example,
might publish a collection of religious experiences he had gathered from
his parishioners.

A constraint like this against making a public thing out of autobiography illustrates some of the assumptions and decorums of the
English literary community at that time. Only an unusually significant
individual or an experience which was somehow exemplary merited
public attention. And since one could not gracefully claim significance
for oneself it was left to posterity or to disinterested authorities to
determine which autobiographies might enter the public domain. Those
who did publish accounts of their own lives usually did so only when
the account was subsumed by some larger project such as a genealogical
history.[2]

But the English literary community was changing; new authors and
new audiences were forming themselves outside of and in partial igno-

rance of the decorums of the High Culture. It was here, among the religious sectarians—the Quakers, the Ranters, and his own Particular Baptists—that Bunyan found his voice and his assured audience. Indeed, the popularity of the kind of intimate spiritual self-relevation Bunyan provides in *Grace Abounding* was so great that more moderate and cultured Puritans such as Richard Baxter became alarmed and protested that the proliferation of these "accounts of heart-occurrences" would obscure the fact that "God deals much the same with all."[3] This was an objection which had little weight, however, with men who held extreme Calvinist convictions; the doctrine of unconditional election was enough to prove to them that God's dealings with the human race were far from universal. Some individuals had been chosen, and as living "saints" they had the sanction of God if not of man to awaken souls who might not perceive the evidences of their own election. "Moses (*Numb.* 33.1,2) writ of the Journeyings of the children of *Israel*, from *Egypt* to the Land of *Canaan*; and commanded also, that they did remember their forty years travel in the wilderness. . . . Wherefore this I have endeavored to do; and not onely so, but to publish it also; that, if God will, others may be put in remembrance of what he hath done for their Souls, by reading his work upon me" (*Grace Abounding*, p. 2). Urgency and the grace of God made strong arguments against an inhibition that was largely a matter of literary good manners.

But one could sensibly claim that John Bunyan had no intention of writing an autobiography—that autobiography was at best a side effect of his actual intention to give witness to abounding grace in the place where he had discovered it. The religion of Calvin and Luther had turned hagiography into autobiography, since it was no longer miraculous works which were the sign of a saint, but faith—a private and personal experience. The drama of salvation was now enacted in terms of individual psychology; the inner life of one man was merely its principal arena.

Bunyan's autobiography is in many ways an act groping for an appropriate form. Because it is connected in a very real way with hagiography, it is not surprising to discover that it has the conventional divisions of a Saint's Life. Its three chapters on conversion, ministry, and imprisonment parallel the traditional description of the conversion, miracles, and persecution of the saint.[4] But Bunyan appears to be seeking some additional value from his choice of form rather than attempting to borrow for his own endeavor the aura of respectability surrounding hagiography. He resorts to other sources as well—for example, to the Pauline epistle, which serves as a model for his preface to the book. Like Paul's letters, *Grace Abounding* is conceived as an address from a distant missionary to the "children" and converts who are separated from him by the flood of other duties and by the walls of his prison.

Children, Grace be with you, *Amen*. I being taken from you in presence, and so tied up, that I cannot perform that duty that doth lie upon me, to you-ward, for your further edifying and building up in Faith and Holiness, etc., yet that you may see my Soul hath fatherly care . . . [I] do look yet after you all. [*Grace Abounding*, p. 1]

My little children, with whom I am again in travail until Christ be formed in you! I could wish to be present with you now. [Galations 4:19–20] [5]

So .eager is Bunyan to win approval for what must seem a novel undertaking that he makes his dependence upon scriptural examples as explicit as possible, so that it cannot fail to be recognized. "It was *Pauls* accustomed manner, *Acts 22.* and that when tried for his life, *Acts 24.* even to open before his Judges, the manner of his Conversion" (*Grace Abounding*, p. 2).

Since his is an act with a religious sanction, it is predictable that Bunyan will—like his contemporaries—see his identity and the stages of his life in terms of the Calvinist doctrines which originally permitted his self-display. Most sectarian autobiographers concern themselves with a threefold pattern of development: "conviction of sin," followed by positive evidence of election or an "effectual call," and a final culmination in "justification," in which faith triumphs over world, flesh, and devil to receive the imputed righteousness of Christ, which is alone sufficient to regenerate the depraved human soul so that it may face the immutable laws of divine justice.[6] *Grace Abounding* does not desert the pattern; its first chapter dutifully recounts "conviction of sin":

from all which I still received more conviction, and from that time began to see something of the vanity and inward wretchedness of my wicked heart. [*Grace Abounding*, p. 25]

"effectual call":

Now had I an evidence, as I thought, of my salvation from Heaven, with many golden Seals thereon, all hanging in my sight. [*Grace Abounding*, p. 40]

and "justification":

By this also was my faith in him, as my Righteousness, the more confirmed to me; for if he and I were one, then his Righteousness was mine, his Merits mine, his Victory also mine. Now could I see myself in Heaven and Earth at once; in heaven by my Christ, by my Head, by my Righteousness and Life, though on Earth by my Body or Person. [*Grace Abounding*, p. 73]

Even Bunyan's designation of himself as the "chief of sinners," in his title, is a conventional touch—other Calvinists who claimed this ostensibly unique distinction for themselves included Oliver Cromwell.[7]

Bunyan's autobiography also bears a resemblance to didactic and controversial pamphlets which circulated in abundance during the stormy seventeenth century. The urgent need of saving souls, under the compulsion of which Bunyan wrote *Grace Abounding*, allowed no gentlemanly generosity with regard to matters of doctrine. Sectarian controversy is as much a part of Bunyan's autobiography as it is of his pamphlets. In fact Bunyan used all his writing, fiction as well as nonfiction, to persuade his audience of their need for the "right" religion; both *Grace Abounding* and *Pilgrim's Progress* give ample narrative space to exposing the errors of rival sects.

the Quakers did oppose his Truth. . . . The errors that this people maintained were: 1. That the holy Scriptures were not the Word of God. 2. That every man in the world had the spirit of Christ, grace, faith, etc. 3. That Christ Jesus, as crucified and dying 1600 years ago, did not satisfy divine justice for the sins of the people. 4. That Christ's flesh and blood was within the saints. 5. That the bodies of the good and bad that are buried in the churchyard shall not arise again. [*Grace Abounding*, p. 39]

They had them first to the top of a Hill called Error, which was very steep on the furtherest side, and bid them look down to the bottom. So Christian and Hopeful looked down and saw at the bottom several men dashed all to pieces by a fall that they had from the top. Then said Christian, "What meaneth this?" The shepherds answered, "Have you not heard of them that were made to err by hearkening to Hymeneus and Philetus, as concerning the faith of the resurrection of the body?" [*Pilgrim's Progress*] [8]

Nor did teaching end with conversion. There was also the task of sustaining the faithful. According to the tenets of the Baptist faith, even the elect could lose their way, become reprobate, and ultimately be damned by committing an unpardonable sin which no amount of faith or imputed righteousness could rectify. There was only one such sin, the so-called sin against the Holy Ghost, but the biblical passage which alluded to it left its nature wholly enigmatic. This potentially terrifying mystery produced scores of tracts aimed at defining the sin against the Holy Ghost, that the faithful might not give way to despair.[9] There is careful discrimination between pardonable and unpardonable sin in both *Grace Abounding* and *Pilgrim's Progress*, as Bunyan depicts the very different character of a weak but normal human condition and total reprobation. Indeed the central issue of the first chapter of Bunyan's autobiography is his own naive fear of having committed the unpardonable offense. After receiving evidence of his election, Bunyan is tormented for months by a demon voice from within, ceaselessly importuning him to "sell Christ." When at last his resistance is exhausted, and he agrees to let Christ go "if he will," he becomes convinced that his is the reprobate condition of Esau, the man who has sold his own birthright, discussed in Paul's Epistle to the

Hebrews. "About this time I took an opportunity to break my Mind to an Ancient Christian; and told him all my case. I told him also that I was afraid that I had sinned the sin against the Holy Ghost; and he told me, *He thought so too*. Here therefore I had but cold comfort, but, talking a little more with him, I found him, though a good man, a stranger to much Combate with the Devil" (*Grace Abounding*, p. 55). It is Bunyan's experience in combat, then, as well as his status as one of the elect, which empowers his autobiographical act, assuring him that it is something his readers truly need and long to hear: "If you have sinned against the light, if you are tempted to blaspheme, if you are down in despair, if you think *God* fights against you, or if heaven is hid from your eyes; remember 'twas thus with your father, *but out of them all the Lord delivered me*" (*Grace Abounding*, p. 3).

When Bunyan returns to the problem of reprobation late in *Pilgrim's Progress*, part one, the Pauline analogy to Esau recurs as well in the parable of "Little Faith" which Christian tells to his traveling companion Hopeful: "But you must put a difference betwixt Esau and Little Faith, and also betwixt their estates. . . . Though faithless ones can for carnal lusts, pawn, or mortgage, or sell what they have, and themselves outright to boot; yet they that have faith, saving faith, though but a little of it, cannot do so" (*Pilgrim's Progress*, pp. 167–68) Christian's solution here is much the same one Bunyan had discovered for himself during the long and trying process of his conversion, and, in delivering his parable, Christian assumes the stance of combat veteran which also appears in the preface to Bunyan's autobiography. "I for my part have been in the fray before now, and though (through the goodness of him that is best) I am as you see alive, yet I cannot boast of my manhood. Glad shall I be if I meet with no more such brunts, though I fear we are not got beyond all danger. However, since the lion and the bear hath not as yet devoured me, I hope God will also deliver us from the next uncircumcised Philistine" (*Pilgrim's Progress*, p. 171).

One can see easily enough how much Bunyan's autobiography has in common with his more famous allegorical novel, not only in source material and imagery but even in didactic goals. Yet Bunyan continued to reissue *Grace Abounding* long after the great success of his novel. Thus, for him and for his reading public, the earlier work achieved something that his fiction could not. The distinction between these two works, written in such close succession and with so many ties of theme and figure between them, exposes the heart of the autobiographical act as conceived by Bunyan and allows us to see the meaning and the purposes that made it unique in his eyes. Both works make use of actual events from the life of their author and both are religious teachings, but only the autobiography changes the value of that life and instructs the author as well as the audience. Bunyan's autobiography is an attempt to prove as much as to memorialize the touch of grace upon his life, and he himself is the party most interested in the sufficiency of his evidence and the validity of his conclusion.

I have wondered much at this one thing, that though God doth visit my Soul with never so blessed a discoverie of himself, yet I have found again, that such hours have attended me afterwards, that I have been in my spirit so filled with darkness, that I could not so much as once conceive what that God and that comfort was with which I have been refreshed. . . . These things I continuallie see and feel, and am afflicted with; yet the Wisdom of God doth order them for my good. . . . They show me the need I have to watch and be sober. [*Grace Abounding*, pp. 102–3]

As a proof, therefore, *Grace Abounding* must be an argument rather than merely an attractive rhetorical display; artful persuasion will not suffice to convince when the goal is to convince the artist himself. The more seductive effects of narrative are often foregone for the sake of minute analysis and logical inference.[10] The stern and unflinching character of Bunyan's sobriety, his refusal to "play" with stylistic adornments or to mitigate in any way his plain dealing, is a reflection of how serious are the consequences of his autobiographical act. Even if one could indulge in fancy when recalling the most deadly afflictions of one's life, there can be no playfulness when the act of writing is itself under judgment and will contribute to the ultimate salvation or perdition of one's own soul. This is the case when Bunyan is writing *in propria persona*, something he does not do in his novel. As autobiographer, Bunyan must suppress the sinful vanities of his own nature and overcome his carnal imagination; for, according to Calvin, "the mind of man is so entirely alienated from the righteousness of God that he cannot conceive, desire, or design anything but what is wicked, distorted, foul, impure, and iniquitous."[11]

Thus *Grace Abounding*, unlike *Pilgrim's Progress*, is a work of the letter as well as the spirit, and its literal quality, its numberings and citations, its scrupulous or even obsessive attention to the naked Word of the scriptures, is possibly its most prominent feature. It is also a work which stresses its empirical foundations, and Bunyan's sobriety is intimately linked with his need to quash anything that could distort his vision or distract his attention. He must strive to remain in a state of receptive watchfulness—empty, earnest, expectant. The mimetic probability of fiction, internal consistency and necessity, is not enough; he must have the actual, the externally verifiable fact. Bunyan stresses, even in his subtitle, that his is a "faithful" account and interrupts his narrative at several points to stress it again. "In these things, I protest *before God*, I lye not, neither do I feign this sort of speech: these were really, strongly, and with all my heart, my desires" (*Grace Abounding*, p. 11).

How different is this strident insistence from the casual and inviting tone Bunyan adopts in the preface to *Pilgrim's Progress*. According to

"The Author's Apology," the later work was begun not in earnestness but as a diversion:

> Neither did I but vacant seasons spend
> In this my scribble, nor did I intend
> But to divert myself in doing this,
> From worser thoughts which make me do amiss.
> [*Pilgrim's Progress*, p. 31]

Bunyan does recognize the need to make an apology for a work of this sort, but the terms of his apology also serve to distinguish the pragmatic value of his novel from that sought for his autobiography. If *Grace Abounding* is a product of scriptural commandment, *Pilgrim's Progress* is the result of biblical and poetic license.

> I find not that I am denied the use
> Of this my method, so I no abuse
> Put on the words, things, readers, or be rude
> In handling figure, or similitude,
> In application; but all that I may
> Seek the advance of Truth this or that way.
> Denied did I say? Nay, I have leave
> (Example too, and that from them that have
> God better pleased by their words or ways
> Than any man that breaketh nowadays),
> Thus to express my mind, thus to declare
> Things unto thee that excellentest are.
> [*Pilgrim's Progress*, pp. 35–36]

Having contracted to instruct by means of his fiction, Bunyan seems to be free to engage in the very play of productive imagination which his autobiography expressly forbids:

> . . . In more than twenty things, which I set down;
> This done, I twenty more had in my crown,
> And they began again to multiply . . . .
> Thus I set pen to paper with delight,
> And quickly had my thoughts in black and white.
> [*Pilgrim's Progress*, p. 31]

But, of course, there is not the problem of self-knowledge interfering with the effort of creation which confronts the autobiographer, nor does Bunyan need to worry in the same way that his efforts will be transparently artificial. Audience and artist, in this case, are distinct:

> Would'st thou divert thyself from melancholy?
> Would'st thou be pleasant, yet be far from folly?
> . . . O then come hither,
> And lay my book, thy head and heart together.
> [*Pilgrim's Progress*, p. 31]

While it may be sinful for Bunyan himself to sink from observation to play, it is commendable for him to improve upon the presumably foolish play of others.

It is possible that Bunyan might never have undertaken *Pilgrim's Progress*, however, if he had not first written *Grace Abounding*. According to Bunyan's editor, Roger Sharrock, the allegory "followed naturally and inevitably on the completion of the spiritual autobiography."[12] In writing about his own life as a religious example, he had already experimented with something resembling allegory, representing "in a single life an idealized pattern of human behavior."[13] Bunyan subsumes his own experiences to scriptural "types," seeking to explain and understand it as a recurrence of experiences recorded in the Bible.[14] His are the struggles of Samson, the responsibilities of Moses and Paul, and, at the penultimate moment when even God seems to have deserted him in his prison cell, his story becomes that of Job:

I was no sooner fixed upon this resolution, but that word dropped upon me, *Doth Job serve God for nought*? as if the accuser had said, Lord, *Job* is no upright man, he serves thee for by-respects, hast thou not made a hedge about him, etc. But put forth now thy hand, and touch all that he hath, and he will curse thee to thy face: How now, thought I, is this the sign of an upright Soul, to desire to serve God when all is taken from him: is he a godlie man that will serve God for nothing rather than give out: blessed be God, then, I hope I have an upright heart, for I am resolved, (God give me strength) never to denie my profession, though I have nothing at all for my pains." [*Grace Abounding*, p. 101]

In much the same way, the pilgrims in Bunyan's dream vision encounter adventures which are typical, and which are often environed by their biblical analogues. Christian and Hopeful overcome their temptation to turn back from their journey to the comforts of "this world" near Lucre Hill, with its proprietor, Demas, drawn from the New Testament and its monument to Lot's wife drawn from the Old. Vanity Fair is another typical experience; an eternally recurrent problem in the lives of religious men, it is appropriately described in the present tense.[15] "Almost five thousand years agone, there were pilgrims walking to the Celestial City, as these two honest persons are; and Beelzebub, Apollyon, and Legion, with their companions, perceiving by the path that the Pilgrims made that their way to the City lay through the town of Vanity, they contrived here to set up a fair . . . the way to the Celestial City lies just through this town, where this lusty Fair is kept; and he that will go to the City, and yet not go through this town, must needs to go out of the world" (*Pilgrim's Progress*, pp. 124–26). Because the events themselves are essentially timeless, it is possible for Christian to observe the entire life histories of Passion and Patience in a single moment as he is shown through the House of the Interpreter. "These two lads are figures, Passion of the men of this world, and Patience, of the men of that which is to come" (*Pilgrim's Progress*, p. 62). When neither dreamer nor character notices the typological parallel, the marginal notes will draw out the universal implications of what might otherwise pass for a singular adventure.

The neighbours also came out to see
him run, and as he ran, some mocked,
others threatened; and some cried
after him to return.

They that fly
from the wrath
to come, are a
gazing-stock to
the world.

[*Pilgrim's Progress*, p. 41]

There is none of the tension between the universal and the particular, between scriptural archetype and individual experience, between afflictions touching the self and what happens to all men in Bunyan's fiction that is so evident in his autobiography. In the earlier work, Bunyan must often interrupt himself to establish the spiritual meaning of the event he is describing. "I will now (God willing) before I proceed any further give you in a word or two, what, as I conceive, was the cause of this temptation" (*Grace Abounding*, p. 74). If Bunyan's life and identity are exemplary, they have become so only through the writing of *Grace Abounding*; typological parallels seem to emerge from autobiographical contemplation, to be earned through incredible interpretive effort rather than given a priori. The ease of *Pilgrim's Progress*, then, is in part the result of an earlier apprenticeship.

One can observe the silent discovery of meaning and meaningful form in Bunyan's conversion narrative. The integrity of this chapter is created by a recurring image of "the condition of the elect" which appears in modified form at each important juncture in Bunyan's spiritual development. At first it is not an image at all, but an actual encounter between Bunyan, then a self-assured formalist in matters of religion, and a group of Particular Baptists.

But upon a day, the good providence of God did cast me to *Bedford*, to work on my calling; and in one of the streets of that town, I came where there was three or four poor women sitting at a door in the Sun; and talking about things of God; and being now willing to hear them discourse, I drew near to hear what they said; for I was now a brisk talker my self in the matters of Religion: but now I may say, *I heard, but I understood not*, for they were far above out of my reach, for their talk was about a new birth, the work of God on their hearts, also how they were convinced of their miserable state by nature. . . . And me thought they spake with such pleasantness of grace in all they said, that they were to me as if they had found a new world, as if they were people that dwelt alone. [*Grace Abounding*, pp. 14–15]

This meeting gives Bunyan his first presentiments that all is not well with his soul, initiating a period of anguished desire to prove himself by performing a miracle or to escape from himself by espousing the extreme antinomian position of the Ranters. But after months of vain effort, the Bedford incident returns to him, transformed, as a waking dream taunting him with a vision of the true life of the blessed. "I saw as if they were set on the Sunny side of some high Mountain, there refreshing themselves with the pleasant beams of the Sun, while I was shivering and shrinking in the cold, afflicted with frost, snow, and dark clouds; methought also betwixt me and them I saw a wall that did compass about this Mountain" (*Grace Abounding*, p. 19). The phenomenology of the original encounter has been heightened—the warmth and light in which the women sit, their communal comfort, even the impression their talk gave of putting them "far above out of his reach," and the emotional implications of Bunyan's own position—the horror of his irremediable isolation and ostracism from all that could help him—have been made definite. But this is vision rather than nightmare. Now that he is convinced of his innate worthlessness and of his powerlessness to save himself, the Bedford experience can begin to take on a larger and more systematic meaning for him. As a chastened observer, he is at last ready to understand and accept what before he could not.

At last I saw as it were, a narrow gap, like a little doorway in the wall, throw which I attempted to pass: but the passage being very straight and narrow. . . . Now this Mountain and Wall, etc., was made out to me; the Mountain signified the Church of the living God; the Sun that shone thereon, the comfortable shining of his face on them that were therein: the wall I thought was the Word that did make separation between the Christians and the world: and the gap which was in this wall, I thought was Jesus Christ, who is the way to God the Father . . . it showed me that none could enter into life but those that were in down-right earnest, and unless they left this wicked world behind them. [*Grace Abounding*, p. 20]

Although years follow before Bunyan's conversion is complete, the form of his quest is now set: he will battle to join the elect from whom he is separated by the wall of the Pauline scriptures on grace, faith, election, and reprobation. But he must first come to understand these doctrines. His struggle with the increasingly difficult concepts of original sin, grace, reconciliation, and imputed righteousness, the progressive stages of his Baptist education, is measured by the recurrence of the visionary dejection and elation associated with the Bedford meeting. "Thus was I sinking, whatever I did think or do. So one day I walked to a neighboring Town, and sate down upon a Settle in the Street, and fell into a very deep pause about the most fearful state my sin had brought me to; and, after long musing, I lifted up my head, but methought I saw as if the Sun that shineth in the Heavens did grudge to give me light" (*Grace Abounding*, p. 58).

Again and again, Bunyan describes his dejection when he cannot understand the scriptures or reconcile his understanding of them with his hopes for salvation. Intellectual assent is not enough; Bunyan must experience a dogma before he can accept it. Each problematic text must become a divine or diabolic visitation which he feels, tastes, is wounded or is called by:[16]

I was in diverse frames of Spirit . . . according to the nature of the several Scriptures that came in upon my mind; if this of Grace, then I was quiet; but if that of *Esau*, then tormented. Lord, thought I, if both these Scriptures would meet in my heart at once, I wonder which of them would get the better of me. . . . Well, about two or three days after, so they did indeed; they boulted both upon me at a time, and did work and struggle strangly in me for a while; at last, that about Esaus birthright began to wax weak, and withdraw, and vanish; and this about the sufficiency of Grace prevailed, with peace and joy . . . for the Word of the Law and Wrath must give place to the Word of Life and Grace. [*Grace Abounding*, pp. 66–67]

This experiential mode of religious learning is in accord with the precepts of Mr. Gifford, the leader of the Bedford congregation, whom Bunyan eventually meets after he has attained enough spiritual sophistication.

This man made it much his business to deliver the People of God from all those false and unsound rests that by Nature we are prone to take and make to our Souls; he pressed us to take special heed, that we took not up any truth upon trust, as from this or that or another man or men, but to cry mightily to God, that he would convince us of the reality thereof, and set us down therein, by his own Spirit in the holy Word; for, said he, if you do otherwise, when temptations come, if strongly, you not having received them with evidence from Heaven, will find you want that help and strength now to resist, as once you thought you had. [*Grace Abounding*, p. 37]

Bunyan renders each step in his religious training according to this pattern; first the "false rest" of apparent belief, then the "storm" of temptations to blasphemy and despair when his superficial acceptance fails him, and finally the resolution in which his doubt and misconception are removed in return for his faithful endurance through temptation. It is thus that Bunyan is driven to test the sufficiency of Grace through contemplating the most heinous sin he can imagine, succumbing, that is, to the "secret thought" that he must sell Christ even as Judas had done. Only a direct experience of the lowest depths of human guilt will allow Bunyan to comprehend the power and meaning of reconciliation; only by becoming the "chief of sinners" can he know the abundance of Grace.

Even what would seem the final achievement of his conversion, his coming to terms with the logic of imputed righteousness, is subject to further tests. He appears to understand the symbolic participation of all men in the "publick person" of Christ; yet only a few paragraphs later he describes an overwhelming blow of spiritual amnesia. "Suddenly there fell upon me a great cloud of darkness, which did so hide from me the things of God and Christ, that I was as if I had never seen or known them in my life; . . . I could not feel my soul to move or stir after grace and life by Christ" (*Grace Abounding*, p. 81). He has been struck down by time and the frailty of his human memory. He recovers only when he is able to overcome time by understanding that election and salvation are things that are timeless, not past or to come. For him, this recovery is the ultimate triumph of his conversion; he can at last freely join the company of the living saints. There is a final echo of the Bedford vision at this point, but once again transformed to converge with a passage from Paul's Epistle to the Hebrews. Now this epistle is no longer the source of Bunyan's agonies over reprobation but the cause of his greatest comfort and joy. "The words are these, 'Ye are come to Mount Zion, to the City of the living God, to the heavenly Jerusalem, and to an innumerable company of Angels, to the general assembly and Church of the first-born, which are written in heaven, and to God the Judge of all, and to the spirits of just men made perfect' " (*Grace Abounding*, p. 82).

These words are the very type of the arrival, the maturity, the assurance and acceptance Bunyan had so long been seeking, but the scriptural analogy has been wrested like a statue from the stony substance of Bunyan's life. The same words appear at the culmination of *Pilgrim's Progress*, as Bunyan attempts to recreate the drama of his personal experience in a more universal form: " 'There,' said they, 'is Mount Zion, the Heavenly Jerusalem, the innumerable company of angels, and the spirits of just men made perfect; you are going there now' "[17] (*Pilgrim's Progress*, p. 200). He has learned how to achieve his climax in writing his autobiography, and he has also learned there how to construct an emotionally resonant landscape. His living saints are placed on unassailable mountaintops, and his road is surrounded with a wall that can legally be penetrated only by passing through a narrow wicker gate—all features reminiscent of his Bedford vision.[18] There can be little doubt that this vision is a prototype of the allegorical technique of Bunyan's novel, a technique which seems to be extended to encompass what was originally realistic, psychological detail in his autobiography. Bunyan's experience, for example, of being "imprisoned" by doubts and moments of despair becomes the imprisoning of the man of despair in Interpreter's house and the dungeons of Doubting Castle.[19] Bunyan also uses the rhythm of false rest, trial, and achievement that formed the epistemological structure of his conversion to give authenticity and dramatic density to Christian's journey. Having surmounted Hill Difficulty and received his scroll of election, Christian falls asleep, "pleasing himself," and nearly loses his certificate of election as a result. Throughout the pilgrimage, tempting opportunities for rest, such as the Enchanted Ground, stand ready to waylay the unwary traveler. But, as in the autobiography, those who merely go along with the general tenor of the journey, taking the easy route through By-Path Meadow, will later have no defense against Diffidence and Giant Despair when they are plunged into the cells of Doubting Castle.

But *Pilgrim's Progress* also goes beyond the experiences recorded in *Grace Abounding*. Its cycle of conversion, ministry, and persecution seems to terminate when Christian is imprisoned in Vanity, with only half of the novel complete.[20] The cycle is repeated in the spiritual development of Hopeful, but most of the latter portions of the novel concern the problems and rewards of Christian's perseverence, long after the drama of his conversion and persecution has subsided. He is sustained through this portion of his journey by Hopeful, who cheers his despondency with promises and memories. "Hopeful also would endeavor to comfort him, saying 'Brother, I see the Gate, and men standing to receive us. . . . These troubles and distresses that you go through in these waters are no sign that God had forsaken you, but are sent to try you whether you will call to mind that which heretofore you have received of his goodness, and live upon him in your distresses' " (*Pilgrim's Progress*, p. 199). His hope, therefore, is what aids him in the trials of the mature saint: dullness in the Enchanted Ground; encounters with the outer world (in the form of Atheist and Ignorance) which jeers at impracticality, legality, and constancy; and the threat of apostasy, in Turn Away and Temporary.

The chief dangers of maturity appear to be society and jaded perception. The private horrors of demonic temptations and secret thoughts which fill *Grace Abounding* give way in the latter half of Bunyan's novel to evils of a public and social nature. The trial at Vanity is one such instance of pettiness and corruption in corporate life. The duties and responsibilities of the good man also become more complex, and the consequences of his sins communal. As it is stated in the marginal notes when Christian persuades his companion to join him in By-Path Meadow, "Strong Christians may lead weak ones out of the way" (p. 149). The danger of becoming hardened and insensate, however, is so great that it calls forth a special note by the dreamer himself, the only such commentary in the entire novel:

> When saints do sleepy grow, let them come hither,
> And hear how these two pilgrims talk together:
> Yea, let them learn of them, in any wise
> Thus to keep ope their drowsy eyes.
> Saints' fellowship, if it be managed well.
> Keeps them awake, and that in spite of Hell.
> [*Pilgrim's Progress*, p. 176]

Thus the potential evils of society are balanced with the potential good of fellowship.

But if the novel does go beyond the autobiography, it does so in part because of problems and possibilities made visible only through the act of writing the autobiography. In *Grace Abounding*, Bunyan encounters his trials alone and his isolation exacerbates his suffering. "Thus being afflicted and tossed about by my sad condition, I counted my self alone" (*Grace Abounding*, p. 28). Bunyan writes his autobiography in part to convince those who are suffering in a similar fashion that they are not alone, that their guilty fears are not without precedent, and that their anxieties, like Bunyan's before them, may be borne if not overcome. The value of fellowship, as communication of one's hopes and fears, and the importance of a vital memory are things which the autobiographical act itself might have revealed to Bunyan. As Hopeful helps keep his companion alert and spiritually strong by recounting the story of his own conversion—a story which closely resembles Bunyan's own—so Bunyan approaches his own audience and cheers himself as well by writing *Grace Abounding.* "I have sent you here enclosed a drop of that honey that I have taken of the Carcase of a *Lyon* (Judg. 14. 5, 6, 7, 8). I have eaten thereof my self also, and am much refreshed thereby" (*Grace Abounding*, p. 1).

Writing the first draft of his autobiography from his prison cell, Bunyan sifts his memory for evidence, for proofs of God's favor that will outweigh what he now experiences. At every stage of the journey to the Promised Land in his later allegory, Bunyan's pilgrims are asked to recall their encounters and to thereby strengthen their hold on the evidences of Grace, reenacting the process Bunyan had learned to value through his own "sad experience." It is significant that Christian forgets to mention the man caged in despair when he recites his experiences at Interpreter's House for the women at the Place Beautiful, since he himself later falls prey to Despair in the dungeons of Doubting Castle. In fact, the time he spends at the Castle exactly parallels the time spent at Palace Beautiful, suggesting that he is being punished not only for straying into By-Path Meadow, but for his earlier failure of memory. The problem of apostasy which dominates the latter half of the novel is also treated as a failure of memory, since apostates "shun the thoughts of guilt and terror, therefore, when once they are rid of their awakenings about the terrors and wrath of God they harden their hearts gladly. . . . They draw off their thoughts from the remembrance of God, death, and judgment to come" (*Pilgrim's Progress,* p. 194).

One can thus also consider *Grace Abounding* as Bunyan's own struggle against such hardening of heart, an *ars memoria* which deliberately inflicts pain upon its author as often as it induces pleasure. Each time he revises and reissues the work, he reawakens the guilt and terror that originally inspired him, and this memory will keep him constant. Remembering, of course, could easily be done in private, but autobiography has the additional advantage of encouraging others to remember as well. "Remember, I say, the Word that first laid hold upon you; remember you terrours of conscience, and fear of death and hell: remember also your tears and prayers to *God;* yea, how you sighed under every hedge for mercy" (*Grace Abounding*, p. 3).

And so John Bunyan becomes exemplary in another sense, not only for what he recalls but for how he recalls it. The very tensions and gaps of his narrative acquire significance as demonstrations of where to seek and what to discount in a pious self-examination. One obvious irrelevancy, judging from how it is treated in the autobiography, is chronology. After a more or less orderly succession of events leading up to his justification, Bunyan's tale suddenly breaks off: "Now I shall go forward to give you a relation of other of the Lord's dealings with me, of his dealings with me at sundry other seasons" (*Grace Abounding*, pp. 78–79). There is no way of telling whether these "sundry other seasons" precede or follow what he has already told, and the chronology becomes even more confused when he moves on to describe his ministry and imprisonment. "I went my self in chains to preach to them in chains" (p. 85), he tells us, suggesting that he is still undergoing the anguish of his conversion, although apparently he became a preacher only after it was complete.

Bunyan arranges his autobiography according to topic rather than time, distributing the events in his life under various headings and assigning a number to each separate paragraph to facilitate cross-reference. His conjunctions, and the plethora of "therefores" and "yets," stress the logical rather than temporal coherence of his work. He thus sees no problem in adding new material out of sequence when he revises it.[21] For Bunyan, his life unfolds in terms of a supermundane sequence of devotional stages rather than in mundane sequences of days, weeks, and years. Events as they are experienced in the chronology of this world are meaningless; at best, time measures only the duration and the quantity of pain, the ongoing process of "my castings down." To achieve their true meaning, experiences must be ripped from their temporal context and reevaluated in terms of a divine scheme. Up to the very end of his book, Bunyan can be seen struggling against the flux and the chaos of the world of appearances, seeking to force it into the fixed and eternal categories of divine logic: "These things I continuallie see and feel . . . yet the Wisdom of God doth order them for my good."

Grace Abounding is the story of Bunyan's increasing capacity for discerning God's order and bringing it to light in appropriate manner. Each stage of his spiritual development features a paragraph or more which illustrates his hermeneutic skill, the kind of analysis reflecting the degree of sophistication the aspiring convert has achieved. We can therefore see Bunyan growing toward the exegetical skill he will need when he finally becomes the itinerant preacher who addresses us from the preface of the autobiography. There are definite levels of interpretive method along the way, as definite as the steps of a Calvinist conversion. When he has reached conviction of human depravity, we see his first halting attempts at biblical exegesis: "I was also made about this time to see something concerning the Beasts that Moses counted clean, and unclean. I thought those Beasts were types of men" (*Grace Abounding*, p. 23).

The method is allegorical, the same he has used in analyzing his vision of the Bedford saints, and the same he will use again in *Pilgrim's Progress*. But while this is a method sufficient for the purposes of inexperienced or unwilling Christians, it will not do for a preacher or for an act in which he displays himself to his fellows and to his God. According to Bunyan's contemporary, the Puritan cleric William Perkins, the preacher must "diligently imprint . . . by the helps of disposition either axiomaticall, or syllogisticall, or methodicall the severall proofs and applications of the doctrines, the illustrations of the applications, and the order of them all. . . . Artificiall memorie, which standeth upon places and images . . . is not to be approved."[22]

It is not until Bunyan has been justified that he achieves this truly methodical, Ramistic hermeneutic.[23] Appropriately enough, the passage he expounds is Paul's discussion of the reprobate Esau which had filled him with overwhelming terror for two years on end. Now, however, Bunyan demonstrates that his terror was the result of his ignorant attempt to reason by analogy rather than axiom:

but now, I say, I began to take some measure of incouragement, to come close to them, to read them, and consider them, and to weigh their scope and tendency. . . . I found their visage changed, for they looked not so grimly on me as before I thought they did: . . . I found that the falling there intended was a falling *quite away*; that is, as I conceived, a falling from, and an absolute denial of, the Gospel of Remission of sins by Christ: for from them the apostle joins his argument, *ver.* 1, 2, 3. Secondly I found that this falling away must be openly, even in the view of the World, even so as *to put Christ to open shame*. Thirdly, I found that those he there intendeth were for ever shut up of God both in blindness, hardness, and impenitency: *It is impossible they should be renewed again unto repentence*. By all these particulars, I found, to Gods everlasting praise, my sin was not the sin in this place intended. [*Grace Abounding*, p. 70]

The text is fragmented, arranged under numerical headings—"secondly," "thirdly,"—and subjected to a rigorous series of proofs and applications point by point. Some eight paragraphs are given over to this demonstration, and Bunyan later argues that the capacity for Ramistic analysis rather than imagistic interpretation was the chief "advantage" gained from his long and harrowing conversion experience. "I was greatly beaten off my former foolish practice, of putting by the Word. . . . Now also I should labour to take the word as God had laid it down, without restraining the natural force of one syllable thereof" (*Grace Abounding*, p. 77).

At the point when he comprehends the scriptures according to their natural force, Bunyan has achieved his identity. Although other trials await him, the man who can thus analyze Hebrews is the same man who writes *Grace Abounding*. The form of the autobiography, in fact, with its numbered paragraphs and topical headings, is another instance of the same interpretive method. The conclusion makes this explicit, as Bunyan reexamines his experiences with "places and images" stripped away, fragmenting his life and applying its lessons as though it were yet another text. Of his afflictions, he now states: "1. They make me abhor myself; 2. They keep me from trusting my heart; 3. They convince me of the insufficiency of all inherent righteousness" (*Grace Abounding*, p. 103).

External and internal, active and contemplative aspects of his life are here reduced to a single plane, personal sensations and private anxieties becoming a newer testament from which Bunyan extracts the message for his autobiographical sermon. Using his life as text, Bunyan earns the right to make typological comparisons between himself and figures such as Samson and Moses, comparisons which might otherwise seem narcissistic or even sinful in their pride. It is proper, given the tendency of his autobiography as a whole, that Bunyan's last chapter should concern his imprisonment, whatever the chronological distortion. As a prisoner for the sake of his religion, Bunyan's entire existence takes on the status of an exemplum: "Indeed, I did often say in my heart before the Lord, "That if to be hanged up presently before their eyes, would be a means to awaken them, and confirm them in the truth, I gladly should be contented" (*Grace Abounding*, p. 87).

In prison, his sphere of action is identical with his sphere of contemplation; he is physically constrained to the passive activities of observation, expectation, and memory—the very activities which go into the autobiographical act itself. His greatest triumph in prison is his discovery that he can cling to his faith through will alone, when no further visitations of Grace come upon him, when he is empty of images and even emotion. "I will leap off the Ladder even blindfold into Eternitie, sink or swim, come heaven, come hell; Lord Jesus, if thou wilt catch me, do; if not, I will venture for thy Name" (*Grace Abounding*, p. 101). The autobiography concludes at that point at which Bunyan's life seems to have achieved some coherent purpose as a lesson for himself and for others. In the paragraphs that immediately follow this triumphant declaration, the lesson is rendered in a form free from all corporeal accidents and carnal imagery, a form that will impress itself upon the memory of those to whom it is addressed.[24] And the chief of these is the autobiographer himself, who must struggle constantly with his own tendency to distraction, despair, and forgetfulness: "I find to this day seven abominations in my heart: 1. Inclinings to unbelief, 2. Suddenlie to forget the love and mercie that Christ manifesteth. . . .5. To forget to watch for that I pray for" (*Grace Abounding*, p. 102).

The strain of effort is visible throughout *Grace Abounding*, down to the very modal verbs Bunyan uses. His capacity and his intense consciousness of obligation, what he "can" and "cannot" express, what he "must" do, is always on display, nor is this inartistic or irrelevant to the purposes of his autobiography. His novel, however, is quite another matter; there a strained or willful narration would intrude between reader and representation. The allegory allows Bunyan to restructure mundane time and space so that it is no longer necessary to impose an extrinsic, spiritual order upon his material. The road upon which the pilgrims travel provides an absolute standard, and the significance of any place or event can immediately be measured with respect to it. There is no need for topical headings or numbered paragraphs, no need to interrupt the narrative to propound the meaning of an event; the religious implications of any action or state of being are evident from the distance one must travel off the road to encounter them or the fate of the characters that represent them. Formalist, Hypocrisy, and By-Ends, for example, are never "seen again in the way" after going over to Lucre Hill. Bunyan can allow far more autonomy to the characters he creates than to the characters he remembers, since they are environed so clearly by the Celestial Journey. As a result, there is far more direct discourse in *Pilgrim's Progress* than in his autobiography. Indeed, during the later stages of their journey, Christian and Hopeful take over the task of narrating the book, telling tales within the larger tale, as they attempt to keep alert crossing the Enchanted Ground. Characters can act out their attributes through the texture and the content of their own directly reported words:

Christian. . . . therefore am I going this way, as I told you, that I may be rid of my burden.
Wordly-Wiseman. Who bid thee go this way to be rid of they burden? . . . I beshrew him for his counsel . . . hear me, I am older than thou! . . . it is happened unto thee as to other weak men, who meddling with things too high for them, do suddenly fall into thy distractions. [*Pilgrim's Progress*, pp. 48–49]

Here, while Christian modestly addresses Wordly-Wiseman with the formal second-person plural, his interlocutor immediately asserts his authority by adopting the familiar mode of address. Bunyan does not trust implicit satire in his autobiography unless the target is his own former self. "I fell to some outward Reformation, both in my words and life, and did set the Commandments before me for my way to Heaven: which Commandments I also did strive to keep; and, as I thought, did keep them pretty well sometimes, and then I should have comfort; yet now and then I should break one, and so afflict my Conscience; but then I should repent, and say I was sorry for it, and promise God to do better next time" (*Grace Abounding*, p. 12). The comedy of manners in this passage, the woefully inappropriate diminutives "pretty well" and the casual obedience of "do better next time," is extremely rare in the autobiography, however. In most cases, the only authorized speakers, aside from Bunyan, are Satan and the scriptures, and with neither of them is joking possible. This is the drama of Bunyan, his tempter, and the literal Word of God; all other voices are swallowed and screened through Bunyan's perception of them. "Wife, said I, is there ever such a Scripture, *I must go to Jesus*? She said she could not tell" (*Grace Abounding*, p. 82).

Thus it is the implications of the autobiographical act, as well as the fictional landscape, which make *Grace Abounding* so different in its narrative technique. The various levels of the text, narrator and narrated, must be welded into the shape of a single personality. In the allegory, Bunyan is free to introduce the portraits of ignorance and knowledge, piety and irreverence in any order he pleases, or to show them at work simultaneously; but in his autobiography ignorance must be shown giving way to spiritual maturity. "But poor Wretch as I was, I was all this while ignorant of Jesus Christ, and going about to establish my own righteousness, had perished therein, had not God in mercy shewed me more of my state by nature" (*Grace Abounding*, p. 14). In the novel, Ignorance, vain of his own moral probity and unconscious of his innate depravity, does perish indeed, thrown to hell at almost the final moment from the very portals of heaven.

The identity between author, narrator, and protagonist which is a necessary part of Bunyan's autobiography is unwoven in *Pilgrim's Progress*; the adventures of Christian and his fellow pilgrims are observed and interpreted by the marginal notes. Bunyan himself transcends the text, replaced by these mediaries. It is because of this that he can indulge his carnal imagination, since the fanciful imagery belongs to another voice, one for which Bunyan is not directly responsible. Images are also sanctioned because the marginal notes assure their appropriate interpretation. No ambiguity, no polysemy is involved; the novel simultaneously describes and expounds. In *Grace Abounding*, however, Bunyan must take great care with his figures of speech: "In my preaching I have really been in pain, and have as it were *travelled* to bring forth Children to God" (*Grace Abounding*, p. 89). This kind of caution is unnecessary when he is no longer speaking in his own person, no longer confined to speaking "as it were": "The man whose picture this is is one of a thousand; he can beget children, travail in birth" (*Pilgrim's Progress*, p. 60).

Moreover, it is in the nature of the dreamer's act that he cannot be made responsible for what he reports. He is merely a faithful and even a somewhat naive observer. The notes must often translate his innocent remarks into more orthodox terminology. What were figurative values in *Grace Abounding* are in a way quite literal in *Pilgrim's Progress*; the

emotional qualities of what are earlier described as "storms" of affliction become actual cloudbursts in the dream. The dreamer does nothing
more that "see" and "hear"—verbs of experience rather than agency,
which cast no reflection on his power of discrimination or selection.
Episodes of the dream succeed one another effortlessly before his eyes.
At times he even seems to disappear from the narrative altogether.

But the autobiography would fall into meaningless fragments without the energies and personality of its author-narrator. He is omnipresent, welding chapter to chapter, forming the bridge between paragraphs and even sentences, constantly calling attention to himself and
the task he performs. As an empirical observer, he must do more than
simply experience; he must deliberately focus his attention and
"watch." Even his memory is treated as a voluntary faculty, while the
name he most frequently applies to his act, "speaking" or "saying,"
makes his grammatical role as an agent unequivocal. This insistence on
seeing himself as able to exert control over his autobiography is in
marked contrast to his perception of himself in other contexts. When
he is not watching or speculating about his fate, Bunyan seems to find
himself the victim of his experiences. "A very great storm came down
upon me, which handled me twenty times worse than all I had met with
before: it came stealing upon me, now by one piece, then by another;
first all my comfort was taken from me, then darkness seized upon me"
(*Grace Abounding*, p. 31).

When much the same sort of storm appears in *Pilgrim's Progress*,
Christian is allowed the luxury of active engagement which Bunyan
himself could not attain. "And now it began to rain, and thunder, and
lighten in a very dreadful manner, and the water rose amain. . . . Yet
they adventured to go back; but it was so dark, and the flood so high,
that in their going back, they had like to have been drowned nine or ten
times" (*Pilgrim's Progress*, p. 151). In the fictional world, it is possible
to confront and combat the demons of humiliation and blasphemous
delusions as things clearly distinct from one's own soul.[25] Bunyan's
reality is far more cruel; the self has more ambiguous boundaries than
the character. Often, unable either to accept or dissociate the "secret
thoughts" he has experienced, Bunyan perceives himself as the ground
of some furious spiritual battle, traversed by alien forces that meet
within him. "They boulted both upon me at a time, and did work and
struggle strangly in me for a while" (*Grace Abounding*, p. 67). "But one
day, as I was passing through a field, and that too with some dashes on
my Conscience, fearing lest yet all was not right, suddenly this sentence
fell upon my Soul, *Thy righteousness is in Heaven*" (*Grace Abounding*,
p. 72).

The transition between the man thus victimized by life and the man
capable of shaping and defining his life in *Grace Abounding* could not

be made unassisted. Bunyan's religious convictions do not artificially circumscribe his identity; rather, they seem to provide the only possible foundation for attaining it. By joining himself with Job and David, Bunyan can experience himself as a martyr rather than as a vague and wounded consciousness. Using the words and the postures of the Bible as his own, he can become heroic rather than helpless. "Many more of the Dealings of God towards me I might relate, but these out of the spoils won in Battel have I dedicated to maintain the house of God, I *Chron.* 26.27" (*Grace Abounding*, p. 101). This is not to say that Bunyan thereby deludes himself into demanding the prerogatives of a Hebrew king. Instead of confusing historical realities, Bunyan uses the analogy to gain detachment from his own reality by reducing it to a piece of biblical text, which he can then interpret. He is no longer a victim but the recipient of a lesson engraved upon his experience. Hallucinations are transformed into communication: "I was much followed by this scripture, *Simon, Simon, behold Satan hath desire to have you*, Luk. 22.31. And sometimes it would sound so loud within me, yea, and as it were call so strongly after me, that once above all the rest, I turned by head over my shoulder, thinking verily that some man had behind me called to me . . . it came as I have thought since to have stirred me up to prayer and to watchfulness. It came to acquaint me that a cloud and a storm was coming down upon me, but I understood it not" (*Grace Abounding*, p. 30).

The dreamer and the marginal notes which jointly conduct the narration of *Pilgrim's Progress* have no natural attachment to the events they relate and the characters they describe, making a strategy for detachment of this sort unnecessary. As a bystander, the dreamer observes Christian's actions but has only indirect access to his subjective reactions: " 'Twas also observed that he was troubled with apparitions of hobgoblins and evil spirits, for ever and anon he could intimate so much by words" (*Pilgrim's Progress*, p. 199). An autobiographer would not need to qualify his statements about his hero's state of mind as the dreamer does: "and I think that Christian fell into a swound." But an autobiographer might, and in Bunyan's case does, experience a certain amount of ambivalence and some difficulty in maintaining a disinterested focus. At times Bunyan is overcome by his past experience to the point of finding his present attempts at description inadequate: "Oh! I cannot now express what then I saw and felt" (*Grace Abounding*, p. 58). The autobiographical act becomes infected with his former point of view, questioning or exclaiming as if that past were still alive. "What? thought I, is there but one sin that is unpardonable? Mercy, and must I be guilty of that? Must it needs be that? Is there but one sin among so many millions of sins, for which there is no forgiveness, and must I commit this? Oh! unhappy sin! Oh unhappy Man! These things would so break and confound my Spirit, that I could not tell what to do, I thought at times they would have broke my wits. . . . Oh! none knows the terrors of those days but myself" (*Grace Abounding,* p. 46). On the other hand, even when Christian is battling for his life in the Valley of Humiliation, the dreamer is not moved to raise his voice: "In this combat no man can imagine, unless he had seen and heard as I did, what yelling, and hideous roaring Apollyon made all the time of the fight; he spake like a dragon: and on the other side, what sighs and groans brast from Christian's heart" (*Pilgrim's Progress*, p. 94).

The emotional proximity between autobiographer and sufferer is also evident in the way temporal adverbs are used, Bunyan constantly using the formula, "now was I . . . " to introduce an adventure as if each isolated moment of his experience were the absolute center of his orientation. Often the narration changes to the present tense, although the events described are long since past. This is particularly true when Bunyan discusses his preaching and ministrations. This is, of course, the place where his past self merges with his present and sacrificial prisoner becomes autobiographer. That Bunyan still sees himself as a preacher and as one who remains engaged in his craft by writing his autobiography is apparent from the way he uses the present perfective: "I have also, while found in this blessed work of Christ, been often tempted to pride and liftings of heart" (*Grace Abounding*, p. 90).

At the close of *Grace Abounding*, it is impossible to distinguish between the self who writes and the self who is written about; the narrator who "finds to this day seven abominations in my heart" has become one with the content of the book. The autobiographer embraces his task and his destiny, almost joyously reaffirming his imprisonment: "I have seen that here, that I am persuaded I shall never, while in this world be able to express. . . . I never knew what it was for God to stand by me at all turns, and at every offer of Satan to afflict me, etc., as I have found him since I came hither" (*Grace Abounding*, pp. 96–97).

The world is contracted to this prison cell, and all movement measured according to it. It is an intensely private world, moreover, a personal space which Bunyan shares with no other man. Even his converts and followers are denied admission. "The Milk and Honey is beyond this Wilderness: God be merciful to you, and grant that you be not slothful to go in and possess the Land" (*Grace Abounding*, p. 4). Resigned and sublimely alone, Bunyan remains behind, gazing on from his own Mount Pisgah as his children pass over into the Promised Land.

The world which the characters of *Pilgrim's Progress* inhabit is just the reverse of this private one. The Way they follow is necessarily open; their success or failure in seeking it out and persisting in it is precisely what marks their spiritual capacity. There can be no question of anchoring the novel's space or time to any one character or even the dreamer—the Way exists before them all, and remains even after the hero has been assumed into heaven and the narrator awakes from his dream. Aside from their mutual journey, in fact, there is no other point where the experience of character and narrator coalesce. And it is a Way equally open to the readers of the novel. The dreamer may naively speak in the past tense, as though of an elapsed event, but the marginal notes make it clear that the rewards and the hazards of this journey are timeless. It is the function of the dreamer's tale to arouse others to the desire for a better world which he himself experienced at seeing the Celestial City; thus the progress of spiritual development must be something that begins afresh whenever the book is read. "This book will make a traveller of thee," according to its Apology, and the notes underscore the value of the allegory as a guide to the questions and problems of all potential wayfarers, not simply those recorded in the dream: "How to carry it to a fool" (p. 163); "How the apostate goes back" (p. 194).

The novel has ample room for its readers and makes ample narrative concessions to their interests. Since it is not an act of direct self-expression, the novel frees Bunyan from a dominant textual concern for the evidence for and against his own salvation. *Pilgrim's Progress* can give greater scope in its scheme of election and greater universality to its treatment of religious experience. More than one valid mode of conversion is possible. Hopeful, though no pioneering spirit, is as true a convert as any, and there are differences even in the awakenings of the patriarchs, Christian and Faithful. Each man experiences his own form of trial in the Valley of Humiliation, according to his individual vulnerabilities.[26] The distinction between these heroes and the narrator of the novel means that there is a bridge between those who successfully complete the journey and those hopeful believers in the audience who are just beginning the pilgrimage or struggling to continue it. The dreamer is escaped alone to tell us, and to prepare and inspire us for what we shall meet.

Unlike Christian, or Bunyan himself in his autobiography, the dreamer has no pretensions to being a seasoned convert with his rite of passage behind him, nor does he speak with the patriarchal voice of a religious leader. He has no apparent history or attributes of his own and experiences nothing that his audience does not experience as well. As a translucent narrator, only his witness and affect stand between us and the story he relates, and neither of these is particularly skillful or idiosyncratic. But if the dreamer has little identity beyond his first-person pronoun, this "I," at least, is always singular and so always distinct from the third person he uses for the characters he sees and the infrequent second person he addresses to his audience. But this is countered by the marginal notes to the novel, in which the inclusive "we" prevails, a first-person plural embracing characters, readers—all of humanity, in fact—as fellow participants in the pilgrimage.

> The pilgrims then, especially Christian, began to despond in his mind, and looked this way and that, but no way could be found by them by which they might escape the River.
>
> Death is not welcome to nature though by it we pass out of this world into glory.
>
> [*Pilgrim's Progress*, p. 198]

These notes are another kind of narration, a second-order observation of both the dreamer and his story, pointing out where, for example, there is "A brief relation of the combat by the spectator" (p. 94). They exist on a level of greater abstraction than that of the dreamer and deliver a more authoritative commentary. But the source of the notes themselves is unnamed, as is the act they perform. If the dreamer is translucent, then they are transparent—the place marks and interpretation they supply are in the public domain and blend imperceptibly into the act of reading itself.

The narrator of *Grace Abounding* cannot be anonymous in this way, nor does Bunyan seem to make any attempt at reducing the distance between himself and his audience. It is his identity, his uniqueness, after all, which is the principal warrant for writing an autobiography. His text is full of references to himself; it is subordinate to self. While the author's Apology to *Pilgrim's Progress* turns attention away from Bunyan and toward "this book," in *Grace Abounding* the focus of attention is always upon "me" and "my discourse." Nor is his identity only that of a narrator and spectator. He is "the chief of sinners," he is minister, martyr, and "God's servant"—any name, in fact, which applies to the religious occupations and roles he has publicly established for himself. As writer, he does not dissociate himself from the man who exists outside the text, but instead attempts to shape and define that extrinsic identity: "My Foes have mist their mark in this their shooting at me. I am not the man, I wish that they themselves be guiltless, if all the Fornicators and Adulterers in *England* were hang'd by the Neck till they be dead, *John Bunyan*, the object of their Envie, would be still alive and well" (*Grace Abounding*, p. 94).

Playing the role of an isolated patriarch, a man whose sufferings and accomplishments have made him exemplary and merged his life with biblical history, Bunyan establishes at best a loose analogy between his own and the reader's potential experience. In fact, he has martyred and made a display of himself in part so that others will avoid his experience. "And I do beseech thee, Reader, that thou learn to beware of my negligence, by the affliction that for this thing I did for days, and months, and years, with sorrow undergo" (*Grace Abounding*, p. 75).

This intimate invocation of the reader in his full individuality never recurs in the autobiography. Unlike the novel, where even the dreamer expresses intimacy and solidarity with his audience—"I have told my dream to thee" (p. 207)—Bunyan most often refers to them as a collective, as his "dear children" or the "weak and tempted People of God." Rather than making them participants in his autobiographical act, he handles them obliquely in the third person. "(And I am very confident, that this temptation of the Devil is more than usual amongst poor creatures then many are aware of, even to over-run their spirits with a scurvie and seared frame of heart, and benumming of conscience" (*Grace Abounding*, p. 11). Although the autobiography would seem to be his opportunity for establishing the communication and companionship he had so long suffered without, he never recognizes the immediate presence of his audience, and his communication is never reciprocal: "that night was a good night to me, I never had but few better; I longed for the company of some of Gods people, that I might have imparted unto them what God had showed me" (*Grace Abounding*, p. 82). Even in this passage, he speaks only of what "might have" occurred.

Of course, remembering is something one can only do for oneself, even if Bunyan intends thereby to encourage others to act in their own behalf. But the readers of the autobiography are rarely treated as potential actors and are instead constantly reminded of what Bunyan has done and continues to do for their benefit. They are "told" and "shown" what he would have them see, and they make no apparent contribution of their own. This is a distinct thing indeed from the treatment he gives the audience of his novel, where at the conclusion each reader is invited to perform his own act of interpretation: "Put by the curtains, look within my veil;/Turn up my metaphors, and do not fail" (*Pilgrim's Progress*, p. 207).

The novel has its own means for regulating the activities of its readers through the unobtrusive device of its marginal notes. Bunyan has no such way of controlling responses in his autobiography, aside from occasionally stepping out of himself to look back at what he has said as though he were the average member of his own audience. "These things may seem ridiculous to others, even as ridiculous as they were in themselves, but to me they were most tormenting cogitations" (*Grace Abounding*, p. 57). Although he recognizes that some portion of his experience must remain incommunicable, he is too urgently involved with it to deny it even for the sake of gaining the trust of his audience. He also recognizes that there are those in his audience who already distrust him. His autobiography will necessarily attract his personal and sectarian enemies as well as his followers and those who are sympathetic to his cause. "So then, what shall I say to those that have thus bespattered me? Shall I threaten them? Shall I chide them? shall I flatter them? shall I intreat them to hold their tongues? . . . beg relief of no man: believe, or disbelieve me in this, all is a case to me" (*Grace Abounding*, p. 94).

It is true that Bunyan does not, indeed refuses to, address his accusers directly, and in the presence of hostility indirection would not seem an unnatural tactic. "The Philistines understand me not," as his preface states darkly (and somewhat incorrectly), invoking the riddles of Samson. Yet though he seldom calls upon his audience or asks them more than an occasional rhetorical question, he is less hesitant to command them. This same riddling preface is full of imperatives directed at friend and enemy alike. His defiance in the face of those he foresees as attacking his work is surely explicit enough. "He that liketh it, let him receive it and he that does not, let him produce a better" (*Grace Abounding*, p. 4).

No doubt, it is partly the anxious self-interest associated with his autobiography which allows Bunyan no possible compromise with his critics that will not also compromise himself. He has no such qualms about placating or even seducing readers in his novel.

> Yet fish there be, that neither hook, nor line,
> Nor snare, nor net, nor engine can make thine;
> They must be groped for, and be tickled too,
> Or they will not be catched, what e'er you do.
>
> [*Pilgrim's Progress*, p. 33]

It is expected, though, that even the most hostile or unworthy reader undergoing the experience of the novel will be transformed by it: "it will make the slothful active be,/The blind also delightful things to see" (p. 37). All that is required of those who come to the allegory is that which can be found in almost any man—curiosity and a healthy concern for his own welfare.

Bunyan therefore feels he can be confident of how the world will receive his fiction, but such is not the case with *Grace Abounding*. Even the response of the godly appears less than certain. "At large I shall not here discourse; onely give you, in a hint or two, a word that may stir up the Godly to bless God and pray for me, and also take encouragement, should the case be their own" (*Grace Abounding*, p. 96). No man but Bunyan himself can possess all the experiences and particular attributes which make his work comprehensible and give it its full emotional and didactic value. But this does not mean that Bunyan has no need for readers. Putting his case before an audience, even if only in imagination, is a test of his evidence and a sign that what he thus lays open to the verification of others has the status of empirical fact. The responsibility he takes on is all the more awesome since he writes in the presence of an omniscient God who "doth know the most secret thoughts of the heart" (p. 76). Bunyan's insistence on "speaking his experience," words which treat his act as an oral public performance, turns autobiography into assailable testimony. At times, the submerged metaphor rises to the surface and becomes nearly literal, as when he challenges those who have charged him with sexual misconduct: "To all which, I shall only say, God knows that I am innocent. But as for mine accusers, let them provide themselves to meet me before the tribunal of the Son of God, there to answer for these things" (*Grace Abounding*, p. 93).

Not merely facts are on trial, but John Bunyan himself. Yet he submits himself willingly, almost eagerly to the slurs and suspicions of his enemies. To be reviled by one's foes is almost as important to the posture of a partriarch as to fulfill the needs of one's followers or one's God. Bunyan derives an identity and an interpretable pattern for his life story by seeing himself surrounded in this way by deliberate animosities and overwhelming want. Divine necessity has transformed him from victim to communicant and example, while human responsibilities have turned his private endurance into a call to speak. "But I at first could not believe that God should speak by me to the heart of any man, still counting myself unworthy; yet those who were thus touched would love me . . . they would also bless God for me (unworthy Wretch that I am!) and count me Gods Instrument that shewed to them the Way of Salvation" (*Grace Abounding*, p. 85).

As God's instrument Bunyan achieves power over his experience, first as a preacher and then as an autobiographer. He is aware that his is only a qualified power, however, and jealously protects his privilege by acting as his own censor. "I think I verily may speak it without any offence to the Lord, nothing hath gone so near me as that" (*Grace Abounding*, p. 88). In addition to watching for what he may and may not speak, Bunyan persistently refers to the brevity with which he must treat the various topics he raises in his autobiography: "A brief relation of the exceeding mercy of God," "A brief account of the author's call," "A brief account of the author's imprisonment." Although this doubtless adds to the flavor of urgency in the text, written by a man who at any moment may be silenced by torture or execution, it is also a tribute on Bunyan's part to the limits of his divine sanction. There is no false humility in these gestures, but a genuine need to reconcile his own rhetorical powers with the omnipotence which alone guarantees them validity and purpose. "Christ can use these gifted men, as with them to affect the Souls of his People in his Church, yet when he hath done all hang them by as lifeless . . . his Gifts are not his own, but the Churches; and that by them he is made a Servant to the Church, and that he must give at last an account of his Stewardship unto the Lord Jesus, and to give a good account, will be a blessed thing!" (*Grace Abounding*, pp. 91–92). There can be no meaningful personal gifts without divine obligation, no certainty of himself and the value of his life without accountability.

Thus, to make *Grace Abounding* a "good account" of himself, Bunyan exerts rigid control over the content and the manner of his presentation. God will be watching. But Bunyan cannot make Him directly a party to his autobiography: "I hope I shall bless God for ever for the teaching I have had" (p. 101). Bunyan does not address the blessing to God; he only expresses his wish to do so. It is after all not for him to presume to impart the lessons of his experience to the power who authored them. Therefore, despite all the witnesses and eventual beneficiaries who are so necessary to his autobiographical act, Bunyan must constantly struggle alone. The "dear Children" of his preface have entirely disappeared from his conclusion, and the final remarks seem applicable only to Bunyan: "7. These things I continuallie see and feel, and am afflicted and oppressed with; yet the Wisdom of God doth order them for my good: 1. They make me abhor myself; 2. They keep me from trusting my heart; 3. They convince me of the insufficiencie of all inherent righteousness; 4. They shew me the necessity of flying to Jesus; 5. They press me to pray unto God; 6. They show me the need I have to watch and be sober; 7. And provoke me to look to God thorow Christ to help me, and carry me thorow this world. *Amen*" (*Grace Abounding*, p. 103). This is both the sketch of a prayer for help and a lesson being committed to memory.

Bunyan cannot achieve here the perfect, transcendental resolution of his fiction, in which the dreamer can actually witness "just men made perfect." Christian is able to leave all carnal inclinations on the far side of the River of Death, but the autobiographer-hero must continue to encounter and abhor these elements in himself. "I can do none of those things which God commands me, but my corruptions will thrust in themselves; When I would do good, evil is present with me" (*Grace Abounding*, p. 103).

Yet there is resolution in *Grace Abounding*, even if it is in the form of a paradox. For prison frees Bunyan by confining those carnal corruptions which frustrate his will to be pure and without spiritual division. Bunyan's punishment is his reward, for it proves his capacity to sacrifice himself and removes forever what he calls the worst of all his temptations, "to question the being of God, and the truth of his Gospel" (p. 102). Here at last he discovers that his faith is sufficient, that he requires no further proof of either God or himself: "How now . . . is this the sign of an upright Soul, to desire to serve God for nothing rather then give out?"

CHAPTER THREE

==

JAMES BOSWELL: GENIUS AND STENOGRAPHY

==

> I find it is impossible to put upon paper an exact Journal of the
> life of Man. External circumstances may be marked. But the
> variations within, the workings of reason and passion, and what
> perhaps influence happiness most, the colourings of fancy, are
> too fleeting to be recorded.
>
> James Boswell

A century after Bunyan had used his autobiography to collect and
display the signs of an upright soul, their value as signs had been largely
eroded. This is not to say that there was no longer an interest in
descriptions of private lives and personal experiences; if anything, the
appetite for these had grown enormously as the reading public in
general, and the audience for English literature in particular, became
less aristocratic. But as one can see from the account James Boswell
gives of his own Calvinist childhood, Bunyan's instrumental psychology
had been superseded: "I shall never forget the dismal hours of appre-
hension that I have endured in my youth from narrow notions of
religion while my tender mind was lacerated with infernal horror. I am
surprised how I have got rid of these notions so entirely. Thank God,
my mind is now clear and elevated."[1] There is no purpose or message
hidden in Boswell's horrors and no divine intervention which has caused
their abatement. Although he attends carefully to his subjective experience, he provides no teleological explanation for either the lacerations
themselves or the attention he now accords them.

For Boswell and the literary community surrounding him, sensibility and sensibilia were interesting in themselves. Affliction could be
observed and its causes pondered without a search for some larger,
transcendental meaning; a particular life could warrant attention without claiming exemplary value. Indeed, the life of a sinner might make
much better reading than the life of a saint for an audience bent more
on sensation than moral enlightenment. Authors like Daniel Defoe, who
had exploited the devices of autobiography while stripping them of
their religious connotations, had taught the reading public to isolate
and appreciate the representational density, emotional vitality, and
illusion of authenticity these devices could produce.[2] Particularity and
immediacy were not necessarily increased by didacticism or teleological

speculations. They might, in fact, be hampered by them, as Boswell points out in distinguishing between biographical fidelity and panegyric in his preface to the *Life of Johnson*. "And he will be seen as he really was: for I profess to write not his panegyrick, which must be all praise, but his Life . . . when I delineate him without reserve, I do what he himself recommended, both by his precept and his example."[3]

Autobiography did not require peculiar literary sanctions, then, if readers existed ready to applaud the skillful transmission of domestic details and curious enough to tolerate almost any sensational revelation. But if autobiography no longer needed divine sanction and was no longer limited to exemplary lives, then much of the meaning of the autobiographical act had been lost. The urgency associated with self-display, the cosmic reassurance it offered a man like Bunyan, disappeared when the empirical facts of one's life could not be treated as evidence of superiority or of divine election. The aesthetic effects of a realistic novel could barely be distinguished from autobiography, and if only these technical achievements mattered, why risk self-exposure? If authenticity and verifiability were the dominant values, then biography would serve as well as autobiography. In the published writings of both Boswell and Samuel Johnson, autobiography and biography are classed together, although autobiography is given a slight advantage because the writer possesses more information about his subject. "Had Johnson written his own life, in conformity with the opinion he has given, that every man's life may be best written by himself; had he employed in the preservation of his own history, that clearness of narration and elegance of language in which he has embalmed so many eminent persons, the world would probably have had the most perfect example of biography that was ever exhibited" (*Life*, p. 19).

In this case, for Johnson and Boswell both, precept did not agree with example. Each may have preached a merely quantitative distinction between autobiography and biography, but in practice neither could accept this simplification. Johnson *had* written his own life; but despite his great skill and eminence as a biographer of literary men much like himself, his "memorials" were deliberately consigned to the flame just before his death. Boswell records receiving the same advice from Johnson with regard to his own journal: "He said indeed that I should keep it private, and that I might surely have a friend who would burn it in case of my death" (*London Journal*, p. 305). If the published remarks of both men treat biography and autobiography as the same phenomenon, then it is a flaw or a gap in the critical vocabulary available to them. As writers, Johnson and especially Boswell were in the midst of acting out what their criticism could not yet articulate.

Autobiography lacked not only a finished critical language but also an appropriate form. Hagiography and Calvinist categories were no longer suitable when the genre lost its religious implications. The journal was an ad hoc solution to this formal dilemma. However unformed journals may seem to a twentieth-century audience, the audience for which they were originally intended often accepted them as finished pieces rather than propaedeutic devices for autobiographies yet to be written.[4] In Boswell's day, journals were perhaps the most common form of autobiographical publication. Since Boswell's journals are therefore in some ways representative of what was already read and produced all around him, his decision to withhold publication of his own journals does not reflect formal embarrassment or the expectation of revising them in some more polished way.

Indeed, Boswell was extremely conscious of the literary merit of his journals, and of his *London Journal, 1762–1763*, in particular. Portions of this journal were dispatched in regular packets to his friend John Johnston in Scotland, and the letters accompanying the serialized journal indicate how severe and disinterested Boswell would like the critical response of his reader to be: "It would oblige me much if you would sit down and write a character of my Journal, just as it would appear to you, if written by an indifferent Person. . . . Tell me when I inadvertently insert things that ought not be written."[5] Although recognizing that it is not reputable literature in the eyes of Samuel Johnson or other members of his father's generation, Boswell cautiously maintains his own position on the subject of journalizing. Johnston serves him as a surrogate public, an audience which must be moved from its indifference by the quality of the work and not by affection for its author.

Boswell shrank from destroying his journal despite Samuel Johnson's personal admonition. "I have at present such an affection for this my journal that it shocks me to think of burning it. I rather encourage the idea of having it carefully laid up among the archives of Auchinleck" (*London Journal*, p. 305). There is even evidence to suggest that he might have attempted publication during his own lifetime had he not feared disinheritance.[6] But he certainly was always aware of writing for some audience, whether Johnston, his heirs, or some larger posterity. The literary autonomy of the *London Journal* is increased by the formal introduction he provides for it, from which one could never infer that this is actually the second in a continuing series of journals kept by Boswell between 1762 and 1765.[7] "A man cannot know himself better than by attending to the feelings of his heart and to his external actions, from which he may with tolerable certainty judge 'what manner of person he is.' I have therefore determined to keep a daily journal in which I set down my various sentiments and my various conduct, which will be not only useful but very agreeable" (*London Journal*, p. 39).

Although a daily record of this sort might seem to be a casual affair, there is ample proof that Boswell engaged in deliberate calculations to maintain his day-by-day perspective. For example, when he writes a post factum account of his first symptoms of a venereal disease, he does not write in the spirit of what he has later discovered but in terms of what he then only feared: "I this day began to feel an unaccountable alarm of unexpected evil: a little heat in the members of my body sacred to Cupid, very like a symptom of that distemper which Venus, when cross, takes it into her head to plague her votaries. But then I had run no risks. I had been with no woman but Louisa; and sure she could not have such a thing. Away then with such idle fears, such groundless, uneasy apprehensions!" (*London Journal*, p. 149). His questions and reaffirmations are oriented in his earlier ignorance. He willfully exposes himself, exclaiming his hyperbolic trust in the honor of his beloved, to the irony of later events. As John Morris remarks in his appreciation of Boswell's autobiographical art: "Often . . . he *does* know a little of the future, for he posts his Journal a week or so at a time . . . but Boswell does not permit that later knowledge to intrude on his record of the past. He is constantly and consciously true to the event as it was. Boswell's deliberate efforts to compel the moment to exist in his pages, no matter how foolish or wrong the record of it may later show him to have been, asserts his intuition of the dignity of the fleeting data of consciousness as the prime, irreducible elements of reality."[8]

Boswell also uses the calendar as a structural device in a work he did publish, his famous biography of Johnson. But here the ironies are never chronological. Instead, he achieves his dramatic effects by manipulating his audience's anticipation of the inevitable Johnsonian response to some word or event.

Mr. Davies mentioned my name, and respectfully introduced me to him. I was much agitated; and recollecting his prejudice against the Scotch, of which I had heard much, I said to Davies, "Don't tell where I come from."—"From Scotland," cried Davies roguishly. "Mr. Johnson, (said I) I do indeed come from Scotland, but I cannot help it." I am willing to flatter myself that I meant this as light pleasantry to smooth and conciliate him, and not as an humiliating abasement at the expense of my country. But however that might be, this speech was somewhat unlucky; for with that quickness of wit for which he was so remarkable, he seized upon the expression "come from Scotland," which I used in the sense of being of that country, and, as if I had said that I had come away from it, or left it, retorted, "That, Sir, I find, is what a very great many of your countrymen cannot help." [*Life*, p. 277]

It is the logic of Johnson's character that controls Boswell's narrative strategies in his biography. Chronology merely helps to assure that the mass of Johnsonian "Memorabilia" and "Collecteana" he has assembled will be evenly distributed throughout the text. Often he violates his system of convenient chronological labels to insert material where otherwise there might be a gap in the narrative. Dating allows a memento of Johnson to be seen against its proper background, as a remark associated with a particularly productive year or behavior taking place during a season of ill health. "To know of what vintage our wine is, enables us to judge of its value, and to drink with more relish: but to have the produce of each vine of one vineyard, in the same year, kept separate, would serve no purpose" (*Life*, p. 753). Apparently Johnson affects the time, rather than time affecting Johnson. Dates are made important by virtue of the use Johnson made of them—what he did or what he wrote. His qualities and capacities do not develop or decay, but simply expose themselves on a particular day: "In 1739 . . . his writings in the *Gentleman's Magazine* were, 'The Life of Booerhaave,' in which it is to be observed, that he discovers that love of chymistry which never forsook him" (*Life*, p. 102).

The quite different use Boswell makes of his calendar in the *London Journal* is one of the marks of a distinction between autobiography and biography. The insistent diurnal rhythm of his journal is better adapted to what he himself called "fleeting variations," to the naked juxtaposition of minor or even trivial events, and to the even more evanescent forms of subjective experience, impressions and Lockean associations. In the journal, each day may serve as a locus of change. The scrupulous register of dates is in fact the journal's only measure of continuity and difference. Boswell prefers to allow implicit development in his autobiography, with only the date to inform us what are the causes and what the effects. He records, for example, a protracted fit of melancholy brought on by a visit to Oxford. In his account of the series of strained adventures following this visit, there is the implication that each is an attempt to throw off his melancholy, but he can overcome it only by forcing himself to attend a public execution and bringing himself to a state of near-total despair. The hanged man reminds him of Captain MacHeath, the hero of Gay's "Beggar's Opera" and Boswell's own personal symbol of urbane gaiety. Thus, when he reports that he is at last again able to see himself playing the role of MacHeath, we recognize that he has recovered indeed: "I toyed with them and drank about and sung "Youth's the Season" and thought myself Captain MacHeath" (*London Journal*, p. 264). But this emotional progress occurs without the announcements and additional commentary one finds in the *Life*; only the sequential schema of the journal itself indicates how the events are connected.

Boswell writes not only of his days but even of parts of each day, subdividing his daily report into an orderly sequence of breakfast, visits, tea, supper, and evening activities. He was a man who loved, or tried to love, regularity, and doubtless his journal is designed to impose as much as reflect an orderly life. "It will give me a habit of application and improve me in expression; and knowing that I am to record my transactions will make me more careful to do well. Or if I should do wrong, it will assist me in resolutions of doing better" (*London Journal*, p. 39). The subdivisions also serve him as mnemonic aids, keeping each day distinct in his mind. "I then called on Lord Eglinton—no, I mistake, it was yesterday that I was there. I am scrupulous to a nicety about truth" (*London Journal*, p. 163).

He does indeed point out each irregularity, zealously rooting up omissions and oversights wherever they occur. But it is more than just brute accuracy which concerns Boswell; it is his ability as autobiographer and man to maintain any plan he has set for himself. "What greater proof need be given of dissipation than my forgetting to mark in my journal of yesterday that the hours between one and three were passed in the Little Theatre in the Haymarket under the auspices of Mr. Foote?" (*London Journal*, p. 255). In the *Life of Johnson*, Boswell suppresses even the slightest indication of error or inaccuracy, and it is hard to imagine any biographer vaunting proofs of his own dissipation. But in autobiography, Boswell implicitly recognized that an admission of one's own objective errors becomes a courageous adherence to subjective truth. The form he has chosen thus serves as a grid upon which his "irregularities" will immediately stand out.

The journal is an instrument for measuring psychology, for catching Boswell unprepared or incapacitated and pondering the causes for this. Long before he openly discusses his anxieties about leaving London for an unfamiliar European environment, one can read his disturbance in the way he begins to misplace more and more events. As his journal draws to a close and he prepares for his upcoming tour of the Continent, he gives up entirely any attempt to record the objective sequence of remarks made by his then-new acquaintance, Samuel Johnson. "After this, I shall just mark Mr. Johnson's *Memorabilia* as they rise up in my memory" (*London Journal*, p. 320). He makes no pretense of writing upon another system; this is plainly a falling away from his system. But it is also an index of his power of memory, and this is as important in autobiography as anything he might actually remember. Again, in the words of John Morris: "On the one hand, there is the order of events as they actually occurred. . . . On the other hand, there is the order of Bowell's ideas at the time that he came to write his Journal . . . we sometimes find in Boswell another temporal dimension, which we may call 'Journal time.' "[9]

The minuteness of Boswell's temporal records, his concern for the juxtaposition of events and his fascination with transitions between states of being, clearly distinguish his autobiography from Bunyan's more abstract account of himself. Boswell is interested in his experiences because they are his, because they are the only things that are his. Lacking transcendental assurances and ultimate goals, his self is a process and never a final achievement. "Could I but fix myself in such a character," he cries at more than one point in his journal. Yet it would be mistaken to claim that there is therefore no pattern to be found in his journal. The structure of his adventures in London has a marvelous and canny narrative coherence—something one can see very well by opposing the journal to Boswell's later account of the same period of his life which appears in his biography of Johnson.

Obviously there are changes imposed by the different subject of each text. Boswell spent ten months in London, from 15 November 1762 until 3 August 1763, and his encounter with Johnson did not take place until the middle of May. In the *Life*, it is Boswell who enters late on the scene, long after Johnson has been established in both his career and the reader's eye. Boswell is but one of the many persons in Johnson's court throughout the rest of the biography, and he is tactfully dismissed from the narrative before the account of Johnson's death: "I now relieve the readers of this Work from any farther personal notice of its author, who if he should be thought to have obtruded himself too much upon their attention, requests them to consider the peculiar plan of his biographical undertaking" (*Life*, p. 1363). Boswell must necessarily omit from the biography all of the extraneous, non-Johnsonian material which fills his *London Journal*, but he goes further than mere omission. The *Life* turns Boswell's entire stay in London into a waiting period, an anguished desire to meet with Johnson or, having met him, to somehow remain in his presence and be constantly near him. The meeting is foreshadowed for several paragraphs describing how Boswell loiters aimlessly about the various homes and shops Johnson normally frequents until "at last" the encounter occurs. Their companionship continues until Johnson accompanies Boswell to the boat which will take him to Europe. But there is hardly a hint that it is actually Boswell who is bound on his own independent adventure. "As the vessel put out to sea, I kept my eyes upon him for a considerable time, while he remained rolling his majestick frame in his usual manner: and at last I perceived him walk back into the town, and he disappeared" (*Life*, p. 334). It seems to be Johnson who is departing from Boswell, while the younger man remains peering after him. In fact, the only motion in the scene belongs to Johnson; it is he who rolls his frame while the ocean itself is static.

Boswell's autobiographical account of his first meeting with Johnson is without foreshadowings, without even a paragraph of its own.

"Temple and his brother breakfasted with me. I went to Love's to recover some of the money which he owes me. But, alas, a single guinea was all I could get. He was just going out to dinner, so I stayed and eat a bit, though I was angry at myself afterwards. I drank tea at Davies's in Russell Street, and about seven came in the great Mr. Samuel Johnson, whom I have so long wished to see" (*London Journal*, p. 260). Although the encounter is only one in a list of Boswell's engagements that day—and not even first in that list—the role Johnson plays in the *London Journal* is actually crucial to Boswell. It is a role, however, subordinated to the rite of passage which Boswell confronts. The "great Mr. Johnson" has a symbolic value in the autobiography arising from his position as a literary giant and moral arbiter in the city to which Boswell has come to seek fame, maturity, and his first independence. The scene of Johnson bidding him farewell at the dock does not even appear in the *London Journal*, since Boswell has classed it with later adventures. This journal must end in the city, since it is the story of his attempt to conquer a great metropolis and to find an autonomous identity away from his family and his homeland.

The *Journal* thus logically begins with a picture of Boswell's departure from Edinburgh, taking the form of a ritual salute to the scenes he associates with his childhood: "I next stood in the court before the Palace, and bowed thrice to Arthur Seat, that lofty and romantic mountain on which I have so often strayed in my days of youth" (*London Journal*, pp. 41–42). Much the same ceremony is repeated at the close of Boswell's stay in London, giving symmetry and a sense of completion to his journal: "In the forenoon I was at a Quaker's meeting in Lombard Street, and in the afternoon at St. Paul's, where I was very devout and very happy. After service, I stood in the center and took leave of the church, bowing to every quarter. I cannot help having a reverence for it" (*London Journal*, p. 331). The site chosen for Boswell's formal farewell is significant, since it is now architecture and the values of urban life that he salutes, replacing his earlier allegiance to the romantic scenery of Scotland. In the Anglican cathedral he reverences as well a more worldly religion than the Calvinism in which he was raised, a church where one can be both "very devout" and "very happy" without guilt or self-mortification. Although he knows that his upcoming Grand Tour will return him to his father's home, eventually to join the Scottish bar and forever lose sight of his cosmopolitan dreams, he is nonetheless satisfied with his stay in the city. His time at London has been a period of development and not a spoiled escape.

Yet development cannot take the form of a simple progress; for Boswell it is always an arduous and perhaps endless dialectic. The thesis, in his *London Journal*, is Scotland: the provincial narrowness and rigid morality of his father, his own childish dependence, and the melancholy Boswell associates with the Scottish world view. The anti-thesis is London: wit, urbanity, and opportunities for "daliance"; an environment for meeting the great and the famous, where Boswell himself may gain fame; the scene of Addison's *Spectator* and Gay's "Opera," in which Captain MacHeath sounds the bold *carpe diem* which the ever-remorseful young Scotsman so envies. (Boswell even comes to London hoping to win his own commission in the Guards and a seraglio to rival MacHeath's.) Throughout the course of the journal, one sees Boswell vacillating between these symbolic oppositions, allying himself now with one group of friends, now with another, as he alternately pursues and disparages various schemes for his life.

I wanted much to be a man of consequence, and I considered that I could only be that in my own country, where my family connections would procure it. I also considered that the law was my plain road to preferment. . . . I would have an opportunity of being of much real use, of being of service to my friends by having weight in the country, and would make my father exceedingly happy. I considered that the law seemed to be pointed out by fate for me. [*London Journal*, p. 200]

The law scheme appeared in another light. I considered it as bringing me back to a situation that I had long a rooted aversion to. That my father might agree to let me be upon the footing of independence, but when he had me under his eye, he would not be able to keep it. . . . That the Guards was a situation of life that had always appeared most enchanting to me, as I could in that way enjoy all the elegant pleasures of the gay world, and by living in the Metropolis and having plenty of time, could pursue what studies and follow what whims I pleased, get a variety of acquaintances of all kinds, get a number of romantic adventures, and thus have my satisfaction of life. [*London Journal*, pp. 201–2]

The British aspirant in Boswell criticizes the Scotsman's provincial-ism, his rudeness of manner and indecorous conversation; the Scots loyalist counters by attacking the extravagence, the sexual debauchery, and the rootless triviality of the Londoner's life. On one hand there is Boswell's father—a man of small universal fame, but respected and powerful in his own circle. On the other is Lord Eglinton, a Scottish member of the British Court—the companion of princes and aristocratic wits, but as a man unreliable and dissipated.

It is into such opposition that Samuel Johnson enters, appearing to Boswell as the very model of a man at once firm in principle and richly cosmopolitan. Johnson offers him the chance for greatness without the need to rely on political favors and without debaucherous ties to men like Eglinton. Frustrated by his attempts to place himself in the shifting world of the Court, Boswell at last finds his opening and gratefully accepts a position in the more stable "court of Johnson": "I considered that I had now experienced how little I could depend on the favour of the great, which, when only founded on personal liking, is very slight. I considered too that I could have no prospect of rising in the Army.

That my being in that way contrary to my parents' advice was uphill work, and that I could not long be fond of it" (*London Journal*, p. 274).

Under Johnson's guidance and example, Boswell attempts to reconcile and strike a rational balance between his goals and his obligations. He will return to Scotland, but to a situation transformed by Johnson's promise of visits and his open invitation to see him in London whenever Boswell wishes. Thus Scotland has been rendered less remote from London and the "elegant pleasures of the gay world." His original plans have been largely destroyed by the end of the *London Journal*, and yet Boswell may justly feel that he has successfully "situated himself" in that city. The tie with Johnson means synthesis rather than total defeat: "I have been attaining knowledge of the world. I came to town to go into the Guards. How different is my scheme now! I am now upon a less pleasurable but a more lasting plan" (*London Journal*, p. 333). In almost the last breath of his journal, Boswell recognizes a world of imposed limitations, but he meets these limitations with a degree of philosophic resignation he has never before achieved. What better companion could he choose at this point than the author of "The Vanity of Human Wishes"?

Even a cursory examination of the *London Journal* would make one aware of how greatly Boswell has altered the meaning of this friendship in writing the biography of Johnson. In the *Life,* he is little more than an enthralled and will-less spectator who must receive Johnson's formal invitation before he dares to call on him. "He again shook me by the hand at parting, and asked me why I did not come oftener to him. Trusting that I was now in his good graces, I answered, that he had not given me much in encouragement, and reminded him of the check I had received from him at our first interview. 'Poh, poh! (said he, with a complacent smile), never mind these things. Come to me as often as you can. I shall be glad to see you' " (*Life*, p. 283). Although Boswell claims to have relied on his journals to create his biography—"From this habit I have been able to give the world so many anecdotes" (p. 307)—this particular anecdote is nowhere to be found. (Indeed, in his *London Journal*, Boswell proudly describes how he deliberately set out to "cultivate" Johnson's acquaintance.) Not only does Boswell ignore irrelevant autobiographical material, he even treats his moments away from Johnson as necessarily culpable. "I was at this time so occupied, shall I call it? or so dissipated, by the amusements of London, that our next meeting was not till Saturday June 25" (*Life*, p. 283). But what the biographer calls "dissipation" is merely concern for his own affairs in his original autobiographical record. The biographical character is allowed no such independent existence. His life is contained totally in Johnson's orbit, from which he is drawn only by duty or contemptible animal weakness.

It could never be said of this slavish fool, this predictable Boswell of the *Life*, what has often been remarked of the autobiographical hero: "one is struck by the lack of solidity and permanence in his idea of himself. . . . What he had to register as the very stock-in-trade of his journalizing was the discordant and gutsy waywardness of his emotional attitudes. . . . He was endlessly fascinated by the mere discontinuity of his orientations towards experience, and regarded the record of these changes as one of the most important features of his self-imposed task."[10] Nor could this be said of the portrait he gives us of Johnson himself. It is not, then, a matter of who is protagonist but of the genre in which he is writing. Without ever deserting biographical fact, Boswell modifies the locus and meaning of fact to reflect his different literary acts.

Biography, according to the preface of the *Life of Johnson*, is "an accumulation of intelligence from various points, by which . . . character is more fully understood and illustrated" (p. 22). Boswell treats "character" as an observable phenomenon, an impression created by an individual on those surrounding him. He even remarks on "how little a man knows, or wishes to know, his own character in the world" (p. 626). Thus, as an object of biographical study, Johnson appears before us as a mass of documents and recorded speeches, and a stock of repeated mannerisms. Through his extreme and almost irreverent descriptions of Johnson's person, his scrofula, distraction, and grotesque wobblings and noddings, Boswell sets his protagonist sharply off from the ranks of normal men—and even from the other persons mentioned in the biography, none of whom seem to have faces worthy of remarking or "characteristic" movements. No matter how extreme, however, it is also a strangely static character Boswell accords his hero. He chooses tenseless and frozen nominals, such as "rigour" and "vivacity," to label its various facets, reducing Johnson at times to a mere collection of qualities: "Such was *Samuel Johnson*, a man whose talents, acquirements, and virtues, were so extraordinary, that the more his character is considered, the more he will be regarded . . . with admiration and reverence" (*Life*, p. 1402). There may be contradictory tendencies, fits of generosity and temper, but these are only highlights and shadows of a character that resembles the Flemish still life to which Boswell compares his biography.

Yet anyone who has read Boswell's final remarks cannot but feel disappointment; something of Boswell's biographical art has been lost in such a summary. His *trompe-l'oeil*, the vivid illusion of life, depends more on creating an affective state in the minds of his readers, similar to what Johnson himself produced in the members of his circle. Most of Boswell's narrative concerns how Johnson's sheer presence affects his acquaintances. Even a sophisticated sensibility like that of Sir Joshua Reynolds cannot remain immune:

Boswell. "His power of reasoning is very strong, and he has a peculiar art of drawing characters, which is as rare as good portrait painting." Sir Joshua Reynolds. "He is undoubtedly admirable in this; but in order to mark the characters he draws, he overcharges them, and gives people more than they really have, whether of good or bad."

No sooner did he, of whom we had been thus talking so easily, arrive, than we were all as quiet as a school upon the entrance of the head-master. [*Life*, p. 978]

But of course the principal and omnipresent barometric device for marking the force of Johnson is the character of Boswell himself. "In a moment he was in a full glow of conversation, and I felt myself elevated as if brought into another state of being" (*Life*, p. 680). Boswell writes not to capture the "being" of Johnson but the experience of "being with" him. He is therefore little concerned with rendering the content of Johnson's consciousness; we learn nothing, in fact, of the subjective life of Johnson that does not appear in his own memoranda. His melancholia is treated as a disease of which Boswell notes only the circumstances and the acuteness of the attack. In his résumé of Johnson's character at the end of the *Life*, Boswell even resorts to anachronism, to theories of "humours" and "ruling passions" which he never uses to explain his own psychology:[11] "in all his numerous works, he earnestly inculcated what appeared to him to be the truth; his piety being constant, and the ruling principle of all his conduct" (*Life*, p. 1402).

Boswell had already raised questions of affective psychology and the aesthetics of representation in his own *London Journal*, and it is to these ideas that he implicitly returns in developing his character of Johnson:[12] "In my opinion, perfect simplicity and intimate knowledge of scenes takes away the pleasing sort of wonder and awe that we have for what is not clear to us: As the seers of old got reverence by concealing the whole of their transactions. People in that case imagine more in things than there really is. . . . When we know exactly all a man's views and how he comes to speak and act so and so, we lose . . . that kind of distant respect which is very agreeable for us to feel" (*London Journal*, p. 176). Deliberately refusing to speculate on Johnson's emotions, while confidently inferring what is on any other mind, Boswell is aiming to provoke imagination, to inspire us with awe through his mystification. Even his most extravagant metaphors are designed to produce these sensations. Johnson is compared to "bears," to "bulls," to "whales," and even to a "rhinocerous"—analogies meant to impress us with size and a slightly predatory menace. The most extended and elaborate of these comparisons portray Johnson as a giant natural force. "Notwithstanding occasional explosions of violence we were all delighted upon the whole with Johnson. I compared him at this time to a warm West-Indian climate, where you have a bright sun, quick vegetation, luxuriant foliage, luscious fruits; but where the same heat produces thunder, lightning, earthquakes, in a terrible degree" (*Life*, p. 953).

The character of Johnson overwhelms the mere senses, to become an almost indefinable force capable of these simultaneously vast and terrifying effects. It is no matter to Boswell whether such comparisons achieve clarity or a consistent image of Johnson, so long as they produce an experience that is suitably sublime. For all their variety and inhuman quality, each of these metaphors accords with the principles of sublimity laid down in Addison's second paper on "the pleasures of the Imagination": "By *Greatness*, I do not only mean the Bulk of any single Object, but the Largeness of a whole View, considered as one entire Piece . . . that rude kind of Magnificence which appears in many of these stupendous Works of Nature. Our imagination loves to be filled with an Object, or to grasp at any thing that is too big for its Capacity."[13] Thus it is almost impossible for Boswell to offer a neat biographical summary. To do so is a violation of his art. The solidity of Johnson's character and the coherence of the "detached particulars" which fill Boswell's *Life* are derived from the way each memento points back to a single, ineffable force. The character of Samuel Johnson is an "Object" at which we grasp, but which is ultimately "too big for our Capacity."

Then Boswell has willfully forfeited the sublime in writing his autobiography, since he knows that his whole practice there is to disclose rather than "conceal the roots of transactions." There are ample illustrations of his own character, but no awe-inspiring analogies. As autobiographer, Boswell aims instead at the relation between interpersonal effect and his private perception and expectation.

I determined to make a trial of the civility of my fellow-creatures, and what effect my external appearance and address would have. I accordingly went to the shop of Mr. Jeffreys, sword-cutter to his Majesty, looked at a number of his swords, and at last picked out a very handsome one at five guineas. "Mr. Jeffreys," said I, "I have not money here to pay for it. Will you trust me?" "Upon my word, Sir," said he, "you must excuse me. It is a thing we never do to a stranger." I bowed genteely and said, "Indeed, Sir, I believe it is not right." However, I stood and looked at him, and he looked at me. "Come, Sir," cried he, "I will trust you." . . . I called this day and paid him. "Mr. Jeffreys," said I, "there is your money. You paid me a very great compliment. I am much obliged to you. But pray don't do such a thing again. It is dangerous." "Sir," said he, "we know our men. I would have trusted you with the value of a hundred pounds." This I think was a good adventure and much to my honour. [*London Journal*, p. 60]

Despite his disclaimer in the biography, it is here clear that Boswell knows a great deal of his own "character in the world" and feels responsible for it, but he knows as well that character is just one element of the far more complex "self" it is the business of his journal to capture. There remains that which wills and desires, approves or blames his character, which can never be fully merged with it. "I had a good opinion of myself, and I could perceive my friend Temple much satisfied with me. Could I but fix myself in such a character and preserve it uniformly, I should be exceedingly happy. I hope to do so and to attain a constancy and dignity without which I can never be satisfied, as I have these ideas strong and pride myself in thinking that my natural character is that of dignity" (*London Journal*, pp. 257–58).

Unlike the character he gives to Johnson, which is designed literally to overpower the viewer's capacity for judgment, Boswell's portrayal of his own character is always open to critical evaluation. The autobiographical character is also subject to change. While the biography compares Johnson with other men, the journal compares a succession of characters, all of them Boswell to some degree. "Since I came up, I have begun to acquire a composed genteel character very different from a rattling uncultivated one which for some time past I have been fond of" (*London Journal*, p. 47). It is hardly surprising, then, that there is far less emphasis on stable qualities of character and far fewer nominalized catalogs. "The sweet elevation of spirits which I now felt is scarcely to be conceived. I was quite in esctasy. O how I admired the objects around me! How I valued ease and health! . . . O why can I not always preserve my inclinations as constant and as warm? . . . surely so delicate a mind as I have cannot be greatly blamed for wavering a little when such terrible obstacles oppose my favourite scheme" (*London Journal*, p. 205). It is the activity of *feeling* his spirits and *preserving* his inclinations that Boswell stresses. Dynamic and fluid experiences, occurring and transforming themselves in time, are the material of his journal. To describe these he needs verbs, with their tenses and progressive aspect for reflecting identity as process. He also needs a different system of cases than those which are appropriate in biography. Character is something Johnson possesses—"such was his inflexible dignity"—something, no matter how fixed and inalienable, which is property once removed from its owner. Boswell is far more free in equating his essence with his emotions and roles. Yet in a record of daily and even hourly inconsistencies, these equations become desperate hyperbole: "When we came upon Highgate Hill, and had a view of London, I was all life and joy" (*London Journal*, p. 43).

His journal remarks: "I have discovered that we may be in some degree whatever character we choose." A discovery, no doubt, which licenses experiment but which also gives a sense of artificiality to whatever he may become. He continually casts his experience in the form of theatrical "scenes." "I felt parental affection was very strong towards me; and I felt a very warm filial regard for them. The scene of being a son setting out from home for the wide world . . . pleased me much" (*London Journal*, p. 41). He plays at various characters throughout his *London Journal*, at MacHeath and at Addison's Spectator, and even at various of his friends. As Bertrand Bronson puts it: "Habitually, he sees himself momentarily as different persons of his acquaintance whom, for one quality or another, he admires . . . he will counsel himself to "be" one of his acquaintances."[14] There is equally joy and despair in this process, protean creativity and the horror of ultimate chaos. "I acquired confidence by considering my present character in this light: a young fellow of spirit and fashion, heir to a good fortune, enjoying the pleasures of London, and now making his addresses in order to have an intrigue with that delicious subject of gallantry, an actress" (*London Journal*, p. 94).

If viewing his identity as an artifice at times gives Boswell confidence and a sense of control over himself, it can only be short-lived. Nothing guarantees his ability to retain that character and nothing makes one character more intrinsically his own than any other. "It is," as he remarks, "very difficult to be keen about a thing which in reality you . . . consider imaginary" (p. 78). In one of his most penetrating moments of self-awareness in the *London Journal*, Boswell states: "I see too far into the system of things to be much in earnest. . . . This being the case, I am rather passive than active in life. It is difficult to make my feeling clearly understood. I may say, I act passively" (*London Journal*, p. 77).

It is difficult indeed to make this, his emerging autobiographical subject and the recurring preoccupation of his journals, clearly understood. Lacking a ready vocabulary and a conscious generic tradition, Boswell is sometimes disturbed by foreign qualities of his own work. "I am vexed as such a distempered suggestion's being inserted in my journal, which I wished to contain a consistent picture of a young fellow eagerly pushing through life. But it serves to humble me, and it presents a strange and curious view of the unaccountable nature of the human mind" (*London Journal*, pp. 205–6). But he knows that he must not falsify the nature of his experience, and he also implicitly recognizes that it is his "passive action" which provides the drama of his story.

As his record focuses ever more closely on his own epistemology and the flavor of his perceptions, the great scene of London almost vanishes and his theatrical flourishes vanish as well. There is nothing artificial about these reflections: he has reached autobiographical fact. "My mind is strangely agitated. I am happy to think of going upon my travels and seeing the diversity of foreign parts; and yet my feeble mind shrinks somewhat at the idea of leaving Britain in so very short a time from the moment in which I now make this remark. How strange must I feel myself in foreign parts. My mind is too gloomy and dejected at the thoughts of leaving London, where I am so comfortably situated and where I have enjoyed most happiness. However, I shall be happier for being abroad, as long as I live. Let me be manly" (*London Journal*, p. 333). The facts of Boswell's journal are unlike the observable facts of biography. His vaguest plans and his unrealizable dreams are legitimate parts of his record. "I could not help indulging a scheme of taking it [Johnson's garret] for myself, many years hence, when its present great possessor will in all probability be gone to a more exalted situation. This was in a strong sense 'building my castle in the air'" (*London Journal*, pp. 311–12). Rather than describing his actions directly, his grammar gives the greater emphasis to the experience of acting: he "feels himself" doing or "sees himself" admired. While one is acutely aware in the *Life of Johnson* of the mannerisms of the great Doctor, one is just as acutely aware in the *London Journal* of the mannerisms of thought and perception. Boswell does describe his external behavior, but the way he qualifies his subjective life is far more unusual.

Indeed, I have a strong turn to what the cool part of mankind have named superstition. But this proceeds from my genius for poetry, which ascribes many fanciful properties to everything. This I have great pleasure from; as I have now by experience and reflection gained the command of it so far that I can keep it within just bounds by the power of reason, without losing the agreeable feeling and play to the imagination which it bestows. I am sure I am happier in this way than if I just considered Holyroodhouse as so much stone and lime which has been put together in a certain way, and Arthur Seat as so much earth and rock raised about the neighbouring plains. [*London Journal*, p. 42]

He does not just see and consider, he sees and considers an object "as" something. He knows that his vision transforms the brute facts of his world, but he also knows that the record of his mode of seeing is as truthful and as relevant to autobiography as brute objective material.

A biographer who announced himself in the manner Boswell does at the opening of the *London Journal* would hardly win his audience's trust. "I shall here put down my thoughts on different subjects at different times, the whims that may seize me and the sallies of my luxuriant imagination" (*London Journal*, p. 39). Self-indulgent and deliberately fantastic narrative tactics would threaten not only distortion but distraction, taking attention away from the protagonist of the biography. But the autobiographer is his own hero and his flights of narrative fancy are an index of the psychology of his subject. As narrator of his autobiography, Boswell looses the very faculties Bunyan had earlier struggled to suppress and in part upends the criteria of reliability. A "Journal of the life of Man" (as he insists in the passage appearing as headnote to this chapter) cannot be "exact" without subjective "colourings." Style and textual order, which exemplified adherence to doctrine and piety for Bunyan, have become illustrations of personal idiosyncrasy. "How easily and cleverly do I write just now! I am really pleased with myself; words come skipping to me like lambs upon Moffat Hill; and I turn my periods smooth and imperceptibly like a skilful wheelwright turning tops in a turning-loom. There's fancy! There's simile! In short, I am at present a genius" (*London Journal*, p. 187).

Given the volatile self which is his subject, style must be equally volatile, variable, even contradictory. There is, for example, his changing treatment of his amorous pursuits. If he sees himself as a successful gallant, his diction is elevated, playfully Latinate, peppered with classical allusions and personifications. "I fanned the flame by pressing her alabaster breasts and kissing her delicious lips. I then barred the door of her dining-room, led her all fluttering into her bedchamber, and was just making triumphal entry when we heard her landlady coming up. 'O Fortune why did it happen thus?' would have been the exclamation of a Roman bard" (*London Journal*, p. 117). The mock-epic touches vanish, however, when he describes his mundane contract with a prostitute. "I went to the Park, picked up a low brimstone, called myself a barber and agreed with her for sixpence, went to the bottom of the Park arm and arm, and dipped my machine in the Canal and performed manfully" (*London Journal*, p. 272). When he at last comes fully under Johnson's influence, he discusses the same topic in yet another tone: "Since my being honoured with the friendship of Mr. Johnson, I have more seriously considered the duties of morality and religion and the dignity of human nature. I have considered that promiscuous concubinage is certainly wrong. It is contributing to one's share towards bringing confusion and misery into society. . . . Sure it is that if all the men and women in Britain were merely to consult animal gratification, society would be a most shocking scene. Nay, it would soon cease altogether. Notwithstanding of these reflections, I have stooped to mean profligacy even yesterday" (*London Journal*, p. 304) This entry reflects Johnson's style as well as his views on subordination—the diction, with its multisyllables and nominalized neologisms ("concubinage") and the rational distance of impersonal pronouns and naked modals ("Sure it is . . .") inverted to make judgment the theme of the sentence are certainly Johnsonian. In the *Life*, Johnson is so dominant that the style is everywhere infected with him; periodical sentences with balanced antitheses become the narrator's chief mode.[15] In the biography, style is will-less homage; in the autobiography, it is method and mask. But since Boswell wears here a series of masks, one succeeding the other, he always remains visible through the waverings of his disguise, and even in his need for disguise.

The terms Boswell has to describe his autobiographical act are equally various and colorful. He "writes" and occasionally "records," as he also does in the *Life*, but he "adorns" and "paints" as well. The latter would obviously cloud the "clearness of narration" which is his ideal for biography. The *Life of Johnson*, Boswell claims, is the product of "collecting" and "assembling" information which has its own, intrinsic shape. "In the chronological series of Johnson's life, which I trace as distinctly as I can, year by year, I produce, wherever it is in my power, his own minutes, letters, and conversation, being convinced that this mode is more lively." His continual apology for trivial accounts creates the impression that he has no control over his facts, that he is literally incapable of omission. "I am therefore exceeding unwilling that any thing, however slight, which my illustrious friend thought it worth his while to express, with any degree of point, should perish. ... I am justified in preserving rather too many of Johnson's sayings, than too few; especially as from the diversity of dispositions it cannot be known with certainty beforehand, whether what may seem trifling to some, and perhaps to the collector himself, may not be most agreeable to many" (*Life*, pp. 25–26). He even refrains from appearing to provide the logic and chronology of his biography. The materials themselves often date an incident and announce new thematic interests. We first learn of the death of David Garrick from a letter. Boswell's introductory remarks in no way prepare us for what follows:

On the 22nd of January, I wrote to him on several topics, and mentioned that as he had been so good as to permit me to have the proof sheets of his *Lives of the Poets*, I had written to his servant, Francis, to take care of them for me.

"Mr. Boswell to Dr. Johnson   "Edinburgh, Feb. 2, 1779
    "My Dear Sir,
    "Garrick's death is a striking event . . ."

[*Life*, p. 1009]

Yet surely the height of deliberate self-effacement is reached in his treatment of Johnson's conversations. The credit, Boswell insists, for this minute reproduction of ipsissima verba belongs to the protagonist, not his biographer. "In the early part of my acquaintance with him, I was so wrapt in admiration of his extraordinary colloquial talents, and so little accustomed to his peculiar mode of expression, that I found it extremely difficult to recollect and record his conversation with its genuine vigour and vivacity. In the progress of time, when my mind was, as it were, 'strongly impregnated with the Johnsonian aether,' I could, with much more facility and exactness, carry in my memory and commit to paper the exuberant variety of his wisdom and wit" (*Life*, p. 297). It is clear in the *London Journal* that precision and verisimilitude require active talents and not a mere tabula rasa. "In recollecting Mr. Johnson's conversation, I labour under much difficulty. It requires more parts than I am master of even to retain that strength of sentiment and perspicuity of expression" (*London Journal*, p. 293).[16]

While the *Life* makes direct quotation of Johnson one of its principal claims and merits—often reserving this honor for Johnson alone when other speakers are cited indirectly—direct discourse does not have the same unquestionable status in the autobiography. Far more important than preserving the substance or quality of past conversation is capturing the immediate mood of the writer. Thus the same dialogue which is quoted directly in the *Life* may be rendered obliquely to serve other needs in the journal:

I mentioned to him how common it was in the world to tell strange stories of him, and to ascribe to him strange sayings. **Johnson.** "What do they make me say, Sir?" **Boswell.** "Why, Sir, as an instance very strange indeed. . . . David Hume told me, you said that you would stand before a battery of cannon, to restore the Convocation to its full powers." Little did I apprehend that he had actually said this: but I was soon convinced of my errour; for, with a determined look, he thundered out "And would I not, Sir? Shall the Presbyterian Kirk of Scotland have its General Assembly, and the Church of England be denied its convocation?" He was walking up and down the room while I told him the anecdote; but when he uttered this explosion of high-church zeal, he had come close to my chair, and his eyes flashed with indignation. I bowed to the storm, and diverted the force of it, by leading him to expatiate on the influence which religion derived from maintaining the church with great external respectability. [*Life*, p. 329]

I last night sat up again, but I shall do so no more, for I was very stupid today and had a kind of feverish headache. At night Mr. Johnson and I supped at the Turk's Head. He talked much for restoring the Convocation of the Church of England to its full powers, and said that religion was much assisted and impressed on the mind by external pomp. My want of sleep sat heavy upon me, and made me like to nod, even in Mr. Johnson's company. Such must be the case while we are united with flesh and blood. [*London Journal*, p. 333]

The focus of the journal account is Boswell's own fatigue and the feverish condition which makes it impossible to attend to more than the bare outline of Johnson's words. Although at many points he does represent both the matter and manner of Johnson's speeches, in scrupulous dramatic detail, it is only the quantity—"he talked much"—which makes an impression on him now. This entry occurs late in the *London Journal*, as Boswell finds himself preoccupied with thoughts of his European tour and ambivalence begins to mar his London attachments. At this point, only those remarks which are directly applicable to his confused situation are rendered directly. Questions of the Convocation of the Church of England cannot penetrate his emotional fog; they seem irrelevant, and so, for the moment, does Johnson. But when he writes in a mood of effortless self-control, his record is utterly different. " 'I assure you, Madam, my affections are engaged.' 'Are they, Sir?' 'Yes, Madam, they are engaged to you.' (She looked soft and beautiful.) 'I hope we shall be better acquainted and like one another better.' 'Come, Sir, let us talk no more of that now.' 'No, Madam, I will not. It is like giving the book in the preface.' 'Just so, Sir, telling in the preface what should be in the middle of the book.' (I think such conversations are best written in the dialogue way.)" (*London Journal*, p. 89).

In a scene like this, the biography would reserve all of its stage directions for the protagonist, doubltess sprinkling his speeches with italicized stress marks to distinguish the "musick" of "his deliberate and strong utterance" from the toneless remarks of his interlocutors.[17] But the autobiographer can be less parochial and distribute his representational detail according to personal whim. Now vividly staged, now remotely remembered, conversation in the *London Journal* is always frankly creative. Boswell is not afraid to destroy the illusion of realistic dialogue by showing us how it is done, since by betraying his skill and even his vanity he writes more realistic autobiography.

We are rarely allowed to forget that the life of the *London Journal* is entirely owed to its author. Without his observation and his "genius" there is nothing, not merely chaos but vacuum. "This day I was rather late at Child's. There was nobody almost there, and no dialogue. So this day must want that garnish, as I am resolved to adhere strictly to fair truth in this my journal" (*London Journal*, p. 128). The significance of what did not and cannot happen is as great in the autobiography as the most dramatic incident it reports. It is Boswell's capacity for truth, and not simply the verifiability of his account, which is the major concern. In fact, for many of the things he reports it would be nearly impossible to propose any objective test of truth. There is only Boswell's word to guarantee that his fears and his joys have such a flavor or such a frequency. The faith we have in this word arises from his confession of failure and frustration as an autobiographer, from his numerous open avowals of his inability to perform. "We had much ingenious talk. But I am dull and cannot recollect it" (*London Journal*, p. 51). Only such an exhibition of candor could make his autobiography convincing. But when it is a matter of biographical authenticity, of facts which exist before and outside of the narrative process, then Boswell must squelch the remotest possibility of personal fallibility. "The labour and anxious attention with which I have collected and arranged the materials of which these volumes are composed, will hardly be conceived by those who read them with careless facility. The stretch of mind and prompt assiduity by which so many conversations were preserved, I myself, at some distance of time, contemplate with wonder" (*Life*, p. 4).

Truth in the *Life of Johnson* depends on a disinterested and almost mechanical intelligence, producing a curious fissure between the narrator of the biography and the man called Boswell who fitfully appears in his account. The narrator coolly exposes Boswell to ridicule, expresses his "wonder" at what Boswell says, and generally stands at a tepid remove from the motives underlying the relationship between

Boswell and Johnson. For example, Boswell's exultant manipulations in achieving the historic encounter of Wilkes and Johnson seem entirely outside the narrator's ken: "I am now to record a very curious incident in Dr. Johnson's Life, which fell under my own observation" (*Life*, p. 764). "When I had him fairly seated in a hackney-coach with me, I exulted as much as a fortune-hunter who has got an heiress into a post-chaise with him to set out for Gretna-Green" (*Life*, p. 767). Although the narrator may dispute, and even defeat, Johnson's arguments on a subject, Boswell is never more than the foil of Johnson's rhetorical powers, the voice whose questions and hasty generalizations arouse Johnson to respond.[18] "When I talked to him of the paternal estate to which I was heir, he said, 'Sir, let me tell you, that to be a Scotch landlord, where you have a number of families dependent upon you, and attached to you, is, perhaps, as high a situation as humanity can arrive at. . . .' His notion of the dignity of a Scotch landlord had been formed upon what he had heard of the Highland Chiefs; for it is long since a lowland landlord has been so curtailed in his feudal authority" (*Life*, p. 290). The biographer is able to assess Johnson critically and expose the ignorance behind his argument, but the man Boswell has nothing to say in reply.

Part of the illusion of objective fact in the *Life* is the impersonality of the narrator. By standing at a distance from himself, Boswell attempts to transcend personality, to avoid "constantly speaking in my own person," as he states in his introduction. When referring to himself as narrator, he prefers to use descriptive titles such as "the author of this work" or "Johnson's biographer." He curtails his identity as much as possible, restricting it to the role of recorder and assembler and making it a shadow with no life beyond the pages of the book or the duties of the biographer. Occasionally, of course, he must individuate himself and speak in the first person singular of an eyewitness. More often the first-person singular is used to signify his accountability for what he reports. "Let me only observe, as a specimen of my trouble, that I have sometimes been obliged to run half over London, in order to fix a date correctly; which, when I had accomplished it, I well knew would obtain me no praise, though a failure would have been to my discredit" (*Life*, p. 4). He is an individual only to the extent that it is necessary to have a responsible reporter rather than anonymous gossip. Usually the biographical act seems to take place of its own accord, with no reference to a human agent. The statement which opens the text, for example, is an infinitive: "To write the Life of him who excelled all mankind in writing the lives of others, and who, whether we consider his extraordinary endowments, or his various works, has been equalled by few in any age, is an arduous, and may be reckoned in me a presumptuous task" (*Life*, p. 19). Johnson may have written biographies, but Boswell is no more than a locus for writing; it is the task and not the man which is the topic and the comment of Boswell's opening sentence.

As an autobiographer, however, Boswell can find no label which adequately describes his role. What he does and who he is are so various and so complex that nothing short of the first-person pronoun has sufficient fluidity and scope. The identity of the journalist is coextensive with his humanity, and it goes without saying that it is one, singular, unique. "What he meant by my being a great man I can understand. For really, to speak seriously, I think there is a blossom about me of something more distinguished than the generality of mankind" (*London Journal*, p. 161). Cases of impersonality or even of universality are rare indeed in the journal. The autobiographical narrator stresses his idiosyncrasy and his isolation from other men. At the same time, he makes clear his vital connectedness to his protagonist. Boswell the autobiographer never repudiates or refuses to comprehend the behavior of Boswell the man—no matter how ridiculous or repugnant they may appear to him as he writes. "When I went home at night, I was tired and went to bed and thought to sleep. But I was still so haunted with frightful imaginations that I durst not lie by myself. . . . I am too easily affected. It is a weakness of mind. I own it" (*London Journal*, p. 254). At the very moment he passes judgment on his weakness of mind, the autobiographer confesses his intimate involvement in that weakness. He owns it in a dual sense, possessing it even as he admits it.

The merger of author and subject matter in the journal is so complete that events become ambiguous, lapsed and past according to tense, yet still here, still "now," according to the demonstratives and adverbs Boswell uses. He is aware of manipulating perspectives: "I have all along been speaking in the perfect tense, as if I was writing the history of some distant period. I shall after this use the present often, as most proper. Indeed, I will not confine myself, but take whichever is most agreeable at the time" (*London Journal*, p. 65). Conscious of the meaning of his grammar, he is conscious as well of displaying a whimsical and spontaneous personality in his shifting prose. The progressive aspect so common in Boswell's recorded experience spills over into the act of recording, making the journal itself a process rather than a product. As his experience of himself continues and mingles with the autobiographical act, the tense of an entry veers suddenly into the present.

At night I fell back into my melancholy mood. . . . Never was any man more upon the fret than I now was. I never thought (or rather would not allow myself to believe) that all these clouds were produced by my sickly confinement. . . . Alas, alas, poor Boswell! to what an abject situation art thou now reduced! Thou who lately prided thyself in luxuriance of health and liveliness of imagination art now a diseased, dull, capricious mortal. Is not this a just punishment for thy offences? It is indeed; I submit to it. Sometimes I thought I would go down to Oxford. . . . But then it would cost me money; and besides I am not fit for travelling. Alas! this sad distemper comes again across me. . . . Perhaps, when I get well again and the fine weather comes in, I may make a trip to it. What is a sure sign of my not being right just now is my having dismal dreams almost every night. I hope to be better ere long. [*London Journal*, pp. 194–95]

The battle between resignation and despair in the face of melancholia is more than the material treated in this entry; it is a struggle in which the journalist is immediately engaged. Writing may be the only way of experiencing despair without capitulating to it and of turning confused self-pity into a more fruitful satiric or even medical observation of his own condition. The way Boswell uses tense in the *London Journal* in fact suggests that a clear perception of the antithetic tendencies which compose his nature may be the only ultimate synthesis of his identity that he can achieve. His various vows to improve himself are marked in the past tense, while his moments of awareness and even self-disgust are in the present tense. His naive introductory claim that his journal will be of important assistance in "resolutions of doing better" becomes less and less credible as the journal progresses. The record is full of his wishes, his intentions, and his hopes, but it is not and cannot be a set of predictions or prescriptions. "Indeed, I sometimes indulge noble reveries of having a regiment, of getting into Parliament, making a figure, and becoming a man of consequence in the state. But these are checked by dispiriting reflections on my melancholy temper and imbecility of mind. Yet I may probably become sounder and stronger as I grow up" (*London Journal*, p. 161).

Since Johnson is dead when Boswell begins his biography, his judgments about character and incident can be far more certain. But there is another kind of change to which Johnson is now subject, and the war against this sort of mutability becomes a principal theme of the biography. Johnson himself described the process in his essay on biography cited in Boswell's introduction: "the incidents which give excellence to biography are of a volatile and evanescent kind, such as soon escape the memory, and are transmitted by tradition. We know how few can pourtray a living acquaintance, except by the grosser features of his mind; and it may be easily imagined how much of this little knowledge may be lost in imparting it, and how soon a succession of copies will lose all resemblance to the original" (*Rambler*, no. 60; *Life*, p. 25).

Boswell's war with time in the *Life of Johnson* takes intricate and subtle forms. In part these are linguistic: Johnson's qualities of character are frozen in tenseless catalogs—or "embalmed," to use Boswell's own word for it, from his introduction. He places continuing emphasis on his act as one of "preservation." By casting the bulk of Johnson's conversation into the form of dramatic dialogues, he thus avoids indicating that the speech took place in the past. There is no discourse frame to qualify the distance between the time when Johnson originally made these remarks and the time at which they are reported or read. It is not a matter of what he "said," but of what we actually witness him saying. The parenthetic stage directions Boswell supplies are also most often tenseless gerunds and prepositional phrases, allowing the entire scene to pass into our immediate present. In addition, keeping his own person subordinate to the biographical record prevents the historical Boswell from forming yet another temporal barrier between Johnson and posterity. The narrator and his text should be as timeless as possible; thus dwelling on the identity of the biographer, which is itself mortal, would only allow further evidence of the inevitability of decay. The illusion of timelessness is far better maintained by infinitives and nouns which refer to the product and not the process of his biographical act. The *Life* is therefore treated as an object—as a "volume" or a "biographical cup" which contains the essence of Samuel Johnson. Although a great deal of time was obviously spent in collecting and constructing it, and another span of time will be required of any audience which reads its more than a thousand pages, Boswell ignores this in favor of spatial metaphors of bulk and monumentality. On the pages of Boswell's scrapbook, the evanescent moments of Johnson's life are transformed into "collecteana" impervious to decay. As the biographer remarks: "Had his other friends been as diligent and ardent as I was, he might have been entirely preserved" (*Life*, p. 22).

Biography can never directly embody its subject, but Boswell can occasionally overcome the arbitrariness of mere report and make his text the shadow or the imprint of Johnson's living force. Johnson becomes the magnetic center of all movement—the entire world of the biography, including the narrator himself, use him as their meridian. Similarly, any city or building in which Johnson is not present seems to lose all realistic dimension. Boswell describes being "in" London or "within" the Johnsonian circle, but he is only "at" Edinburgh or "at" his ancestral home, Auchinleck. Lacking the presence of Johnson, any place is reduced to a mere point on a map, as though it were his character alone which carved out an inhabitable space for himself and his followers. And of course since language is the medium both of the biography and of Johnson's art, the gap between narrative and protagonist can be bridged by including his letters, his documents, and specimens of his poetry and prose. Boswell always discusses Johnson's writings in the present tense. Here is the eternal Johnson, the voice and the sentiments that cannot die: "His moral precepts are practical; for they are drawn from an intimate acquaintance with human nature. His maxims carry conviction; for they are founded on the basis of common sense, and a very attentive minute survey of real life" (*Life*, p. 1401). By drawing his biography to a close with the focus upon these durable facets of Johnson's character and fame, Boswell earns the right to speak confidently of the future as well as the past. His Johnson is immortal, forever relevant: "Such was **Samuel Johnson**, a man whose talents, acquirements, and virtues, were so extraordinary, that the more his character is considered, the more he will be regarded by the present age, and by posterity, with admiration and reverence (*Life*, p. 1402).

There is probably no form less suited to creating an illusion of permanence than the one Boswell chooses for his autobiography. As a string of discrete entries reflecting the variations of daily experience and the momentary quality of inspiration, it is too erratic to be statuesque: "**Thursday 21 July.** I remember nothing that happened worth relating this day. How many such days does mortal man pass!" (*London Journal*, p. 316). Boswell cannot allow the requirements of an extrinsic form to obscure the shape of self emerging on the pages of his diary. Even the arbitrary device of the calendar acquires a personal meaning, becoming a symptom of his will and perseverence. "I sat up all last night writing letters and bringing up my lagging journal, which, like a stone to be rolled up a hill, must be kept constantly going" (*London Journal*, p. 324). His scrupulous accuracy about matters few other men could verify or would even care to challenge is similarly an index of personality: "I am resolved to adhere strictly to fair truth in this my journal. . . . I do think a love of form for its own sake is an excellent qualification for a gentleman" (*London Journal*, p. 128). It is less the nature of truth than his own nature which obliges his scrupulous measures.

A record so full of self can be neither autonomous nor inert. The journal is always "my" journal, reminding one of his later essay in *The Hypochondriack* where he called it "a part of my vitals."[19] Boswell would like to so reduce the distance between experience and expression that journalizing might become a kind of thinking on paper. Only by achieving total immediacy can Boswell hope to catch himself "in the act," to see what is otherwise invisible to him because it is inextricably bound up with the very process of perception. "I now see the sickly suggestions of inconsistent fancy with regard to the Scotch bar in their proper colours. Good heaven! I should by pursuing that plan have deprived myself of felicity when I fairly had it in my power, and brought myself to a worse state than ever. I shudder when I think of it" (*London Journal*, p. 205). Unlike biography, which is a work of preservation, autobiography must be an act of exploration and an opportunity for fresh discoveries.

This means that Boswell must be his own reader, whoever else eventually may come upon his journal. At times his double role becomes vivid and explicit: "I don't think this is all bad. My simile of the hares (my metaphor, rather) is pretty well. They might have answered me, 'Suppose a man went out to shoot a hare for dinner, and not only shot that but a brace of patridges. The lord of the manor sees him, and is offended at him, and wants to take them all from him. Don't you think he is very well off if he gives the lord the patridges and trudges peaceably home with his hare on his shoulders, which is all he wanted?' " (*London Journal*, p. 76). He assesses his performance and becomes his own interlocutor, instantly perceiving what might have been said in reply by an opponent. At other times the change of role is so swift that lines in the dialogue are left unspoken. "I take pleasure in recording every little circumstance about so great a man as Mr. Johnson. This little specimen will serve me to tell as an agreeable story to literary people. He took me cordially by the hand and said, 'My dear Boswell! I do love you very much.'—I will be vain, there's enough!" (*London Journal*, p. 303). The question or the accusation raised by this display of vanity is never stated outright, but it need not be. The writer hears the reader's protestations because he is that reader, and his reaction is immediate and triumphant.

Yet if he would truly trap his prey unawares, he must suppress his own awareness that he is under observation. The illusion must be that of a soliloquy rather than an exchange. Thus he counsels himself, "Let me be manly," rather than adopting the second-person "Be manly," which he uses in notes to himself.[20] Although dispatching the *London Journal* directly to John Johnston, his references to him are always oblique. "I hope it will be of use to my worthy friend Johnston, that while he laments my personal absence, this journal may in some measure supply that defect and make him happy" (*London Journal*, p. 40).

Boswell does make concessions to a Scottish reader, carefully sketching introductions to any person or scene unfamiliar to Johnston and filling his language with Scottish idioms and analogies.[21] "It was just one of the worst Edinburgh tea-drinking afternoons" (*London Journal*, p. 20). "To tell the plain truth, I was vexed at their coming. For to see just the plain *hamely* Fife family hurt my grand ideas of London" (*London Journal*, p. 61). But however much he may rely on Johnston's associations to supply the full effect of these descriptions, Boswell never addresses Johnston, never questions him or orders him in the text of his journal.

Johnston's exclusion from direct participation becomes even more apparent when Boswell is engaged in describing himself rather than his social scene. He would seem to compliment his friend with a confidence his elders specifically advise him against: "He said he would trust his journal to no man, from which I saw that he had no idea of people being so connected that they were but one person" (*London Journal*, p. 310). Yet the connection is far more tenuous than these idyllic words would suggest. Johnston is at best the goal of Boswell's autobiographical act, someone to whom the journal is shown or entrusted but otherwise denied immediate engagement. His function is to be symbolic target, the man in whose name Boswell undertakes the task of rendering his private moments public. "Ideas which gave me exquisite sensations at the time but which are so very nice that they elude endeavours to paint them. A man of similar feelings with me may conceive them" (*London Journal*, p. 201). These feelings are so ephemeral and so deeply personal that Boswell allows only the possibility that another man "may" conceive them. More often, he stresses the singularity of his experience so intently that communicating it seems to be impossible. "I wish I may make myself understood upon this subject. The ideas are perhaps odd and whimsical; but I have found them with respect to my own mind just and real" (*London Journal*, p. 77).

As a biographer, however, Boswell's eye is always on his audience and his open regard for the success of his communication in no way detracts from the value of his work. It seems rather to enhance it. An important part of his attempt to preserve Johnson is saving him from being "transmitted by tradition." Thus Boswell is deeply engaged in a polemical confrontation throughout the *Life of Johnson*, doing battle with his rival authors who threaten to bury the authentic Johnson in a "succession of copies" increasingly remote from the original. "Sir John Hawkins guesses vaguely and idly, instead of having taken the trouble to inform himself with authentick precision" (*Life*, p. 240). His bellicose gestures toward Hawkins and Mrs. Piozzi fill the footnotes and even enter into the text of the biography. This is not merely a contest of literary quality or even personal vanity; Boswell feels himself involved in something resembling a legal battle with the life of his client at stake. Much of his language for his biographical particulars suggests that he is assembling "evidence" for his case. Unlike the casual and belletristic mode of his rivals, whom he derisively calls "other pens," Boswell's text is an argument, a rebuttal of distortion and gossip. He styles his own act as "attesting" and "witnessing" in preference to the less strictly accountable act of "writing." Boswell wants to be seen struggling, so his immense "labour" will convince us that his facts are proved and his argument precise and valid.

Yet though he has undertaken a singular obligation to biographical truth, an obligation which is constantly before us in his frequent reference to what he "must" perform, he takes equal pains to show that the actions of his readers are vital to the success of his task. By effacing himself whenever he is not directly engaged in an argument, he purports to let us judge the evidence for ourselves. He speaks of his audience as often as he speaks of himself; indeed, their roles are often difficult to distinguish. The inclusive first person makes reader and writer coparticipants and partners in the biographical act. Although Boswell had been an intimate of his protagonist and has exerted unusual zeal in collecting Johnsoniana, he treats his role as that of an observer who is in no way superior to other observers who first encounter Johnson intimately in the context of his book. "To us who have long known the manly force, bold spirit, and masterly versification of this poem, it is a matter of curiousity to observe the diffidence with which its author brought it forward into publick notice" (*Life*, p. 90). The biographer takes for granted that his audience is already familiar with the figure and fame of Johnson and lacks only his own peculiar opportunities for more extended observation. He almost appears to apologize for the uniqueness of his own circumstances:

As I had the honour and happiness of enjoying his friendship for upwards of twenty years; as I had the scheme of writing his life constantly in view; as he was well apprised of this circumstance, and from time to time obligingly satisfied my inquiries by communicating to me the incidents of his early years; as I acquired a facility in recollecting, and was very assiduous in recording his conversation . . . and as I have spared no pains in obtaining materials concerning him, from every quarter where I could discover that they were to be found, and have been favoured with the most liberal communications by his friends; I flatter myself that few biographers have entered upon such a work as this, with more advantages; independent of literary abilities, in which I am not vain enough to compare myself with some great names who have gone before me. [*Life*, pp. 19–20]

The implication here is that any man with similar advantages might have produced the same biography. This is not only deference to the members of the jury who will decide his case, it is also a subtle argument for the undistorted quality of the material he presents. Any other person, exerting similar effort, would have presented the same evidence in the same perspective. He appears to extend and develop whatever knowledge his audience already has, whether of Johnson or of human nature. In portraying Johnson's qualities, he begins from the generic and only then discusses how Johnson was specific: "Man is, in general, made up of contradictory qualities; and these will ever shew themselves in strange succession. . . . In proportion to the native vigour of the mind, the contradictory qualities will be the more prominent . . . and, therefore, we are not to wonder that Johnson exhibited an eminent example of this remark which I have made upon human nature" (*Life*, p. 1399).

In the rhetorical stance adopted for the purpose of his biography, Boswell treats his audience as at once a public mass and a group of his familiars. He calls upon them personally as "my readers," yet for all his affectionate possessiveness, imagines that the entire "present age" and much of posterity may be included in their number. Part of Johnson's granduer, then, is the true universality of the reaction he inspires. "We may feel indignation that there should have been such unworthy neglect; but we must, at the same time, congratulate ourselves, when we consider, that to this neglect . . . we owe many valuable productions" (*Life*, pp. 216–17). Since the narrator shares in a response that is common to such an immense and divergent mass of men, he becomes an unspeakably average man, his viewpoint undistinguished but "normal," and of course credible. Not only seeing what any man would, but also seeing it in the same emotional terms, the narrator seems merely to join in voicing the exclamations and questions the audience has already formulated for itself: "How must we feel when we read such an anecdote of Samuel Johnson!" (p. 56).

There must of course be some persons in so vast an audience who would dispute with the biographer, but these are immediately relegated to the periphery of the biographical act. Boswell disdains to treat them as full participants, to address them as "you"—let alone include them in the universal "we" which embraces the biographer and the sympathetic members of his audience. The infidels who challenge his formulation are handled distantly, in the third person, and given titles such as "men of superficial understanding." Those who object to either Boswell's mode of presentation or his standard of emotional evaluation of the character of Johnson are implicitly abnormal, even explicitly depraved. "Here let the profane and licentious pause; let them not thoughtlessly say that Johnson was an *hypocrite*" (*Life*, p. 1376).

Even in this imperative, the narrator refuses to engage in a direct exchange with the dissidents in his audience. But when issuing commands to those who are in sympathy with his task, he places himself in the same position and under the same obligation. "Let it be remembered . . ." and "Let us not wonder . . . ," for example, are orders that both addressor and addressee must obey. The narrator does not need to coerce this audience, but like them, he is forced to adhere to the norms of morality and common sense.[22] Since both in role and in capacity the biographer is nearly identical to the average member of his audience, it is a simple matter to predict how the readership will behave. "The character of **Samuel Johnson** has, I trust, been so developed in the course of this work, that they who have honoured it with a perusal, may be considered as well acquainted with him. As, however, it may be expected that I should collect into one view the capital and distinguishing features of this extraordinary man, I shall endeavour to acquit myself of that part of my biographical undertaking, however difficult it may be to do that which many of my readers will do better for themselves" (*Life*, p. 1398). His own achievement is only possible, but of his readers he is serenely certain: he knows what they "will" be able to do. It is this assurance about the capacity of his audience, once they have been acquainted fully with the facts of Johnson's life and the amazing force of his character, that underlies Boswell's ultimate certainty of immortalizing Johnson. Johnson will be preserved because each new reader of the biography will recreate his own acquaintance with Johnson. The result of such exposure to the "Johnsonian aether" can be nothing less than to make Boswells of them all. As he states in the "Advertisement to the Second Edition" of his *Life of Johnson*: "In reflecting that the illustrious subject of this Work, by being more extensively and intimately known, however elevated before, has risen in the veneration and love of mankind, I feel a satisfaction beyond what fame can afford. We cannot, indeed, too much or too often admire his wonderful powers of mind" (*Life*, p. 7).

There is no such certainty about how even Boswell himself will eventually respond to the *London Journal*. His plans are not clearly formulated, and his hopes that he will find it "a store of entertainment for my after life" (p. 40) are tentative-sounding indeed. And so there is no little sophistry in entrusting the *London Journal* to a friend because they are "so connected that they are but one person." Boswell of all men is surely aware how problematic the connections and unity of one person are. He shows his caution and uncertainty about the man he will turn out to be in his "after life." Actually, it is the entire business of his journal to collect and conjoin the disparate aspects of a self that has otherwise little integration. Here at least the fragments of character and consciousness are united within the framework of a single, unending inquiry. "Am I not too vindictive? It appears so; but upon better consideration I am only sacrificing at the shrine of Justice; and sure I have chosen a victim that deserves it" (*London Journal*, p. 175).

In undertaking a journal, Boswell has added another determinant to his life. Even in this brief passage, for example, one can see how the autobiographical act becomes a dialectic, modifying the views of the man who performs it. The final statement—"sure I have chosen a victim that deserves it"—is a more emphatic and more "considered" position than that with which he began. It is also a new embodiment of himself and a new, less purely psychological explanation of his actions. Boswell had certainly hoped that maintaining a journal might change him. But the changes he had hoped to effect—"fixing" himself in a character, "preserving" his inclinations "constant and warm"—were intended to bring stability to the uncertain, shifting mass of his identity. Instead of imposing a positive and final form on himself, his journal has become another unknown entailing even greater uncertainty. He cannot predict how the discoveries he makes as a journalist will ultimately affect him. "The great art I have to study is to balance these two very difficult ways of thinking properly. It is very difficult to be keen about a thing which in reality you do not regard, and consider as imaginary. But I fancy it may do, as a man is afraid of ghosts in the dark, although he is sure there are none; or pleased with beautiful exhibitions on the stage, although he knows they are not real" (*London Journal*, p. 78).

The subjective facts he examines are inherently conditional, and giving them explicit form is an alteration of conditions. Here, the difficulties of the "great art" he must practice gain greater clarity, the result being a diminution of Boswell's original commitment and an increased ambiguity in the spectral effects he had hoped to achieve. Rather than simplifying his experience, he finds that he is engaged in complicating it, as each new entry in the journal exposes previously unsuspected or unperceivable material to his observation. Each may be the locus of emergent phenomena. Moreover, each time he records, he leaves behind fresh traces of his mind and character which must in turn be analyzed and entered into his record. The process is potentially interminable. "I am vexed at such a distempered suggestion's being inserted in my journal, which I wished to contain a consistent picture of a young fellow eagerly pushing through life. But it serves to humble me, and it presents a strange and curious view of the unaccountable nature of the human mind. I am now well and gay. Let me consider that the hero of a romance or novel must not go uniformly along in bliss, but the story must be chequered with bad fortune. Aeneas met with many disasters in his voyage to Italy, and must not Boswell have his rubs? Yes, I take them in good part" (*London Journal*, pp. 205–6).

Yet the man who here discovers that he "has his rubs" and "takes them in good part" will crumble within the space of only a page or two and find himself looking back to his gay assurance before adversity with peevish incomprehension: "I was much vexed and fretted, and began to despair of my commission altogether and to ruminate whether it would not be better to lay aside thoughts of it" (*London Journal*, p. 210). As the journal swells the quantity, the subtlety, and the sheer inconsistency of the facts about himself he must simultaneously hold in view, Boswell's dependency upon it increases. The journal can encompass what he himself cannot, can even tolerate those things in himself that he oftentimes finds unbearable. "But I cannot find fault with this my journal, which is far from wishing for extravagant adventures, and is as willing to receive my silent and serious meditations as my loud and boisterous rhodomontades" (*London Journal*, p. 269).

Animated by Boswell's need for indulgence, approval, and forgiveness, the journal becomes a companion and confessor. It is personified as well by the fact that the pages confronting the autobiographer seem to speak with his own accent. Only this wayward mirror could receive and recognize the idiosyncratic nature Boswell struggles to express.

Since the journal, and it alone, keeps pace with his fluid self, Boswell can address it directly without shattering the utter privacy of his act: "And now, O my journal! Art thou not highly dignified? Shalt thou not flourish tenfold? No former solicitations or censures could tempt me to lay thee aside; and now is there any argument which can outweigh the sanction of Samuel Johnson?" (*London Journal*, p. 305). The intimacy is genuine, since we are overhearing Boswell speaking with himself. His identity is necessarily composed of more than one voice. It has the unity of a process rather than a single role or image, a synthetic integrity which is nonetheless natural. Because it is an identity forged within and by means of his journal, it is spontaneous and ever open to amendment. "And now I swear that this is the true language of my heart. O why can I not always preserve my inclinations as constant and as warm? I am determined to pursue it with unremitting steadiness . . . surely so delicate a mind as I have cannot be greatly blamed for wavering a little."

CHAPTER FOUR

=====================================

THOMAS DE QUINCEY: SKETCHES AND SIGHS

=====================================

> Vast numbers of people, though liberated from all reasonable
> motives of self-restraint, *cannot* be confidential—have it not in
> their power to lay aside reserve; and many, again, cannot be so
> with particular people. . . . If he were able really to pierce the
> haze which so often envelop's, even to himself, his own secret
> springs of action and reserve, there cannot be a life moving at all
> under intellectual impulses that would not, through that single
> force of absolute frankness, fall within the reach of a deep,
> solemn, and sometimes even of a thrilling interest.
>
> Thomas De Quincey

The status of Boswell's autobiography was uncertain, a compromise
between literary experiment and social discretion. Boswell could neither accept Johnson's critical strictures nor forego the sanction of the
literary community to which he aspired. He at last resorted to an
audience of his own creation, a half-imaginary readership capable of
recognizing autobiography as literature rather than sensationalism. Yet
in less than a century, autobiography was to become an almost banal
literary event. Thomas De Quincey could speak of confidentiality as an
ability rather than a failure of restraint. De Quincey was almost as
prolific an autobiographer as Boswell himself, but without the same
need for clandestine measures. Indeed, according to Aileen Ward: "De
Quincey's major and in effect his only real literary work was his
autobiography, which he spent his whole career in writing, rewriting,
and never quite finishing."[1]

The interdependence of the autobiographical and the near-autobiog-
raphical in De Quincey's writing is also similar to Boswell. But in De
Quincey's case, it is his strictly autobiographical work which is derivative, written late in his career, and partially made up of material
excerpted from his other writing. The *Autobiographical Sketches* are
secondary in literary importance as well as in order of composition.[2]
De Quincey assembled them into a single text only under the pressure
of publishing his collected edition, and his "General Preface" makes
only a modest claim for the *Sketches*, placing them in: "that class
which proposes primarily to amuse the reader; but which, in doing so,
may or may not happen to occasionally reach a higher station, at which
amusement passes into an impassioned interest."[3] Since all of De

Quincey's writing is to some extent occasional, it is not simply the circumstances of composition which cause him to scant the *Autobiographical Sketches*. In reading the "General Preface" to the collected edition, one becomes aware that a consistent but extremely subtle distinction is being evolved between autobiography *simpliciter* and works such as the *Confessions of an English Opium-Eater* and the *Suspiria de Profundis* which, despite their autobiographically colored material, form "a far higher class of compositions." The *Autobiographical Sketches* are deficient to the extent that they remain no more than autobiography, while the *Confessions* and "more emphatically" the *Suspiria* transcend autobiography to become "modes of impassioned prose ranging under no precedents that I am aware of in any literature" (p. 14). De Quincey is struggling (as had Boswell before him) to find an adequate critical language for a new kind of literature, but it is no longer autobiography which is the alien and unprecedented act.

Boswell's private glorification of an art which bears the immediate imprint of a sensibility, supple enough to be the index of the fleeting variations of an emotion, has become a public norm. For De Quincey, it is an aesthetic principle, a desideratum of all art, the very soul of anything to be dignified as "style." "The skill with which detention or conscious arrest is given to the evanescent, external projection to what is internal, outline to what is fluxionary, and body to what is vague,—all this depends entirely on the command over language as the one sole means of embodying ideas; and in such cases the style, or, in the largest sense, *manner*, is confluent with matter."[4] "Impassioned prose" not only emulates but surpasses the expressionistic force of autobiography because it embodies a purer subjectivity.[5] "Those who rest upon external facts, tangible realities and circumstantial details—in short, generally upon the *objective*, whether in a case of narrative or of argument,—must forever be less dependent upon style than those who have drawn upon their own understandings and their own peculiar feelings for the furniture and matter of their composition."[6] The factual and the individual which are inextricably part of the autobiographical act now appear to bar the way to deeper subjective levels.

De Quincey's position is the result of the increased attention accorded to subjective phenomena in the later eighteenth and early nineteenth centuries. The casual study of mind had given way to systematic speculation by the German Idealists, and the object of their study had taken on a more systematic appearance as well. Epistemology was no longer contingent upon external impressions; in Kant's treatment, the accidents of association had been replaced by fixed and irreducible categories of perception and judgment. Since these were universal categories and constituted the primary ground for all human experience, psychology was no longer a matter of idiosyncrasy and caprice. De Quincey, the intimate of the great English Romantics Wordsworth and Coleridge—and like Coleridge, himself a popularizer of German thought—recognized a hierarchy of mental powers. His "passions" are not simply desire and rage but resemble what Coleridge had called the faculty of Imagination. As he states in one of his essays: "It is concerned with what is highest in man; for the Scriptures themselves never condescend to deal by suggestion or co-operation with the mere discursive understanding: when speaking of man in his intellectual capacity, the Scriptures speak not of the understanding, but of *"the understanding heart,"*—making the heart, *i.e.* the great *intuitive* (or non-discursive) organ, to be the interchangeable formula for man in his highest state of capacity for the infinite."[7]

Thus a too-minute attention to individual differences in men would lose sight of the universal process of intuition which is highest in man. A facility for observing and rendering objectively verifiable details would fail to develop a capacity for the infinite in either author or audience. In fact, the "secret springs of action and reserve" could never be uncovered by this kind of superficial observation. These springs are too deeply buried to be perceived directly. The truth is subliminal, arriving at the surface through complicated refractions and a series of weird angles which utterly changes its appearance.

Great is the mystery of Space, greater is the mystery of Time. Either grows upon man as man himself grows; and either seems to be a function of the godlike which is in man. In reality, the depths and heights which are in man, the depths by which he searches, the heights by which he aspires, are but projected and made objective externally in the three dimensions of space which are outside of him. He trembles at the abyss into which his bodily eyes look down, or look up ... by an instinct written in his prophetic heart feeling it to be, boding it to be, fearing it to be, and sometimes hoping it to be, the mirror to a mightier abyss that will one day be expanded in himself.[8]

The most profound subjectivity is paradoxically selfless, or at least escapes an easy appropriation by the mundane conscious mind. Pursued far enough, subjective experience becomes ineffable and identity breaks down in mystery. The transcendental categories of mind merge with the infinite and questions of individuality become meaningless.

Challenged by these new formulations of what had been its subject matter and by a new, more rarefied claimant for its aesthetic values, autobiography was forced to modify its purpose and its scope. For De Quincey and the literary community with which he allies himself, the act becomes increasingly concerned with circumstantial matters. The autobiographer must rely on his audience's curiosity about the surfaces and peculiarities of his life; the nexus between self and institution, self and history, self and society is now the distinguishing feature of his work. Private experience could occasionally provide the grounds for lyrical effusion as well, but the connection is contingent and the value of lyrical expression does not actually derive from the particularities of event or personality. De Quincey's *Confessions of an English Opium-Eater* is a case in point of "impassioned prose" that springs from the materials of personal history. But as the "General Preface" reminds us, it is *Suspiria de Profundis*, with its mingled reminiscence, dream, and fiction, which "more emphatically" embodies De Quincey's ideal of impassioned prose. Thus, although his greatest renown as an autobiographer comes from the *Confessions*, it is not here but in the oppositions between his less well-known *Sketches* and *Suspiria* that one may find the best evidence of the status of the autobiographical act. These are the polar types and the purest instances of what is mixed in the *Confessions*. By comparing these two works, one can see how the transcendental passion of the lyric has come to rival, define, and set an upper limit to the empirical passions, and how the newly glimpsed profundity of spontaneous subjective life trivializes autobiography as a genre.[9]

So despite substantial overlapping in material, the generic convergence of De Quincey's *Autobiographical Sketches* and his *Suspiria de Profundis* is only apparent and is almost accidental. The opening chapter in both works is the same account of De Quincey's personal history and has the same title—"The Affliction of Childhood"—in both works.[10] Yet in the autobiography, this chapter is followed by fourteen other sketches of an equally personal nature, whereas the lyric immediately departs from De Quincey's own life for its subsequent materials. Since there are exactly fifteen sketches, the book opening immediately with the "Affliction" without comment or introduction, and since the final sketch concerns De Quincey's life from his fifteenth year until his departure for Oxford, it is obvious that some care has been exercised in balancing narrative chronology and textual form. Not that the *Autobiographical Sketches* provide a neat, year-by-year chronicle of De Quincey's childhood and adolescence—far from it. The first sentence of the book makes it clear that his autobiographical record is composed, instead, of developmental stages and divided according to the distinct epochs of the young man's life. "After the close of my sixth year, suddenly the first chapter of my life came to a violent termination; that chapter which, even within the gates of recovered Paradise, might merit a remembrance" (*Sketches*, p. 28). Explicit evidence of formal parallels like this are reassuring in a text which at times appears to wander rather far from its mark and to discuss things which have only a tenuous connection with De Quincey himself. Portions of two chapters, for example, are given over to an account of Irish history through the turn of the eighteenth century, and another chapter follows the adventures of De Quincey's younger brother, "Pink," recounting his life at sea during a period long after De Quincey reached manhood. One could dismiss such interpolations as further instances of De Quincey's notorious habit of digressing, but if so they are digressions suited to the nature of his act—as are the quite different digressions in his *Suspiria*. Autobiography for him necessarily includes elements which are neither subjective nor even totally personal, external objects and events which have touched upon a life in particular ways, as the history of Ireland eventually touched De Quincey when his schoolboy tour happened to coincide with the end of Irish home rule. De Quincey's peculiarities of experience and identity have been shaped by the nature of his encounters and his participation in the institutions surrounding him: his role within the family and the nation, the church and the school. Moreover, since autobiography is for him a developmental study, his digressions are useful analogies for the process of his own growth. He interpolates a discussion of Irish revolutions and fraternal rebellions at a point when he is describing his own restless transition from childish confinement to young manhood. Throughout the *Sketches*, De Quincey reiterates a sense that his life has mirrored the historical process and been influenced by the zeitgeist of the period in which he has lived. He speaks, for example, of the changes in public transportation in the first half of the nineteenth century, and how they have affected his experience: "The revolution in the whole apparatus, means, machinery, and dependencies of that system—a revolution begun, carried through, and perfected within the period of my own personal experience—merits a word or two of illustration in the most cursory memoirs that profess any attention at all to the shifting scenery and moving forces of the age, whether manifested in great effects or little" (*Sketches*, p. 270).

De Quincey gradually broadens his focus to include more and more of these "moving forces" surrounding personal identity and influencing the direction of growth as his autobiography progresses. His first chapter, the "Affliction of Childhood," is rather static, however, although it does establish the point of departure for all later development and progress. It is the incident recounted in this chapter which confers upon De Quincey the possibility of identity, an isolated existence which is wholly his own. He awakens suddenly to his individuality and the fact that he is forever and utterly alone when his protective older sister, Elizabeth, dies. Beginning at this point, when De Quincey is already six years old, the autobiography implies that neither self nor time existed for De Quincey in the Eden from which this death has so precipitately expelled him. As J. Hillis Miller describes it: "Before, De Quincey, his sister, and the divine love which he possessed through her formed a charmed circle of warmth and intimacy. . . . He was not aware of himself because self and world interpenetrated one another and overlapped. There was no problem of communication, for his feelings were understood by his sister almost before they were spoken."[11]

De Quincey portrays his first consciousness of self and the ambiguous gift of individuality in a scene in which he stands over his sister's body, laid out in ceremonial readiness amid the paradoxical warmth and refulgent life of a summer afternoon. As he stares at her and struggles to comprehend the implications of her death, he is thrown into a trance in which he experiences a visionary conflict between life and death, infinite and finite modes of being. His vision is a direct encounter with psychological and metaphysical horror, as he sees himself in a futile pursuit of the endlessly receding throne of God, vanishing ever farther into the vaults of heaven. In each subsection of the chapter, the elements of the trance reappear, first as a vision occurring at a church service a few months after Elizabeth's death, then as a dream during his student days at Oxford, and finally as a fantasy ostensibly composed in the act of writing the autobiography itself. This repeated vision represents the core and changeless center of De Quincey's identity—in his hopeless pursuit of a vanished divine presence the primary rupture between subject and object, self and other, infinity and mortality is symbolically reenacted. Later in his autobiography, De Quincey explains that every man's life possesses such a still point at its center: "Man is doubtless *one* by some subtle *nexus*, some system of links, that we cannot perceive, extending from the new-born infant to the superannuated dotard: but as regards many affections and passions incident to his nature at different stages, he is *not* one, but an intermitting creature, ending and beginning anew; the unity of man, in this respect, is co-extensive only with the particular stage to which the passion belongs" (*Sketches*, p. 43).

As the first chapter of his autobiography, then, De Quincey approaches this "nexus" and gives it a token examination. Whatever else changes within and around him, he will continue to be that dreamer and that mourner, his consciousness a product of a wound that cannot heal. But autobiography cannot fully explore the "system of links that we cannot perceive" without ceasing to be autobiography, and so De Quincey passes on to a consideration of the superficial changes and the various stages of his public life. "Infancy, therefore, is to be viewed not only as part of a larger world that waits for its final complement in old age, but also as a separate world itself; part of a continent, but also a distinct peninsula" (*Sketches*, p. 121). His true subject is the "intermitting creature" which nonetheless must always bear his name, a series of transient appearances and accidents bound together only by his conscious recollection and his willingness to claim them as his own. The loose assembly of sketches which makes up his autobiography reflects this evanescence and discontinuity. As he writes, De Quincey stresses the tension between individual stages and expresses his present wonder at the alien quality of some of his childish adventures. "Most fraudulent. it seemed of all things, when looked back upon as some mysterious parenthesis in the current of life, 'self-withdrawn into wondrous depth,' and alienated by *every* feature from the new aspects of life that seemed to await me" (*Sketches*, p. 55).

His second chapter therefore represents a shifting of attention away from subjective experience toward relationships between a conscious self and others, exploring the agonies of a sibling rivalry with a much older brother, William. The "rustic solitude" and "gentle sister" which were the matter for his first chapter are supplanted by a "pugilistic brother" who makes De Quincey his slavish accomplice in battles with the laboring children at a newly constructed textile mill. All the negative aspects of childish weakness and an overwhelming sense of powerless responsibility are developed in this sketch. There is the nightmare, for example, of De Quincey's competition with William over their respective imaginary kingdoms. The younger child listens with helpless conviction to William's arguments that the natives of Gombroon—De Quincey's chosen island domain—must be so backward that they have not evolved to the point of losing their vestigial tails. He is equally the helpless observer of the actual persecution and eventual death of his tutor's deaf twin daughters. His sense of impotence culminates in a scene in which his brother tries to lure a rabid dog across a stream and onto the family lawn where De Quincey and his other brothers and sisters look on in uneasy but naive compliance.

The third chapter, however, provides the counterbalance to this picture of the miseries of childhood. The same weakness and overly developed sensitivity which were the source of his anxiety are also a source of power. "Childhood . . . in the midst of its intellectual weakness, and sometimes even by means of this weakness, enjoys a privilege of strength. The heart in this season of life is apprehensive; and, where its sensibilities are profound, is endowed with a special power of listening for the tones of truth" (*Sketches,* pp. 121–22). The wordless and indistinct sensitivity to the emotional ambience of his tutor's home which had been a torture to De Quincey is also what makes it possible for him to respond to the tragic dimensions of great literature and to feel the rapture of what he calls the "moral sublime" in his aesthetic responses.

De Quincey's circle widens in chapter four, when he reports his first encounter with a stranger in his own home, an infamous lady atheist, as it happens, whose profligacy and eventual ruin implicitly shatter his childish faith, based only on his experience of his mother and his sisters, in the virtue of all women. In chapter five it is De Quincey who is the stranger, leaving the family fold to attend his first public school and meeting there with the organized hostility of older students who are put to shame by his precocious intelligence. At school in Bath he also achieves his first awareness of national events, when he sees a prisoner who has escaped from Napoleon's prisons to return to England. As he observes this man, his capacity for empathy with another human being is awakened. Until this point, he had felt only a diffused and uncomprehending sympathy for others. Chapter six is entitled "I Enter the World," and indeed his autobiographical account does become more worldly, here and throughout the remainder of the book. After chapter six, we also see him almost constantly in motion, traveling through time and space in his physical adventures and his intellectual speculations. But the real crux of the autobiography is in chapter seven—"The Nation of London"—where De Quincey experiences, in the urban sprawl surrounding him, the minuteness of his individual impact on the world. "You become aware that you are no longer noticed; nobody sees you; nobody hears you; nobody regards you; you do not even regard yourself. In fact, how should you at the moment of first ascertaining your own total unimportance in the sum of things—a poor shivering unit in the aggregate of human life" (*Sketches*, p. 181). It is at this point, near the middle of his book, that De Quincey begins making his narrative excursions into Irish history and into adventures not immediately connected with his own life, as though the autobiographical record can no longer "regard . . . a poor shivering unit."

De Quincey returns to his personal history in chapter thirteen, after treating Irish politics, the Industrial Revolution, and progress in the field of education (speculations induced by the contrast between the brutality which sent his brother Pink to sea and more enlightened modern methods). His "premature manhood" is just beginning, but the manner in which he treats this developmental stage in his own life is not especially personal. He groups himself with others experiencing versions of the same phenomenon—two in particular, whom he visits in the next chapter—and uses the same language of vast and ineluctable historical processes which he used to trace the growth of nations and the rise of technology. "A premature development of my whole mind was rushing in like a cataract, forcing new channels for itself and for the new tastes which it introduced" (*Sketches*, p. 327). The fact of change erupts into De Quincey's awareness when he feels his first sexual attraction to a young woman. The forces of intellectual, moral, and tacitly sexual development gather strength in chapter fourteen, as the young man indulges himself by playing the adult in a prolonged visit to the home of family friends. Here he is allowed to conduct the after-dinner conversation and to act as the teacher of the mistress of the house, knowing that at any moment his guardian may demand that he return to the life of a mere grammar-school student.

In the final chapter, the crisis point is reached. Unable to bear the confinement of school, he runs off to London—precipitating the adventures described in his *Confessions of an English Opium-Eater* (omitted here as already familiar to readers of this autobiography). When he at last returns home to confront those in authority, these figures, his mother and his guardian-uncle, are brought to the foreground of the narrative for the first and final time. Home is now "The Priory," a house De Quincey renders as miniature in every detail: "insulated . . . from the tumults of life . . . an atmosphere of conventional stillness and tranquility brooded over it and all around it for ever." The insulated eternality of this setting is almost a parody of the stillness of the infant paradise described in the first chapter of the autobiography. Parody because it can no longer comfort or even contain the adult energies of De Quincey's uncle, on leave from the colonial army in India, and of De Quincey himself. In this now stifling atmosphere there is an inevitable explosion, as De Quincey enrages both mother and uncle with exercises of his new-found polemical skill.

One book, which one day fell to my share by accident, was De Foe's "Memoirs of a Cavalier." This book attempts to give a picture of the Parliamentary War, but in some places an unfair, and everywhere a most superficial account. I said so: and my uncle, who had an old craze in behalf of the book, answered me with some asperity; and in the course of what he said, under movement of ill temper he asked me, in a way which I felt to be taunting, how I could consent to waste my time as I did . . . and the result was that, within seven days from the above conversation, I found myself entering that time-honoured University [Oxford]. [*Sketches*, p. 416]

The *Autobiographical Sketches* reach their abrupt termination with these words; the young De Quincey seems literally thrown from his home to Oxford by the force of the familial eruption.

But in spite of the abruptness, the autobiography has reached a logical termination, for the final two chapters clearly demonstrate emerging skills and preoccupations which are common to the adolescent and the man who now is writing. The younger man's polemics still resonate in the footnotes to the *Sketches* and the theology and political positions which engage the teenager are treated as alive and relevant by the autobiographer. "I even startled myself, with distinctions that to this hour strike me as profoundly just and as undeniably novel" (*Sketches*, p. 368). The final form of De Quincey's identity has thus been reached when he concludes his record. For the purpose of his autobiography, his ultimate identity is what the contemporary reading public now ascribes to him—an audience which knows him as a periodical polemicist, an intellectual, and an opium sufferer. Trusting that his public image will be recognized, De Quincey ends upon this note.

While there are few substantial changes in the material transferred from *Suspiria de Profundis* to the opening of De Quincey's autobiography, the account of his sister's death and the visions induced by it has nonetheless a radically different significance in its original context. "The Affliction of Childhood" is the title of the entire first half of the lyric, including not only what later became the first chapter of his autobiography but three other pieces associated with it: a meditation on the "palimpsest of the human brain" and a series of dream visions— "Levana and Our Ladies of Sorrow," "The Apparition of the Brocken" (which does appear in a modified form in the autobiography), and the Finale, "Savannah-La-Mar."[12] Strictly autobiographical material is surrounded by these essays and reveries on the one hand and by a long and ornate "Introductory Notice" on the other. This preface, which might almost be an independent essay in its own right, stresses the universal application of each of the narratives to follow and explains the entire *Suspiria* as "a record of the third or final stage of opium" (p. 451), as phantom projections of a drugged mind. If the incidents recounted in the "Affliction" were indeed the actual experience of a six-year-old De Quincey, this experience is now mediated by the power of the hallucinogen—with untold damage to clarity and historical accuracy. But more important than brute fact is the emotional coloring which the incidents originally possessed and which now undergoes a drug-induced revival. The death of a favorite sister is an individual catastrophe, but the mood of "absolute ruin" it produces, like the ruinous condition of the opium addict, is something any man might experience. These emotions, and the purity of expression they inspire, are more central to the lyricist than the circumstances leading to the ruin. "The sentiment which attends the sudden revelation that *all is lost* . . . too deep for gestures or for words. . . . The voice perishes; the gestures are frozen; and the spirit of man flies back upon its own centre. I, at least . . . spoke not, nor started, nor groaned. One profund sigh ascended from my heart" (*Suspiria*, p. 451).

The reader of *Suspiria de Profundis* encounters the visions, meditations, reveries, and fictions the narcotic produces but never the objective details of the third stage of De Quincey's own addiction. Between these events in one man's life and the egotistical sublime of the *Suspiria* there intervenes what the preface calls the mysterious "language of dreams." "During this third prostration before the dark idol, and after some years, new and monstrous phenomena began slowly to arise. . . . Or, in the imagery of my dreams, which translated everything into their own language, I saw through vast avenues of gloom those towering gates of ingress which hitherto had always seemed to stand open, now at last barred against my retreat, and hung with funeral crape" (*Suspiria*, p. 450). De Quincey as a person is ancillary to this transcendental language. His "constitutional determination to reverie" and solitary habits which allow the ordinarily "too much dissipated and squandered ... action of thought and feeling" to be "reconcentrated" are fortunate accidents, important only because they make it possible "to reveal something of the grandeur which belongs *potentially* to human dreams." Even his addiction to opium is nothing more than an efficient cause which "assists the faculty of dreaming," overwhelming more mundane preoccupations and the superficial operations of the conscious mind to expose the nether layers of a purer subjectivity.

Following from such an introduction, the story of De Quincey's afflicted childhood must have a greatly altered mien; the grief which individuated him in the *Autobiographical Sketches* is presented here "not for the mere facts ... but because these facts move through a wilderness of natural thoughts or feelings." It becomes a grief less personal than instrumental, a means of entrance into a strange, less finite mode of being: "the grief which I passed through drove a shaft for me into the worlds of death and darkness which never again closed" (*Suspiria*, p. 453). In the *Suspiria*, the visionary gleam imparted to De Quincey in his trance at his dead sister's bedside is submitted to a further act of interpretation. Instead of a symbol of his individual loss and insuperable isolation, his trance is treated as the "hieroglyph" of some higher reality, an instance of the mantic power his preface claims for the subconscious, dreaming faculty. "The machinery for dreaming planted in the human brain was not planted for nothing. That faculty, in alliance with the mystery of darkness, is the one great tube through which man communicates with the shadowy. And the dreaming organ, in connection with the heart, the eye and the ear, compose the magnificent apparatus which forces the infinite into the chambers of the human brain, and throws dark reflections from eternities below all life upon the mirrors of that mysterious *camera obscura*—the sleeping mind" (*Suspiria*, p. 448).

While the *Autobiographical Sketches* are often bemused or quizzical in their attitude to things past, the lyric is almost diffident in its translation of a private experience into the terms of a universal dream language. A footnote to the "Affliction" makes the mediated quality of the report clear—a footnote carefully excised from the autobiography: "The reader must not forget, in reading this and other passages, that, though a child's feelings are spoken of, it is not the child who speaks. *I* decipher what the child only felt in cipher" (*Suspiria*, p. 476 n). It is not and cannot be the purpose of the *Autobiographical Sketches* to decipher or otherwise reduce out the personal qualities of the experience related, but the lyric need have less respect for origins. The language of dreams may be derived as easily from revery as from actuality. Ignoring private meanings, the *Suspiria* turns the same interpretative attention on De Quincey's reminiscences and on a fresh, poetic creation like "Levana and Our Ladies of Sorrow." "*They* wheeled in mazes; *I* spelled the steps. *They* telegraphed from afar; *I* read the signals. . . . *Theirs* were the symbols; *mine* are the words" (*Suspiria*, p. 516). Thus all portions of *Suspiria de Profundis* are equally mysterious, equally remote from individual consciousness. The lyric is an assembly of occult messages transmitted by means of any situation rich enough to arouse emotions so profound that the human voice is stifled and all sublunary motion frozen. Only in such circumstances will a transcendental language become momentarily audible through the din of mortal living.

The depiction of tragic situations in fact becomes redundant, with the result that what was pathetic in the life of an individual becomes problematic in the context of the *Suspiria*. The concern becomes the explanation, the reason or the purpose for suffering.[13] The structure of each narrative is the same, proceeding to a point, just before the anagnorisis, at which all action ceases and the dramatic irony of lurking fate becomes most palpable. The helplessness of character and audience alike, suspended in this insecure tableau outside of time, exploits to its fullest the affective horror of the "indefinite approach of a loitering catastrophe." Yet the reiteration of this structure—which would have been even more pronounced in the ultimate expansion De Quincey had planned for the *Suspiria*—has an entropic effect.[14] "The eye is wearied with the eternal wheelings. . . . Grecian simplicities of motion, amidst a labyrinthine infinity of curves that would baffle the geometry of Appolonius" (*Suspiria*, p. 493). Even the "Affliction of Childhood," in its original form, consists of three complete cycles of grief. De Quincey lists these "phases of revolving affection": "1st, for instance, in its immediate pressure, so stunning and confounding; 2dly, in its oscillations, as in its earlier agitations, frantic with tumults . . . diseased impulses of sick languishing desire, through which sorrow transforms itself to a sunny angel . . . third . . . where the affliction, seemingly hushing itself to sleep, suddenly soars upwards again upon combining with *another* mode of sorrow, namely, anxiety without definite limits" (*Suspiria*, pp. 492–93).

In its original triadic pattern, the "Affliction" was well suited to the dialectical design of the *Suspiria* as a whole. Interlocking triads recur at several levels of the text: three stages of opium addiction, three oscillations of childish sorrow, three personified sorrows appearing in one of three dream sequences in the first part of the lyric, and three tales of human strife (two biographical and a third of an ambiguous, half-fictive nature) in the second and concluding part, "Vision of Life." The structural logic is pendular rather than linear, superficially aberrant yet subliminally sound.

Here pause, Reader! Imagine yourself seated in some cloud-scaling swing, oscillating under the impulse of lunatic hands; for the strength of lunacy may belong to human dreams, the fearful caprice of lunacy, and the malice of lunacy. . . . Seated in such a swing, fast as you reach the lowest point of depression, may you rely on racing up to a starry altitude of corresponding ascent. Ups and downs you will see, heights and depths, in our fiery course together, such as will sometimes tempt you to look shyly and suspiciously at me, your guide, and the ruler of the oscillations. [*Suspiria*, p. 502]

Although the direction of De Quincey's autobiography is less than straightforward, it is certainly not lunatic; the *Sketches* move steadily ahead in time and become steadily broader in social and historical scope. But chronology is confused in the *Suspiria*. De Quincey's experiences as infant, as schoolboy, as Oxonian, and ultimately as addict are interspersed irrationally in an antitemporal pattern. The psychological processes of memory and dream which are kept distinct in the autobiography merge and blend chaotically. The lyric mimics, in the way chronologically separate scenes lie together in the text, the workings of a subconscious mind. *Suspiria de Profundis* is an enactment of a dream, whereas the *Autobiographical Sketches* is only the report of certain dreams.

The "profound sigh" for which the lyric is named is actually the middle term in the triadic chain which gives the text its order and momentum. Beginning in the "Introductory Notice" in a state of will-less resignation to sorrow which is the product of the final stage of opium, the lyric then moves back to explore, in part one, a childish grief in which total resignation is not yet reached. There is a description of how De Quincey resisted capitulating to his sorrow, omitted from the later autobiography, where it would be irrelevant.

In what world was I living when a man (calling himself a man of God) could stand up publicly and give God "hearty thanks" that he had taken away my sister? But, young child, understand—taken her away from the miseries of this sinful world. O Yes! I hear what you say; I understand *that*; but that makes no difference at all. . . . I did not presume, child though I was, to think rebelliously against *that*. The reason was not any hypocritical or canting submission where my heart yielded none, but because already my deep musing intellect had perceived a mystery and a labyrinth in the economies of this world . . . it was a benignity that pointed far ahead; such as by a child could not have been perceived, because then the great arch had not come round. [*Suspiria*, pp. 481–82]

Rather than submit, the child looks outside himself, questions and accuses his elders and, in a later passage, the heavens themselves. But though there is no answer or reconciliation, and though this stage of sorrow diffuses into "anxiety without definite limits," the way to redemption remains open in the lyric as it was not in the autobiography. The irreparable loss can here be healed, but the loss cannot be made good in the person of De Quincey or his sister Elizabeth. There is an explanation and a meaning to this sorrow, but it is not a meaning the conscious mind can accept. It is a mystery revealed only to the "deep musing intellect."

From this potent but ultimately unconsummated childish grief, the *Suspiria* returns to adult sorrows, to the state of resignation described in the preface in which no resilience or innocence remains and "the spirit of man flies back upon its own centre." Examining the "palimpsest of the human brain," it explains how ineradicable memories persist within this centre, beneath the level of consciousness, and by way of demonstration presents a series of "dreams or noonday visions" which recapitulate the earlier affliction under the influence of opium. In the first vision, the "Ladies of Sorrow" portray various modes of grief, the childish "Lady of Tears" giving way to the resigned "Lady of Sighs." But she is in turn succeeded by another and more demonic form of sorrow, "Our Lady of Darkness." The lyric has now progressed from the state of emotion with which it began, but the movement is inward as well, into an abyss of sinister and schizophrenic doubt. The next vision, "The Apparition of the Brocken," also appears as a dream in chapter one of the autobiography, but there it is abbreviated and on the whole rather playful. In the lyric, this strange apparition, mimicking every human movement, becomes instead a symbol for the ambiguity of the subconscious and the phenomenology of dreams. De Quincey identifies the specter with what he calls "the Dark Interpreter": "Such a relation does the Dark Interpreter, whom immediately the reader will learn to know as an intruder into my dreams, bear to my own mind. He is originally a mere reflex of my inner nature. But . . . the Interpreter sometimes swerves out of my orbit, and mixes a little with alien natures. I do not always know him as my own parhelion . . . in dreams there is a power not content with reproduction, but which absolutely creates or transforms" (*Suspiria*, p. 525).

The mockery of the spectral reduplication of each gesture of sorrow, which is the peculiar property of the Apparition of the Brocken and also of dream life, begins to take on a new meaning. What might have seemed obsessed and futile repetition of a tragedy in dream after dream is shown to be a subtle mode of transformation: "in dreams there is a power not contented with mere reproduction." The remorse of opium addiction has given rise to the visionary Levana, goddess of education, and her ministers, the Ladies of Sorrow. "By the education of Levana, therefore, is meant,—not the poor machinery that moves by spelling books and grammars, but by that mighty system of central forces hidden in the deep bosom of human life, which by passion, by strife, by temptation, by the energies of resistance, works forever upon children,—resting not day or night, any more than the mighty wheel of day and night themselves, whose moments, like restless spokes, are glimmering forever as they revolve" (*Suspiria*, p. 514). Repeated agony at last exhausts the ability and will to evade its lessons. The figures of the dream turn upon the dreamer "to plague his heart until we [Levana and her Sorrows] had unfolded the capacities of his spirit." The force of Levana is everywhere in the dreams and sorrowful tales which compose the lyric, and the demonic Dark Interpreter, linked to the *Mater Tenebrarum* or third Lady of Sorrow, is another of her agents. It is he who expounds upon the nature of transcendental justice envisioned by the dreaming mind as the ruined city of "Savannah-La-Mar." The alien wisdom of his interpretation of the vision both comforts and confounds one who can no longer recognize in the Interpreter's command of the involuted logic of providence a "mere reflex of my inner nature." "O, deep is the ploughing of grief! But oftentimes less would not suffice for the agriculture of God. . . . Upon the sorrow of an infant he raises oftentimes from human intellects glorious vintages that could not else have been" (*Suspiria*, p. 527).

As the *Suspiria* unfolds, then, the emotional effects and implications of that original remorseful sigh take shape before our eyes, generating new categories of emotion and new capacities of intuition. The education of Levana is carried out within and by means of the lyric itself, making static recollection a dynamic process. In the final segment of the text, the autobiographical world is upended, memory becomes prophecy and the problem of death and things past becomes the problem of birth and things to come: "Heavens! When I look back to the sufferings which I have witnessed or heard of, even from this one brief London experience, I say, if life could throw open its long suites of chambers to our eyes from some station *beforehand*,—if, from some secret stand, we could look by *anticipation* along its vast corridors . . . what a recoil we should suffer of horror in our estimate of life" (*Suspiria*, p. 544). This is the "Vision of Life" which the *Suspiria* provides in its second part, charting the calamities of three successive generations. Each narrative predicts the suffering of a young woman, but the anticipated events are never actually described. The final words of the lyric are not a statement about what has happened but a question about what might: "Seeing such things in so short a space of years . . . we say,—Death we can face: but knowing, as some of us do, what is human life, which of us is it that without shuddering could (if consciously we were summoned) face the hour of birth?" (*Suspiria*, p. 551).

Suspiria de Profundis thus achieves its reconciliation with death, "the great arch" has ultimately "come round." It has also reached a new concern and a new kind of fear and pity, a depth of emotion beyond the personal privations of a child or the private horrors of an opium addict. But this deeper and more universal agony trembles paradoxically on the verge of exultation. Paralysis and will-less silence have become art and motion, and the questions of the heaven-accusing child have been turned inward to excavate and explore an infinity beneath superficially finite and unique experiences. Self-pity has been replaced by an inexhaustible compassion for the entire race of men and the human condition. Moreover, at the *Suspiria*'s close, human suffering is balanced against a mysterious but justifying providence. Awareness of this comes only in dreams, but despite intervening material between the visionary segments and the conclusion, it is a subliminal awareness even here. It must be, according to what we have earlier been told about the cumulative powers of the human brain: "Everlasting layers of ideas, images, feelings, have fallen upon your brain softly as light. Each succession has seemed to bury all that went before. And yet, in reality, not one has been extinguished" (*Suspiria*, p. 510). Long before the work concludes, the dreams have hinted that human suffering is potentially endless but at the same time have created a priceless recognition that infinite emotion implies an infinite capacity in the human spirit.

The *Autobiographical Sketches* never achieve because they never aspire to such a tragic resolution. De Quincey claims no universality for his experiences, and sentimentality and whimsy are alone within his reach. There is a marked egocentricity in his autobiographical treatment of even fairly public and observable affairs. Take, for example, two small but telling changes made in transferring the account of his sister's funeral from *Suspiria de Profundis* to his autobiography:

There is exposed once again, and for the last time, the coffin. All eyes survey the record of name, of sex, of age, and the day of departure from earth,—records how useless! and dropped into darkness as if messages addressed to worms. . . . The coffin is lowered into its home; it has disappeared from the eye. [*Suspiria*, pp. 472–73]

All eyes survey the record of name, of sex, of age, and the day of departure from earth—records how shadowy! and dropped into darkness as messages addressed to worms. . . . The coffin is lowered into its home; it has disappeared from all eyes but those that look down into the abyss of the grave. [*Sketches*, p. 44]

In the *Sketches*, the record on the coffin lid is no longer "useless" but "shadowy," suggesting that, however vaguely, it still remains within the scope of a human observer. Moreover, the coffin no longer simply disappears from the general eye; a privileged few—among them De Quincey himself—are still able to see into the abyss into which it has been lowered. Much of the terror and all of the universality of the original perspective has been lost. The scene of his sister's burial has become, in a phrase added to the autobiographical account, "a sweet and solemn farewell." The funeral ceremony thus becomes the only possible amends for the "mutilated parting" he had earlier attempted to effect at his sister's bedside; custom and tradition repair, albeit imperfectly, the farewell which had been flawed by an interruption and left incomplete. A rational and sentimental acknowledgment of death replaces the savage mystery and disappearance into darkness no human eye can delve which had been the burden of the original description.

The same tendency to take himself as his exclusive point of orientation lurks beneath the surface of most of De Quincey's autobiographical scenes, no matter how meticulously he details the position of other features of the setting:

On the centre of the lawn stood my eldest surviving sister, Mary, and my brother, William. Round *him*, attracted (as ever) by his inexhaustible opulence of thought and fun, stood, laughing and dancing, my youngest sister, a second Jane, and my youngest brother, Henry ... whirling round on his heel, at a little distance, and utterly abstracted from all around him, my next brother, Richard. ... And, finally, as regards myself, it happened that I was standing close to the edge of the brook, looking back at intervals to the group of five children and two nursemaids who occupied the centre of the lawn. [*Sketches*, p. 117]

The order of presentation and the eccentricity of De Quincey's own position conceal the fact that he is actually the focus of the account. It is his own backward glance that catches and groups the children and servants into their various constellations, positioning them in the still and moving circle at the geometric center of the lawn. The orientation becomes more evident when the tableau is suddenly shattered by the approach of a mad dog:

So standing, and so occupied, suddenly we were alarmed by the shouts as of some great mob manifestly in rapid motion, and probably, at this instant, taking the right-angled turn into the lane ... within one minute, another right-angled turn in the lane itself brought the uproar fully upon the ear ... and it became evident that some imminent danger ... must be hastily nearing us. We were all rooted to the spot. ... In a few seconds, a powerful dog, not much above a furlong ahead of his pursuers, wheeled into sight. We all saw him pause at the gates; but, finding no ready access through the iron lattice-work ... he resumed his course along the outer margin of the brook. Coming opposite myself, he made a dead stop. [*Sketches*, pp. 117–18]

In a few sentences, the world beyond the suburban landscape has been opened to our view, revealing that what had seemed to be the center was actually the periphery and that De Quincey alone occupies the point on which the maze of right-angled turns will at last converge.

Similarly, when the *Autobiographical Sketches* quote speakers other than De Quincey, the ostensibly direct and unmediated report of what was said is actually not that at all:

It was the understood necessity of the case, that I must passively accept my brother's statements so far as regarded their verbal expression; and, if I would extricate my poor islanders from their troubles, it must be by some distinction or evasion lying *within* this expression, or not blankly contradicting it.

"How, and to what extent," my brother asked, "did I raise taxes upon my subjects?" [*Sketches*, p. 90]

Despite the disclaimer and the quotation marks, this is not what his brother said but what De Quincey heard—since William is not posing a question to himself but interrogating and bullying his younger brother on his policies as regent of Gombroon. De Quincey himself rarely speaks in his recollections, and when he does his speech is reported indirectly. Especially in the closing chapters and as he matures, the indirect reports of his youthful disputations become more numerous and lengthy. By citing his former remarks indirectly in this way, the words of the younger man overlap with those of the older and mingle with the autobiographical act itself. "I even startled myself, with distinctions that to this hour strike me as profoundly just. . . . Two out of many I will here repeat; and with the more confidence, that in these two I can be sure of repeating the exact thoughts" (*Sketches*, p. 368).

There follows a list of points, all in indirect discourse: "my own assertion to Lady Carbery, that all religion amongst the Pagans resolved itself into a mere system of ceremonial worship . . . was expressly insisted on in 1800" (p. 372). The original words have passed through a process of analysis, preserving only the propositional content of the assertion. When, however, the autobiographer is less eager to assimilate what he once had said and wishes to destroy the identification between the writer and the speaker, quasi-direct report techniques are used, capturing in caricature the mannerisms of voice. "Still there was one resource: if I 'didn't like it'—meaning the state of things in Gombroon—I might 'abdicate.' Yes, I knew *that*. I might abdicate; and, once having cut the connection between myself and the poor abject islanders, I might seem to have no further interest in the degradation that affected them. After such a disruption between us, what was it to me if they had even three tails apiece?" (*Sketches,* p. 99). De Quincey ridicules his childish anxiety by placing snatches of his original idiom and mood—his hyperbolic interrogative, for example—in the context of words far above what any child could have spoken. He uses the same mixed direct and indirect report for the speech of his former tutor, a man whose scholarship and constitutional indolence bring him uncomfortably close to the autobiographer, and a man whose guilty complicity in the mistreatment of his daughters makes the identification abhorrent to De Quincey: "But with a nature that sought for peace before all things, in this very worst of its aggravations was found a cure—the effectual temptation to willful blindness and forgetfulness. . . . Could he be pinned on, morning, noon, and night, to his wife's apron?" (*Sketches*, p. 107).

The contrast between indirect and quasi-direct renderings is vital to the effect of the autobiography's conclusion. "He asked me, in a way which I felt to be taunting, how I could consent to waste my time as I did. Without any answering warmth, I explained that my guardians, having quarrelled with me, would not grant for my use anything beyond my school allowance of £100 per annum. Upon that opening, he spoke to my mother; and the result was that, within seven days from the conversation, I found myself entering that time-honoured University" (*Sketches*, p. 416). In his exchange with his uncle—with whom he still "occupied the position of a reputed boy"—it is the older man who is reduced to the status of a child. Whereas De Quincey's uncle petulantly questions, the cool and neutral response of his nephew is a sentence too complex in its embedded clauses and too technical in its diction to have actually been spoken. The indirect report is the restrained rhetoric of a writer, of the man who now is writing this account, while the quasi-direct quotation of his overwrought uncle appears infantile in contrast. No matter what the outcome of his original confrontation, De Quincey clearly wins the day in retrospect.

The progress of the young De Quincey is a clearly measured one; all the resources of language reflect his triumphant march toward adulthood. In the earliest stages of his youth, De Quincey sees himself consistently acted upon and never acting, the helpless victim of forces and persons larger than himself. "About this time, my brother began to issue . . . a regular gazette. . . . I suppose that no creature ever led such a life as *I* did in that gazette. Run up to the giddiest heights of promotion on one day, for merits which I could not myself discern, in a week or two I was brought a court-martial for offences equally obscure. I was cashiered; I was restored. . . . I was threatened with being drummed out of the army . . . and then, in the midst of all this misery and degradation, upon the discovery of some supposed energy that I had manifested, I was decorated with the Order of the Bath" (*Sketches*, p. 85). At times he is so inert that he seems hardly human, and his role as mere object serves as topic of the sentence: "On these visits it was that I, as a young pet whom they carried about like a doll from my second to my eighth or ninth year, learned to know them" (*Sketches*, p. 359).

Even when he has left his infancy and earlier childhood behind him, he assumes at best a limited mobility and control over his own actions. He is "sent" on his visits or to his schools and "directed" to perform a good part of his deeds. Until the final chapter of the autobiography, the forces which compel him go unnamed. But when he abandons public school of his own accord, flees to London, and eventually returns to his home, he at last confronts directly the source of all these orders and directives, his widowed mother. Oxford is, significantly, the first school to which De Quincey sends himself; the sheer irritation he arouses with his constant, pedantic quarrels forces his mother to capitulate to his desire for early college entrance. The young man who thus becomes the architect of his own fate, and who does so through his powers of argument, now coincides with the writer who manipulates his life within his autobiography.

The same process of growth appears in other dimensions as well. Much of the autobiography's comedy comes, for example, from dwelling on discrepancies between appearance and reality, on what "seems" to be the case to the naive child or adolescent. "It seems I owed eternal deference to one so much older than myself, so much wiser, stronger, braver, more beautiful, and more swift of foot" (*Sketches*, p. 71). As the autobiography progresses, however, one sees the ability to gauge the motivation of others develop in De Quincey. The increasing use of modals which reflect certainty or necessity becomes another axis for displaying his relative maturity. "I—contemplating the idea of that gloomy academic dungeon to which for three long years I anticipated too certainly a sentence of exile—felt very much as in the middle ages must have felt some victims of evil destiny" (*Sketches*, pp. 330–31). When the child becomes capable of this kind of certain anticipation of what others "must have felt," the autobiographical record of the growth of judgment is complete.

Suspiria de Profundis is an accumulation rather than a progression, reconciling rather than abandoning various stages of interpenetrating emotion. There is no a priori condition such as adulthood which it must reach, no externally circumscribed identity with which it must converge. In fact, it is so far from egocentricity that it appears to have no perfectly stable center of orientation. As in the autobiography, but far less casually, apparently innocent geographies will suddenly burst open, distend into vague and irrational perspectives. A lunatic maze becomes visible around the point where we had at first been situated, destroying our sense of distances and relationships, threatening our balance.

Behold a lawn islanded with thickets. How perfect is the verdure, how rich the blossoming shrubberies that screen the verdurous walls from the possibility of intrusion, whilst by their own wandering line of distribution they shape and umbrageously embay what one might call lawny saloons and vestibules, sylvan galleries and closets! Some of these recesses, which unlink themselves as fluently as snakes, and unexpectedly as the shyest nooks, watery cells, and crypts, amongst the shores of a forest lake, being formed by the mere caprices and ramblings of the luxuriant shrubs, are so small and so quiet that one might fancy them meant for *boudoirs*. [*Suspiria*, p. 549]

De Quincey toys briefly with a setting "unlinking" itself and snaking off into indefinable distances in his *Autobiographical Sketches*, when he describes his first impressions of arriving in London: "The great length of the streets in many quarters of London; the continual opening of transient glimpses into other vistas equally far-stretching, going off at right angles . . . the murky atmosphere which, settling upon the remoter end of every long avenue, wraps its termination in gloom and uncertainty" (*Sketches*, p. 182). This expanding universe is too threatening, however, when orientation centers on an individual person, and the description is quickly terminated before the vertiginous sense of "Babylonian confusion" becomes unbearable. Although he may be peripherally aware of things lurking just beyond the edges of his vision, the autobiographer holds fast to his limited point of view. Forces may gather where he cannot see them, but he registers them only as they coalesce around himself, as when the mad dog's mazing path takes him centripetally and inevitably toward De Quincey at the center.

The *Suspiria* deliberately creates a sense of disorientation, not only spatial but temporal. When a sufficiently deep layer of subjectivity is reached, time and space in fact are one. This merger of the mazing space of infinity and the "spiralling time" of eternity is a central metaphor of the lyric.[15] "If life could throw open its long suites of chambers to our eyes . . . we could look by *anticipation* along its vast corridors, and aside into the recesses opening upon them from either hand . . . simply in that narrow tract of time, and no more, where we ourselves shall range" (*Suspiria*, p. 544). The more superficial experiences and subjectivity recorded in the autobiography can of course never arrive at this transcendental connection.

It is the Dark Interpreter, as one might expect, who reveals how very distorted is the mundane view of time. A second is the smallest conventional unit of time, yet a second may be segmented into 100 separate drops passing through a Roman clepsydra. "When the fiftieth of the hundred is passing, behold! forty-nine are not, because they have perished; and fifty are not, because they are yet to come. You see therefore, how narrow, how incalculably narrow, is the true and actual present. . . . Yet even this approximation to the truth is *infinitely* false. For again subdivide that solitary drop . . . and so by infinite declensions the true and very present, in which only we live and enjoy, will vanish into a mote, distinguishable only by a heavenly vision" (*Suspiria*, p. 526). In its concluding "Vision of Life," the lyric attempts to recreate just such a sensation, leaping dizzily from moment to moment, dissolving time into a chimera of unrelated moments which are all equally present and not-present. "Shall we, then, after an interval of nearly two years has passed over the young lady in the boudoir, look in again upon *her*? You hesitate, fair friend; and I myself hesitate. For in fact she also has become a wreck. . . . On consideration, therefore, let us do this.— We will direct our glasses to her room at a point of time about six weeks further on. Suppose this time gone; suppose her now dressed for her grave, and placed in her coffin" (*Suspiria*, p. 548). This giddy process continues for the length of several pages, ending only with the conclusion of the *Suspiria* itself. The present seems to become coterminous with each passing word, a sickening instability meant to drive us from the delusions of consciousness to the infinite truth of dreams. "All is finite in the present; and even that finite is infinite in its velocity of flight towards death. . . . Therefore, it follows, that for God there can be no present. The future is the present of God, and to the future it is that he sacrifices the human present" (*Suspiria*, p. 527).

God has a topological view of time, a simultaneous awareness of contemporary suffering and its eventual redress. But there is a "god-like" power in human intuition which reconciles experience and providence. *Suspiria de Profundis* simulates this intimation of immortality in its architectural metaphors and in its inverted and pendular narrative perspectives. The interlocking logic of the work means that the end is already implied in the beginning; that no part is really separate or prior to another. The text explicitly folds back upon itself in its final moments: "recesses . . . being formed by the mere caprices and ramblings of the luxuriant shrubs. . . . Here is one that in a less fickle climate would make the loveliest of studies for a writer of breathings of some solitary heart, or of *suspiria* from some impassioned memory! And opening from one angle of this embowered study, issues a little narrow corridor, that, after almost wheeling back upon itself, in its playful mazes, finally widens into a little circular chamber; out of which there is no exit (except back again by the entrance. . .)" (*Suspiria,* p. 549). The circle closes seamlessly, the beginning now implied within the end, a perfect structural analogue of eternity.

There are hints earlier on that the text is actually spiraling back upon itself, becoming a self-sustaining artifact from which there is no referential exit. For example, the subjunctive mood of the "Affliction of Childhood" portrays the rupture between what "might have been" and what really has occurred. "Thus perished the vision, loveliest amongst all the shows which the earth has revealed to me; thus mutilated was the parting which should have lasted forever" (*Suspiria,* p. 469). The subjective realm of wish and pure potentiality is opposed and defeated by objective factors beyond its control. But in the sequence of reveries which follow this piece of personal history, will is triumphant. The subjunctive gives way to the indicative; what "could" or "should" be becomes what is. In the elaborate analogy between the human brain and the many-layered palimpsest, this shift in mood is particularly noticeable. "Had *they* been better chemists, had *we* been worse, the mixed result, namely that dying for *them*, the flower should revive for us, could not have been effected" (*Suspiria,* p. 507). Simultaneous possibilities—apparently inconsistent with each other—have been realized; what might have been both is and is not the case. As the lyric moves into the vortex of the dreams, the language ever more strongly reflects an act of will. "I wish to have these abstractions presented as impersonations" (p. 515), breathes the narrator, and immediately that wish is effected by the appearance of the Ladies of Sorrow.

It is in the "Vision of Life," however, that dream possibilities become indistinguishable from realities.

Suppose her now dressed for her grave, and placed in her coffin. The advantage of that is, that though no change can restore the ravages of the past, yet . . . the expression has revived from her girlish years. The child-like aspect has revolved and settled back upon her features. The wasting away of the flesh is less apparent in the fact; and one might imagine that in this sweet marble countenance was seen the very same upon which, eleven years ago, her mother's darkening eyes had lingered to the last. . . . Yet, if that were in part a fancy, this at least is no fancy,—that not only much of a child-like truth and simplicity has reinstated itself . . . but also that tranquility and perfect peace, such as are appropriate to eternity. [*Suspiria*, pp. 548–49]

Here, narrator and audience hover over the coffin, in a scene that parallels the child standing over his dead sister, and the interrupted farewell is restaged. It is accomplished only in imagination, and the characters are no longer the same, but within the charmed circle of the lyric, the moment of parting is perfected and no alien force from the outer world can intrude upon the scene. Although "no change can restore the ravages of the past," some subjective efforts are strong enough to make what "one might imagine" into something which is "no fancy." "Tranquility" has been achieved, a momentary nexus between humanity and eternity established, as the comfort of imagination bypasses the superficial intellect to penetrate mysteriously the "understanding heart."

A seamless work of art, a simulacrum of the infinite, cannot appear to be dependent on an extrinsic power—even the power of its author. Quite the opposite occurs in the *Suspiria*: the narrator appears to be absorbed into the text. One cannot even tell when the narrator is speaking or when it is his "parhelion" and sardonic double, the Dark Interpreter. "This dark being the reader will see again in a further stage of my opium experience; and I warn him that he will not always be found sitting inside my dreams, but at times outside, and in the open daylight" (*Suspiria*, p. 525). Originally, of course, the Dark Interpreter was nothing more than a projection. His first incarnations are treated as the narrator's invention—the "Mother of Darkness"—or as a mirage troubling his vision—the "Apparition of the Brocken." It is he who invests them with the power of movement and speech: "Do they talk, then? O no! Mighty phantoms like these disdain the infirmities of language. They may utter voices through the organs of man when they dwell in human hearts . . . *mine* are the words" (*Suspiria*, p. 516).

But in the landscape of the dreams the distinction between artifice and reality becomes harder and harder to sustain. The words of the Dark Interpreter are rendered as direct discourse, as quotations of autonomous remarks which are addressed to the dreamer and not created by him. "What he says, generally, is but that which *I* have said in daylight. . . . But sometimes, as his face alters, his words alter; and they do not always seem such as I have used, or *could* use" (*Suspiria*, p. 524). After "Savannah-La—mar," the Dark Interpreter seems to disappear; yet as readers we have been warned that he will be seen again, outside dreams, and that he may be altered beyond all recognition. A queasy sensation of doubt has been engendered by these words, a sensation that becomes all the more intense when one reads a casual remark about the enchanted gardens appearing in the final scene of the "Vision of Life": "however caused and supported, the silence of these fanciful lawns and lawny chambers is oftentimes oppressive" (*Suspiria*, p. 550). One cannot be at all certain who or what is in control, behind this oppressive silence and winding maze of hedges from which, as we are told, there is now "no exit." A wordless energy seems to enclose the narrator, making his words echo strangely in the lawny chamber—"the loveliest of studies for a writer of suspiria"—which suddenly surrounds him. It is almost as if he himself were now being quoted, reduced to a character within his own ostensible creation.

The impression of a miraculuos creation ex nihilo is woven deeply into the texture of the lyric. Visions and memories are personal materials, and yet, for all their intensity, the narrator treats them as foreign visitations. "It is a fact that this pertinacious life of memory for things that simply touch the ear, without touching the consciousness, does in fact, beset me. Said but once, said but softly, not marked at all, words revive before me in darkness and solitude; and they arrange themselves gradually into sentences, but through an effort sometimes of a distressing kind, to which I am in a manner forced to become a party" (*Suspiria*, p. 480). The thematic focus is not, as in the autobiography, on the passive individual but on the "pertinacious life of memory" which seems to overwhelm him and use him to effect its own designs. The inverted syntax which appears here and elsewhere in De Quincey's "impassioned prose" has aroused a good deal of comment[16] for the rhythmic qualities of its anaphoric repetitions[17] and its decorative parallel clauses.[18] But inversion also has a semantic dimension as a means for selectively attending to some factors while omitting others. In the passage cited here, the omission of an agent of the inverted clause—"said but once"—creates a momentary uncertainty about who it is that speaks and who is listening, thus heightening the awe and universality of the reported subjective process. The self-begetting life of memory is situated in a voided, pure subjective space that has been cleared of all the accidents of time and place, identity and personality.

Despite the fact that the narrator's responsibility for subjective acts has been so much reduced, these remain almost the only duties or capacities the lyric will allow him. De Quincey's avatar in the *Suspiria* has all of the contemplative but nothing of the active life of De Quincey in the *Sketches*. He is also a far more shadowy and indefinite figure, often identified only by his titles: "a lover of open-hearted sincerity," "a sufferer," or simply "the man who reports." These impersonal labels obviously contribute to the ambiguous blurring of the narrator with his Dark Interpreter. In the sections of the *Suspiria* which reappear in his autobiography, De Quincey carefully expunges these remote designations, replacing "a lover of open-heared sincerity," for example, with "myself." The autobiographer is never reduced to playing the simple functionary of his text, and the link between De Quincey and his narrator is never impersonal. "Now began to unfold themselves the consolations of solitude, those consolations which only I was destined to taste; now, therefore, began to open upon me those fascinations of solitude, which when acting as co-agency with unresisted grief, end in making out of grief itself a luxury; such a luxury as finally becomes a snare, overhanging life itself, and the energies of life, with growing menances" (*Sketches*, p. 45).

When the same emotional moment is reported in the lyric, amid the cycles and epicycles of so very many griefs, it loses its privacy, and "I" is changed to "you" and finally to "we." "Witchcraft has seized upon you,—nympholepsy has struck you. Now you rave no more. You acquiesce; nay, you are passionately delighted in your condition . . . when we stretch out our arms in darkness, vainly striving to draw back the sweet faces that have vanished, slowly arises a new strategem of grief, and we say,—'be it that they no more come back to us, yet what hinders but we should go to them?' " (*Suspiria*, pp. 483–84). In the autobiography, I and "only I" taste those emotions; a shared subjective experience is never contemplated. Principles of psychology may indeed be much the same, but these are treated as objective "agencies of grief." The *Sketches* reserve "you" and "one," or the inclusive "we," for matters which are capable of being literally shared, phenomena of modern life, urban flurry, modes of travel, national events. The author's past and his private sensations are not open to the mystical participation of others.

The voice of the autobiography, then, speaks with individual accent while the voice of the lyric is almost disembodied. Even when he is forced to use the first person, the narrator of the *Suspiria* insists that: "I do not mean to lay a stress upon any idiosyncrasy in myself. Possibly every man has an idiosyncrasy . . . what I point to are not peculiarities of temperament or of organization, so much as peculiar circumstances and incidents through which my own separate experience had revolved. Some of these were of a nature to alter the whole economy of my mind" (*Suspiria*, p. 452). De Quincey's idiosyncrasies at best have an instrumental value; his suffering has meaning only because it has given him access to the roots of human pain. He penetrates other afflictions using his own as a wedge, and it is with these others that the lyric finally ends. (In De Quincey's fully expanded version of the lyric, there would have been an even smaller proportionate role for the narrator's own experiences.) This is a voice that speaks of its own painful memories with neither more nor less sympathy than those of any other person, seeming actually to report as the result of patient inference rather than recollection. "Henceforeward, the character of my thoughts must have changed greatly; for so representative are some acts, that one single case of the class is sufficient to throw open before you the whole theatre of possibilities in that direction" (*Suspiria*, p. 460). The child's mind is entered via the laws of epistemology, as though only thus can the narrator determine what must have been the case. To this transcendental ego, the universal processes of mind are more familiar than the facts of one man's life. But there is no such qualification on self-knowledge in the *Autobiographical Sketches*, the modal "must" is pruned to give the parallel to this passage the sound of something spoken directly from experience.

The power of universal sympathy which underlies *Suspiria de Profundis* moves the narrator to "look indulgently upon the errors of understanding, or limitations of view which now he has long survived." Sublime disinterest can afford greater benevolence than an autobiographer who cannot avoid self-conscious worries about his own appearance. "Frantic were the clamours as I concluded my nonsense. . . . I look back on that state of mind as an almost criminal reproach to myself" (*Sketches*, p. 396). Speaking as an autobiographer, De Quincey feels himself compelled to censure or to praise, to defend or to quarrel with what even a long-past performance might imply about himself. He thus becomes defensive about his mistaken first impressions of Irish politics: "I wrote, therefore, originally under a jealousy that partially I might have been duped. . . . Duped, perhaps, I was myself: and it was natural that I should be so under the overwhelming influences oppressing any right that I *could* have at my early age to a free independent judgment" (*Sketches*, pp. 265–66 n).

The strain between a mute sense of identity and a perception of difference, the art of forming an acceptable whole from moments which are alien and shameful as well as familiar or proud—which is the chief preoccupation of the autobiography—is treated in a summary fashion and casually dismissed in the lyric's preface. "Though relating to a man's proper self, it is a self so far removed from his present self as to wound no feelings of delicacy or reserve. It is privileged, also, as a proper subject for the sympathy of the narrator. . . . He acknowledges the deep, mysterious identity between himself, as adult and as infant, for the ground of his sympathy; and yet, with this general agreement and necessity of agreement, he feels the differences between his two selves as the main quickeners of his sympathy" (*Suspiria*, p. 452). The discussion of this task is discharged coolly, in a businesslike third person all the more remarkable for its context in "impassioned prose." There is so little pressure toward the kind of convergence of character and narrator found in the *Sketches* that the two become, if anything, increasingly remote. As the lyric begins to withdraw palpably into itself, the narrator is detached from what the victim undergoes, the experiences of the latter becoming to the former "the image, the memorial, the record, which for me is derived." In the midst of terrifying dreams, the narrator begins to feel redeemed—at one level a martyr to opium, at another level beneficiary of the visions it creates: "suddenly, at a silent command, at the signal of a blazing rocket sent up from the brain, the pall draws up, and the whole depths of the theatre are exposed. Here was the great mystery: now this mystery is liable to no doubt; for it is repeated, and ten thousand times repeated, by opium, for those who are its martyrs" (*Suspiria*, p. 512).

When the single narrative consciousness becomes fragmented, dissolving into a multiple and involuted presence, we recognize that mundane identity is as infinitely divisible and ultimately as delusive as our mortal sense of time. De Quincey must also recognize this, but his autobiography cannot transcend mundane delusions, since it must be faithful—or at least responsive—to the things (including vulgar conceptions of identity) which elemented it. His "impassioned prose" is self-contained, generating its own narrative intelligence and a set of experiences and memories coterminous with the work itself. It can achieve therefore what autobiography cannot, the ideal aesthetic condition where "manner is confluent with matter." "The whole course of this narrative resembles, and was meant to resemble, a *caduceus* wreathed about with meandering ornaments, or the shaft of a tree's stem hung round and surmounted with some vagrant parasitical plant. The mere medical subject of the opium answers to the dry, withered pole, which shoots all the rings of the flowering plants and seems to do so by some dexterity of its own; whereas, in fact, the plant and its tendrils have curled round the sullen cylinder by mere luxuriance of *theirs*" (*Suspiria*, p. 454). The "Introductory Notice" alludes to the mysterious organic life of the lyrical process, but on the whole, *Suspiria de Profundis* maintains an air of secrecy about its inner workings. Self-consciousness would wither the appearance of organic growth and prevent the full flowering of subconscious expression. "The preparation pregnant with the future; the remote correspondence; the questions, as it were, which to a deep musical sense are asked in one passage, and answered in another; the iteration and ingemination of a given effect, moving through subtle variations that sometimes disguise the theme, sometimes fitfully reveal it, sometimes throw it tumultuously to the blaze of daylight: these and ten thousand forms of self-conflicting musical passion."[19]

De Quincey's essay on "Style" obviously captures the program of his impassioned prose. His *Suspiria* does indeed exalt rhythmic meaning over concept, emergent and spontaneous beauties over classical control. The structure of the work seems to hang on a certain subtle nexus where the energy of one emotion modulates into a new subjective key:

> Then it was plain that despair, that the anguish of darkness, was not *essential* to such sorrow, but might come and go. . . .
>   Yes! the light may come and go; grief may wax and wane; grief may sink; and grief may rise, as in impassioned minds oftentimes it does, even to the heaven of heavens; but there is a necessity that, if too much left to itself in solitude, finally it will descend into a depth from which there is no reascent; into a disease which seems no disease; into a languishing which, from its very sweetness, perplexes the mind, and is fancied to be health. [*Suspiria*, p. 483]

The intonation mimes the pendular swing of the emotion: first up from the tone of quiet meditation in the preceding paragraph, then inexorably down as the phrases run on and on, out of breath, to meet with the negative conjunction "but" and there languish. Anaphoric exclamations of this sort which look back to and repeat elements of a former paragraph as the opening of a new one do create a sense of musical correspondence and crescendo. Images and situations are reiterated until they have defined themselves and create their own appropriate classification. The process of the lyric is even called a "tumult of images" or a "musical chorus," something to be experienced and intuitively apprehended rather than rationally understood. The narration is a product of "desire" and "want," a breath that has escaped almost unnoticed to betray the sorrows of the soul.

There is never the slightest attempt to hide the machinery behind the *Autobiographical Sketches*, however, or to pretend that they are not consciously directed to a waiting world. What we see are after all deliberate representations, "sketches," and not involuntary sighs. The autobiographer continually shows himself at work, "looking back," "mentioning," "illustrating," and "demonstrating." Whereas the narrator of the *Suspiria* may occasionally "remember," the narrator of the *Sketches* insists on conscious control: "I recapitulate and gather under abstractions." He has subjected the material of the autobiography to analysis and separated it into appropriate "periods," "episodes," and "classes of experience" rather than allowing its organic shape to show itself. De Quincey also draws attention to the literal, the verbal quality of his act, to his "words" and "pages," and especially his "chapters." Indeed, it is the formal division into chapters, rather than any natural divisions in his life, which seems to fascinate him and to provide the cohesion necessary to the text. Chapters correspond to areas of time or space, and De Quincey enjoys informing his readers of how a clever author can impose his order on even the most arbitrary matters. "My last two chapters, very slenderly connected with Birmingham, are yet made to rise out of it; the one out of Birmingham's own relation to the topic concerned (viz., *Travelling*) and the other (viz., *My Brother*) out of its relation to all possible times in my earlier life, and therefore, why not to all possible places. . . . Pretending only to amuse my reader, or pretending chiefly to *that* . . . I enjoy a privelege of neglecting harsher logic, and connecting the separate sections of these sketches, not by ropes and cables, but by threads of aerial gossamer" (*Sketches*, p. 316).

The barrier between experience and its presentation is frequently made absolute; space contracts from three dimensions to a point within the linear unfolding of the book. De Quincey portrays adventures "at" geographical centers, rarely inviting us to enter "in" or be with him "within" them. He makes an elegant but obtrusive artifice out of his most harrowing adventures, such as his escape from a mad dog: "Not only was the Chapter of *Infancy* thus solemnly finished for ever, and the record closed; but—which cannot often happen—the chapter was closed pompously and conspicuously, by what early printers through the fifteenth and sixteenth centuries would have called a bright and illuminated Colophon" (*Sketches,* p. 120). One is allowed to relish his skill and to admire his erudition, but entrance into his life is ultimately denied.

This glossy barrier between his public act of self-display and his inviolable past is also evident in the strict alternation between the perfective of the performatives and the imperfective of events and experience. There is frequent mention of what "has been said," or what the narrator "has always maintained," but episodes in De Quincey's life are always and irrevocably severed from the present. This is the discrepancy one sees most clearly in the book's concluding sentence, where no attempt is made to bring the past to its fulfillment in the present. The autobiography concludes as he "was entering" Oxford, and there it will always remain, left dangling in unresolved progressive.

The progressive appears near the end of the *Suspiria* as well, but there it coincides with the pulsing of the text itself: "Now and just as we are speaking, you may hear her joyous clamour . . . now she comes dancing into sight" (*Suspiria*, p. 550). The process of the report and the process of experience are perfectly isomorphic. The progressive is far more widely used in the lyric than in the later *Sketches*, no doubt because it reflects organic dynamism and because it merges with the "-ing" form of the gerund which is also prevalent. The lyric does not speak of singular actions but of iterated, cyclical phenomena or of activity in its eternal potentiality. The city of "Savannah-La-Mar," ruined yet preserved beneath the sea, is an emblem of this ceaseless motion without either beginning or end. "The city, therefore, like a mighty galleon with all her apparel mounted, streamers flying, and tackling perfect, seems floating along the noiseless depths of the ocean . . . she fascinates the eye with a *Fata-Morgana* revelation, as of human life still subsisting in submarine asylums sacred from the storms that torment our upper air" (*Suspiria*, p. 525). This is the simulacrum of memory, activity preserved without actuality. The palimpsest of the human brain is filled with such records, remote and unapproachable, yet perfectly alive in each detail. From the mortal point of view this kind of memory is torture, but from eternity the present is no less fantastic and no more real. Thus within the lyric, past exists with present and even future. "But love, which is *altogether* holy, like that between two children, will revisit undoubtedly by glimpses the silence and the darkness of old age . . . that final experience in my sister's bed-room, or some other in which her innocence was concerned, will rise again for me, to illuminate the hour of death" (*Suspiria*, p. 470).

The pure subjectivity which has its past and future enclosed within the *Suspiria* may easily engage in prophecy. But the autobiographer, whose existence is only partly within his art, cannot predict the future in this way: "But love, which is altogether holy like that between two children, is privileged to revisit by glimpses the silence and the darkness of declining years; and, possibly, this final experience in my sister's bedroom, or some other in which her innocence was concerned, may rise again for me" (*Sketches*, p. 43). This tentative remark seems hollow in a context where there is generally so little confidence or respect for potentiality; in the *Sketches*, what merely "can" or "could" occur is associated with fancy and hyperbolic play—"we could have backed to the North Pole." Playfulness is not sustained creation, and willfully imposed coherence cannot achieve true, organic continuity. Thus the *Sketches* cannot aspire to what De Quincey has called the "self-revolving" condition of music; they cannot be really "eloquent." As De Quincey says in his appraisal of Hazlitt's art: "Hazlitt was not eloquent, because he was discontinuous. . . . Eloquence resides not in separate or fractional ideas, but in the relation of manifold ideas, and in the mode of their evolution from each other. It is not enough that ideas should be many, and their relation coherent."[20] De Quincey constantly alludes to the discontinuity of his autobiographical effort, and does so with a degree of condescending diminution: "this little trait" or that "little parenthetical record." Since autobiography can neither penetrate to the subliminal levels where all subjective life is one nor invent its own, autonomous unity, it has only what his "General Preface" calls "that sort of amusement which attaches to any real story . . . moving through a succession of scenes sufficiently varied, that are not suffered to remain too long upon the eye."[21]

Self-consciousness and an eye eternally on the effect he is making distract the autobiographer from a total unconstrained involvement in even the most profound of the experiences he reports. De Quincey is on guard in his *Autobiographical Sketches*, ready to prove that he is not blinded by self-interest, willing to turn his sorrows into jokes. "On returning to our own frontiers, I had an opportunity of displaying my exemplary greenness. That message to my brother, with all its *virus* of insolence, I repeated as faithfully for the spirit, and as literally for the expressions, as my memory allowed me to do: and in that troublesome effort, simpleton that I was, fancied myself exhibiting a soldier's loyalty to his commanding officer" (*Sketches,* p. 79). There are temptations to ridicule overblown childish anxieties in the *Suspiria* as well, but they are quickly cut off by a powerful empathy which breeds respect for any human pain: "O heavens! that the misery of a child should by possibility become the laughter of adults!—that even I, the sufferer, should be capable of amusing myself, as if it had been a jest, with what for three years had constituted the secret affliction of my life" (*Suspiria*, p. 501).

Irony touches every level of the *Sketches*, undercutting any immediacy of expression, protecting the autobiographer from ridicule or public rebuff. De Quincey does not scruple to parody his own impassioned prose: "Forty and four years have passed since then. Almost every body connected with the case has had time to assume permanently the horizontal posture ... —that unhappy pony of eighteen (now, alas! sixty-two, if living; ah! venerable pony, that must (or musteth) now require thy oats to be boiled)" (*Sketches*, pp. 405–6). Obviously no passion could sustain itself amid such studied self-ironies. In the lyric, De Quincey carefully confines his *cri de coeur* to moments of intense, high seriousness. His apostrophes there are limited to cases in which a sympathetic reception is at least possible, since he knows, as his "General Preface" states, that "a single false note, a single word in a wrong key, ruins the whole music" of impassioned prose. He must not overuse exclamatory rhetoric, and therefore makes a few prominent exclamations do the work by distributing them to key moments when individual experience gives way to transcendental mystery. "The writer would command how sweet a bedroom, permitting him to lie the summer through, gazing all night long at the burning host of heaven. How silent *that* would be at the noon of a summer night—how grave-like in its quiet!" (*Suspiria*, p. 549).

Since the writer is overcome by some more elemental presence, there is no self-consciousness about this "lyrical outcry."[22] But passion this delicate and shy requires a sensitive and unobtrusive audience. "The very idea of breathing a record of human passion, not into the ear of the random crowd, but of the saintly confessional, argues an impassioned theme."[23] Close enough to overhear what is hardly a communication, to perceive the symptoms of passion without the need to be told, the reader of *Suspiria de Profundis* must become almost the narrator's other self. The reader endures the very same process of grief, shares the identical emotions and memories: "Such a palimpsest is my brain; such a palimpsest, oh reader! is yours" (p. 510). Although at the beginning the reader is outside and merely adjacent to the lyrical brooding of the text, familiarity evolves as the work unfolds. In the dream sequences, the reader is admitted as a full participant, as "you," and by the conclusion, references to the reader are always in the inclusive first person. In the "Vision of Life," the text becomes a mutual undertaking of narrator and reader—"just as we are speaking." Here, also, the always definite and individualized reader becomes clearly and exclusively female: "As the hastiest of improvisations, accept, fair reader (for reader it is that will chiefly feel such an invocation of the past), three or four illustrations from my own experience" (*Suspiria*, p. 544).

In this mode of address one can identify traces of the original relationship between the young boy and his sister in the "Affliction of Childhood." "Never but to thee only, never again since thy departure, *durst* I utter the feelings which possessed me. For I was the shyest of children; and a natural sense of personal dignity held me back at all stages of life, from exposing the least ray of feelings which I was not encouraged *wholly* to reveal" (*Suspiria*, p. 463). The communion of narrator and reader has restored the possibility of exposing feelings buried since childhood. The new bond of artistic sympathy reincarnates a dead sister and projects her features onto the audience. But even this identity is too limiting, for the reader must have a nature as unbounded as the narrator's own. The reader of the lyric is not a particular female, but the "receptive" female principle itself, released from all its former transient incarnations: "The rapture of life (or anything which by approach can merit that name) does not arise, unless as perfect music it arises . . . by the confluence of the mighty and terrific discords with the subtle concords. Not by contrast, or as reciprocal foils, do these elements act, which is the feeble conception of many, but by union. They are the sexual forces in music: "male and female created he them"; and these mighty antagonists do not put forth their hostilities by repulsion, but by deepest attraction" (*Suspiria*, p. 528). Thus the great synthesis of the lyric is achieved only in its final moments, after the repetition of the past has made it lose all narrowly personal meaning and the obsessed soliloquy of sorrow becomes the musical harmony of interacting principles, joy and agony, expression and reception. For De Quincey, there can be no passion without relationship.

There is certainly a relationship at the root of the *Autobiographical Sketches*, but the passion is all on the side of the audience, and it is a crude sort of passion at that. De Quincey writes his autobiography as a response to interests and questions which are imposed on him, which surround him and inhibit him from attaining that "severe abstraction" which lyricism requires. "What was the Priory like? Was it young or old, handsome or plain? What was my uncle the captain like? Young or old, handsome or plain? Wait a little, my reader; give me time, and I will tell you all" (*Sketches*, p. 400). This is the appetite of the "random crowd," the mass reading public, which wants to use the autobiography for its own satisfaction, rather than the desire of the intimate reader the *Suspiria* shapes for itself. De Quincey seems almost to resent the demands they make of him, demands for "dazzling display," in the words of his "General Preface." Writing his autobiography to allay mere curiosity will do nothing to develop his own higher faculties, and yet this is what a novel-reading public—accustomed only to the lurid pleasures of suspense—seems to require.[24] "Yet, perhaps, it is injudicious to have too much excited the reader's expectations; therefore, reader, understand what it is that you are invited to hear—not much of a story, but simply a noble sentiment" (*Sketches*, p. 131).

It is from this kind of audience that De Quincey protects himself and seals off his more intimate experiences. His distrust of their capacities and their intentions as readers is everywhere in evidence. "For what purpose have I repeated this story? The reader may, perhaps, suppose it introductory to some tale of boyish romantic passion for some female idol clothed with imaginary perfections" (*Sketches*, p. 326). He must summon all his firmness to dispel their false impressions, direct and hold their wandering attention. "The reader must do for me the favour to fix his attention upon the real questions at issue" (*Sketches*, p. 371). Although at times indulging his reader's childish span of attention, he can barely veil his contempt in doing so. "I am disposed to concede a few words to what modern slang denominates his 'antecedents'" (*Sketches*, p. 402).

The audience of the *Autobiographical Sketches* is indifferently singular and plural; when treated as an individual, it remains the personification of the lowest common denominator of the random mass. De Quincey becomes familiar with them without becoming familiar himself. They are "my readers," but he is not "your author." It is they who have created the public mask of periodical polemicist and humorist he now must wear.[25] Knowing that he is responding to their wishes, he has no need to woo them. He may treat them imperiously: "Be not offended, compatriot of Birmingham, that I salute your natal town with these disparaging epithets" (*Sketches*, p. 268). He knows what this predictable public must be thinking but does not feel the need for true apology.

The *Autobiographical Sketches* have an occasion and a steadfast public sanction, and yet the very nature of the sanction limits them. De Quincey is confined by an extrinsically imposed identity. Yet from within the *Sketches*, he recalls wistfully a dance he once had seen in which there glimmered for him the promise of a more organic art: "The life, the motion, the sea-like undulation of heads, the interweaving of figures, the . . . self-revolving, both of the dance and the music, "never ending, still beginning," and the continual regeneration of order from a system of motions which for ever touch the very brink of confusion . . . capable of exciting and sustaining the very grandest emotions of philosophic melancholy to which the human spirit is open" (*Sketches*, p. 198).

CHAPTER FIVE

=====================================

VLADIMIR NABOKOV: ILLUSIONS OF REALITY AND
THE REALITY OF ILLUSIONS

=====================================

> In this life, rich in patterns (a life
> unrepeatable, since with a different
> cast, in a different manner,
> in a new theater it will be given),
>
> No better joy would I choose than to fold
> its magnificent carpet in such a fashion
> as to make the design of today coincide
> with the past, with a former pattern . . .
>
> to bend and discover in my own childhood
> the end of the tangled-up thread . . .
>
> And carefully then to unravel myself
> as a gift, as a marvel unfurled,
> and become once again the middle point
> of the many-pathed, loud-throated world.
>   Vladimir Nabokov

Autobiographers as heterogenous as Bunyan, Boswell, and De Quincey have at least the common assumption that their work reflects and transmits something that exists outside the act of composition. The events, objects, and relationships they describe are there whether or not they are written about, even if they are nothing more than memories or fleeting observations, even if they are known only to God or scarcely believed by the writer himself. However much autobiography may deliberately qualify or inadvertently complicate the scope of their identity, despite the new precision it may give to their knowledge of themselves, it remains in essence the record of a self with its own autonomous existence. It is only because of this, in fact, that autobiography can be a mode of discovery or relevation. Even De Quincey accepts this notion of autobiography, although he uses it to disparage the genre for its false worship of empirical truth.

From a twentieth-century point of view, however, this must seem a naive sort of empiricism, assuming as it does a realm of "fact" that is independent of description. Even the sciences now admit to possibilities of "indeterminacy," to the role of the experiment itself in determining

127

the shape of the discovery.[1] The techniques and equipment which both the physicist and the writer bring to bear upon their materials distort— or better, in part constitute—the behavior of the object under study. For a contemporary author like Vladimir Nabokov, a man who is both artist and scientist, a naive faith in facts damages either sort of observation. As he says in describing the artistic decline of Gogol: "He was in the worst plight that a writer can be in: he had lost the gift of imagining facts and believed that facts may exist by themselves. The trouble is that bare facts do not exist in a state of nature, for they are never really quite bare."[2]

Facts are never "bare": they are the trajectory of the questions with which one began and the needs which initiated the inquiry. It is not simply a matter of impurities. Observation would be impossible without some initial guide for recognizing similarities and significance. Lacking an informing interest or intention, experience is chaotic and data are meaningless. Categories are the prior condition of perception and knowledge, not the natural outgrowth of experience. Nor is Nabokov inclined to ascribe a transcendental status to such categories. Even the Kantian absolutes of time and space are no more than convenient fictions—what he calls elsewhere "our pseudo-physical agreements with ourselves."[3]

But exposing the necessary fiction at the roots of fact and the interests behind disinterested empiricism places autobiography in a difficult position. What is it that autobiography actually captures? How much does it record and how much does it create? Identity can no longer seem impermeable to the conditions and techniques of the autobiographical act. Doubt is cast on the relationship between the nexus of self and character which develops within the text and that which otherwise exists. Perhaps there is no other nexus—De Quincey's lyric prose had already illustrated how perfectly a disembodied voice mimics the accents of passionate experience. Sincerity can offer no guarantee, since it is a creation of will and appearance, and may be as easily feigned or as much a chimera as anything else. Sincerity, moreover, is consciously unconscious of its own effects, ignoring the artificial condition of a self forever being watched and probed. It is no solution but a futile, even laughable evasion.

Nabokov confronts the fictions in autobiography in less general terms as well. His novel *Lolita* explores the quirks and excesses of the genre by means of parody. A parody as thorough and extreme as *Lolita* becomes possible only with long familiarity and the contempt it breeds. Of course, neither Nabokov nor the object of his travesty is unique in the context of modernist literary heterodoxy. Conscious experimentation and deliberate violation of literary codes and models have accelerated the slow and largely accidental process of literary history in this century. This paradoxical convention of the unconventional has naturally touched autobiography as well as poetry and the novel—giving us, along with free verse and the *nouveau roman, Anti-Memoirs* as well. But since Nabokov writes both an autobiography (*Speak, Memory*) and an autobiographical burlesque, there is no question that the genre retains its vitality for him and for the members of his literary community. Its life has, however, been made more subtle, its claims less naive, and the delicate balance between truth and fiction, tradition and possibility, has been brought into sharper focus.

Lolita is the ostensible autobiography of one Humbert Humbert, although there is a good deal of indecision on the part of the autobiographer and his editor, John Ray, Jr., Ph.D., about the status of the completed work. Humbert's manuscript was left behind at his death with two alternate titles: "Lolita," or the "Confession of a White Widowed Male." To his pedantic editor, its "strange pages," while not without artistry, are best regarded as a psychiatric case history or an unwitting sociological record of "dangerous trends" in modern life. During the course of his narrative, Humbert exhausts a string of categories, including "confession" and "trial notes," "case study" and "memoir," "tragic tale" and "novel." The mock-autobiographer apparently cannot see his own disconcerting oscillation between different centers of attention—Lolita and himself—and contradictory genres— fiction and nonfiction, informal notes for his own use and free-standing narrative art. The suggestion that neither Humbert nor Ray can see what he is about is an important aspect of Nabokov's sabotage of his creatures. Humbert Humbert of course richly deserves this kind of merciless exposure, but in many ways he is no worse than the classical autobiographer. Humbert's confessions parallel in ways too numerous for accident the confessions of Jean Jacques Rousseau.[4] There is the same elegaic sense of childhood lost and the same paranoid suspicions emerging as the work progresses. Nabokov simply gives another turn to the screw of Rousseau's attempt to justify himself and disarm his tormentors by means of absolute and sensational sincerity. He also travesties more technical aspects of the autobiographical act, found not only in the *Confessions* but in almost all conventional representatives of the genre. Humbert Humbert calls attention to the problems of self-representation and self-imaging, and by doing so makes a shambles of the very effects he had hoped to achieve:

I do not know if in these tragic notes I have sufficiently stressed the peculiar "sending" effect that the writer's good looks—pseudo-Celtic, attractively simian, boyishly manly—had on women of every age and environment. Of course, such announcements made in the first person may sound ridiculous. But every once in a while I have to remind the reader of my appearance much as a novelist, who has given a character of his some mannerism or a dog, has to go on producing that dog or that mannerism every time the character crops up in the course of the book. . . . My gloomy good looks should be kept in the mind's eye if my story is to be properly understood.[5]

Not only does Humbert unwittingly alert us to the essential artificiality of all attempts at representation, he also displays how gross and hackneyed are the fictions he uses in constructing his image of himself. His physique, his character, his charisma are obviously appropriated from conventional portraits of the dark, romantic hero, from *Wuthering Heights* and *Manfred*. An element of the Byronic, or at least the self-dramatic, is frequently a part of classical autobiography. The autobiographer is torn between observing and being himself; his object is forever just beyond his grasp, contemporaneous with the act of composition and undergoing changes even as he writes. Usually the act is terminated at the point, implicit or explicit, where the character merges with the narrator in a solidified and ostensibly permanent personality and role. But to Nabokov, this coincidence and completion is a fiction, and the three-dimensional wholeness of the person thus constituted is a trick of perspective. To identify and unite aspects of being may be artistic, but to accept an artifact, an impersonation, without qualification is either a delusion or a lie. (And in the case of Humbert Humbert, perhaps both.) *Lolita* does achieve an ironic resolution by allowing its narrator to die just as the book ends. The record is complete only because the life is over: with his death, Humbert is reduced to fit exactly the dimensions of the character he created.

One sees through Humbert's ploys more clearly than those of the ordinary autobiography, of course. Nabokov has provided excess of it, and made the twists and changes in self-impersonation visible through their sheer violence. The man that Humbert observes himself to be, with alternate love and loathing, is treated with ostensible distance and dispassion. Of his past self in particular, Humbert speaks in the third person, using titles and even calling himself by name: "What a foolish Hamburg that Hamburg was! Since his supersensitive system was loath to face the actual scene, he thought he could enjoy a secret part of it" (*Lolita*, p. 264). But this is a sham objectivity, not so much naming as name-calling. Humbert's self-representation is far from disinterested.[6] By alienating certain moments and certain actions he has performed, he is able to become his own judge, thereby condemning part of himself while he saves another part from condemnation. Both the manipulation of grammatical person and the epithets he chooses become the tools of his selective self-censure. "I have toyed with many pseudonyms for myself before I hit on a particularly apt one. There are in my notes, "Otto Otto" and "Mesmer Mesmer" and "Lambert Lambert," but for some reason I think my choice expresses the nastiness best" (*Lolita*, p. 310).

Humbert's mode of representing himself as "other" is yet another instance of his obsessional Tom-peeping. It would appear that autobiography appeals to him as a way of sustaining what had always been his chief preoccupation: "I used to review the concluded day by checking my own image as it prowled rather than passed before the mind's red eye. I watched dark-and-handsome, not un-Celtic, probably high-church, possibly very high-church, Dr. Humbert see his daughter off to school. I watched him greet with his slow smile and pleasantly arched thick black ad-eyebrows good Mrs. Holigan" (*Lolita*, p. 190). The autobiography of a voyeur is itself voyeuristic. Even, or perhaps especially, in relation to himself, Humbert savors his spectator sport, objectifying his self-image for the sake of perverse, narcissistic pleasure, hoping to "enjoy a secret part" just as he did when he returned to the scene of his first seduction to search through old newspapers for a picture of himself on his way to Lolita's hotel room.

Humbert Humbert's hyperbolic flaws as an autobiographer are only a logical extension from what one can observe in actual autobiographies, however. The struggle against unwitting self-revelation—or its encouragement, in the case of Boswell—is a concomitant of the structure of the act. The gaps and incongruities, the continuity and perfection, of the narrative surface become a symptom and a way of reading hidden information. Humbert awkwardly shows himself at every turn, intruding to confess his peculiar difficulties of composition and noting suddenly how his objectives have been transformed without his notice. The story of *Lolita* is as much the story Humbert refuses to impart as anything he manages to say. Nabokov knows this underside of the autobiographical act intimately, not only as a reader of Rousseau but also as a writer of his own autobiography. *Lolita* follows immediately upon the heels of the first version of *Speak, Memory*; according to Alfred Appel's preface to *The Annotated Lolita*: "As a book about the spell exerted by the past, *Lolita* is Nabokov's own parodic answer to his previous book the first edition of *Speak, Memory*."[7] And subsequent to the writing of *Lolita*, Nabokov returns to *Speak, Memory* to make of it "An Autobiography Revisisted."[8]

What are the things, then, that betray Humbert Humbert and how does Nabokov cope with his disillusioned view of autobiography when he returns to his own text? Primarily there is Humbert's refusal or inability to recognize the fruits of his own imagination and to take responsibility for them. Humbert is a literalist of the imagination, willfully clinging to what he knows to be limited perspectives and evanescent realities. Lolita herself is his creation, a nymphet only to his nympholepsy, a deliberate forgery of his lost childhood love. "She was Dolores on the dotted line. But in my arms she was always Lolita. . . . In point of fact, there might have been no Lolita at all had I not loved, one summer, a certain initial girl-child" (*Lolita*, p. 11). Humbert's first love was "Annabel Leigh," thus making his obsession with Lolita an illusion of an illusion. Nabokov emphasizes the madness of this by making the memoirist a professional student of American literature, a man who therefore ought to recognize when his own case begins to resemble a famous poem by Edgar Allan Poe. Humbert describes his adventures, before encountering Lolita, at Melville Sound and Pierre Point, without turning a hair. At the climax of his book, when he murders his nympholeptic double and rival for Lolita's charms, Clare Quilty, the scene reduplicates an earlier catalog of Lolita's favorite films: "musicals, underworlders, westerners" (p. 172). The successive stages of Quilty's death agony involve first stopping to sing at his piano, then doing an imitation of an "underworld numbskull," and finally grappling with Humbert hand to hand in "the obligatory scene in the Westerns" (pp. 299–304).

Although he consciously toys with the jargon of psychoanalysis, thus managing to rebut the classical Freudian theories by showing a perfect and lucid awareness of what should be repressed sexual desires, Humbert cannot prevent certain subliminal manifestations of his madness from leaking into his narrative without his notice. These parapraxes diminish his claims to accuracy and flawless deduction, for one is constantly surprising Humbert in the act of chasing and fleeing acknowledged fictions and dubious private phantoms. "Oh, I am quite sure it was not a delusion" (p. 229), he exclaims, destroying credibility as he tries to bolster it by introducing evidence that he and Lolita really were pursued by mystery cars on the final, fateful portion of their journey. The conflict in his soul between desire and disgust shows plainly through erratic structure and the wild and heedless changes in his diction. Aspects of his "slippery self" appear to battle for control as Latinate euphemisms give way to childish monosyllables within a single page. "Here is Virgil who could the nymphet sing in single tone, but probably preferred a lad's perineum" (*Lolita*, p. 21). "Humbert Humbert tried hard to be good. Really and truly, he did" (*Lolita*, p. 21). At times an open break in the narration juxtaposes one sentence in schizophrenic condemnation of another. "In a princedom by the sea. . . . About as many years before Lolita was born as my age was that summer. You can always count on a murderer for a fancy prose style" (*Lolita*, p. 11).

Throughout the manuscript, brief parentheses puncture the most elevated and grandiose expression, deflating formal beauty with crude actuality. "The fatal gesture passed like the tail of a falling star across the blackness of the contemplated crime. . . . But what d'ye know, folks—I just could not make myself do it!" (*Lolita*, pp. 88–89). Humbert's narrative seems incapable of sustaining itself in either plot or style. His sentences fall apart, his narrative becomes fragmented and confused, especially when he is recounting painful situations. "This daily headache in the opaque air of this tombal jail is disturbing, but I must presevere. Have written more than a hundred pages and not got anywhere yet. My calendar is getting confused. That must have been around August 15, 1947. Don't think I can go on. Heart, head—everything. Lolita, Lolita, Lolita, Lolita, Lolita, Lolita. Repeat till the page is full, printer" (*Lolita*, p. 111). This is actually an entire chapter: chapter 26, book I. The same kind of confusion overcomes the narrative in chapter 26 of book II, Humbert again recounting a visit to the small town of Briceland. "I notice that I have somehow mixed up two events, my visit with Rita to Briceland on our way to Cantrip, and our passing through Briceland again on our way back to New York, but such suffusions of swimming colors are not to be disdained by the artist in recollection" (*Lolita*, p. 265).

Thus despite all his attempts to create a reasonable, or at least an unassailable case for himself, Humbert is plagued by pathological slips of the pen. He may use performatives which stress judicious probity— "prove," "explain," "analyze," and "itemize"—but the performance itself rarely bears him out. "With the passage of the Children and Young Person Act in 1933, the term 'girl-child' is defined as a 'girl who is over eight but under fourteen years.' . . . Hugh Broughton, a writer of controversy in the reign of James the First, has proved that Rahab was a harlot at ten years of age. This is all very interesting, and I daresay you see me already frothing at the mouth in a fit; but no, I am not; I am just winking happy thoughts into a little tiddle cup" (*Lolita*, p. 21). He cannot even fulfill his promise for a "clear, frank account of the itinerary" of his travels with Lolita without becoming distracted in autistic play: "*Nous connûmes* (this is royal fun) the would-be enticements of their repetitious names—all those Sunset Motels" (*Lolita*, p. 148). By his casual but overwhelmingly frequent allusions to dreams during his initial infatuation with Lolita and to nightmares during his hopeless attempt to retain her after her seduction, Humbert demonstrates the instability of his perception of events.[9] "Whether or not the realization of a lifelong dream had surpassed all expectation, it had, in a sense, overshot its mark—and plunged into nightmare" (*Lolita*, p. 142).

The dividing line between dream and nightmare seems, in fact, to motivate the partition of the manuscript into two parts, the second a grotesque anticlimax to the first, with mania turned into phobia and realistic surfaces distorted by ever more baroque twists of plot and design. Throughout the book, but especially in book II, the names and even the natures of the characters undergo the metamorphic transformations of a dream, the process culminating in the figure of Humbert's private nemesis, "Detective Trapp," which suddenly dissolves into that of the man responsible for stealing and ultimately ruining Lolita, Clare Quilty.[10]

Humbert's madness is not really a perverse desire for little girls but a willful attempt to copulate with his own dreams and to murder his own nightmares in his vengeful guilt and disappointment. All the women who become involved with him, save only Rita, are ultimately killed by the effects of his attentions, as though he robbed them of vitality by combining them with his fantasies. Both his first wife and, later, Lolita herself, die in childbirth, as though to indicate the essential and murderous sterility of Humbert's love. So confirmed is Humbert in his voyeurism that even in the pit of his most desperate remorse he remains unable to conceive the error of his ways. He still confuses the carnal reality of his beloved with the phantom shapes of photography and film: "No hereafter is acceptable if it does not produce her as she was then, in that Colorado resort between Snow and Elphinstone, with everything right. . . . Idiot, triple idiot! I could have filmed her! I would have had her now with me, before my eyes, in the projection room of my pain and despair" (*Lolita*, pp. 232–33). There is some suggestion that the reformation and change of heart which Humbert undergoes while pondering Lolita in his prison (resulting in the transformation of trial notes into a tribute to his love), is merely an exchange of one delusion for another—a willed sacrifice of both lover and beloved for the sake of artistic immortality. Humbert's manuscript is simply another attempt to capture Lolita,[11] with all the lurking ambiguity that term implies, and his famous outburst—"Oh, my Lolita, I have only words to play with!" (p. 34)—echoes dangerously when one recalls his diseased capacity for erotic play. In his memoirs, Humbert hopes to construct a timeless space he may share with his nymphet, a shrine no doubt, but a tomb as well, recalling the necrophiliac closure to the fable with which Humbert began, the tale of Annabel Lee.

Thus, neither of us is alive when the reader opens this book. . . . I am thinking of aurochs and angels, the secret of durable pigments, prophetic sonnets, the refuge of art. And this is the only immortality you and I may share, my Lolita. [*Lolita*, p. 311]

> And so, all the night-tide, I lie down by the side
> Of my darling, my darling, my life and my bride
> In her sepulchre there by the sea—
> In her tomb by the sounding sea.[12]

In love with his own demons and unwilling to be awakened from even his worst dreams, Humbert Humbert can be heard pleading, from time to time, to be left alone with his fantasies. And this may be the ultimate purpose of the memoir, to environ himself more firmly in delusion and to defend his shadowy Humberland from intruding realities. Humbert's penchant for Tom-peeping at remote, gauzy windows, his love for a girl-child surnamed Haze, are the emblems of an underlying horror of anything too sharply seen, too stubbornly defined to become the stuff his dreams are made on. *"Mes fenêtres!* . . . grinding my teeth, I would crowd all the demons of desire against the railing of a throbbing balcony . . . whereupon the lighted image would move and Eve would revert to a rib, and there would be nothing in the window but an obese partly clad man reading the paper. Since I sometimes won the race between my fancy and nature's reality, the deception was bearable" (*Lolita*, p. 266).

Humbert Humbert cannot bear the recognition of deception, but Nabokov's own autobiography, *Speak, Memory*, is a celebration of the consciousness of illusion. Nabokov prefers flaunting his "dazzling insincerity" to engaging in Humbert's glib confessions, what Appel calls the "solemn introspection . . . the diarist's compulsive egotism, candid but totally self-conscious self-analysis, carefully created 'honesty,' willful irony, and studied self-deprecation."[13] Andrew Field sees more artwork than personal history in *Speak, Memory*, since "the past is not searched out. It is, rather, carefully selected—the changing form may be likened to breathing—and poetically fixed."[14] Each of Nabokov's fifteen chapters carefully evokes a rich and delicately worked chimera of the past, only to shatter it as the chapter ends:

I witness with pleasure the supreme achievement of memory, which is the masterly use it makes of innate harmonies when gathering to its fold the suspended and wandering tonalities of the past. I like to imagine, in consummation and resolution of those jangling chords, something as enduring, in retrospect, as the long table that on summer birthdays and namedays used to be laid . . . exaggerated, no doubt, by the same faculty of impassioned commemoration. . . . Through a tremulous prism, I distinguish the features of relatives. . . . In the place where my current tutor sits, there is a changeful image, a succession of fade-ins and fade-outs; the pulsation of my thoughts mingles with that of the leaf shadows. . . . And then, suddenly, just when the colors and outlines settle at last to their various duties . . . some knob is touched and a torrent of sounds comes to life . . . like a background of wild applause.[15]

The optical tricks, the description of a memory which feeds on and is fed by the imagination—composing rather than resurrecting the setting—and the final "background of applause," leave little doubt about the status of this scene. It will not be forgotten by any reader of these memoirs that the memory summoned by the title's epic invocation is the mother of all the other arts. Nabokov has said as much in an interview: "I would say that imagination is a form of memory. . . . When we speak of a vivid individual recollection we are paying a compliment not to our capacity of retention but to Mnemosyne's mysterious foresight in having stored up this or that element which creative imagination may use when combining it with later recollections and inventions."[16]

Far from characterizing himself as "handsomely simian" or even dwelling on any sort of self-representation, Nabokov fills his autobiography with the portraits of others. There are his parents, his governess and tutors, even the ancestors whom he never knew, but whose existence has somehow contributed to the pattern of family traditions and possessions, of aristocratic codes of conduct and education which have shaped his own life. The most intimate and important private moments in his life, the assassination of his father, the courtship of his wife, are merely hinted at, anticipated, or mentioned only when they have already taken place offstage. He treats his life in exile—the period in which he met and married his wife and had his only child—by focusing upon the chess problems he composed for émigré journals:

I remember one particular problem I had been trying to compose for months. . . . It was meant for the delectation of the very expert solver . . . (who) would start by falling for an illusory pattern of play . . . which the composer had taken the greatest pains to "plant." . . . Having passed through this "antithetic" inferno the by now ultrasophisticated solver would reach the simple key move (bishop to c2) as somebody on a wild goose chase might go from Albany to New York by way of Vancouver, Eurasia, and the Azores. The pleasant experience of the roundabout route (strange landscapes, gongs, tigers, exotic customs, the thrice-repeated circuit of a newly married couple around the sacred fire of an earthen brazier) would amply reward him for the misery of the deceit. [*Speak, Memory*, p. 292]

The chess discussion itself is an "illusory pattern of play," for hidden within it is a masked account of a marriage ceremony, and immediately following this passage one encounters the first reference to Nabokov's wife and son. "All of a sudden, I felt that with the completion of my chess problem a whole period of my life had come to a satisfactory close. . . . Sleeping in the next room were you and our child" (*Speak, Memory*, p. 292).

A similar camouflage covers his father's death:

This final dachshund followed us into exile, and as late as 1930, in a suburb of Prague (where my widowed mother spent her last years . . .) he could still be seen. [*Speak, Memory*, p. 48]

On the night of March 22, 1922, around ten o'clock, in the living room where as usual my mother was reclining . . . I had just got to the end of the little poem about Florence . . . and as she was saying over her knitting, "Yes, yes, Florence does look like a *dimniy* iris, how true! I remember—" when the telephone rang.
    After 1923, when she moved to Prague . . . . [*Speak, Memory*, p. 49]

The telephone message reporting that Nabokov senior had been shot is deliberately blotted out, and only the attentive reader who recalls Prague as the site of his mother's widowhood will recognize what has occurred. The agony of Nabokov's loss is never expressed, although it may be inferred from various statements about his father scattered throughout the book. Nabokov refuses to collect this rich scattering of emotion and memory into one convenient category or to turn a father's death (as Humbert turns Lolita's disappearance) into the locus for his own display of grief. Open trickery is less deceitful than the covert manipulations of sincerity.

Of course, this constant magic and stunning sleight of hand requires a magician, and so it is hardly surprising to find the narrator so often intruding on his tale. The interruptions are even more prominent than in *Lolita*—too prominent, in fact, to be experienced as distractions or digressions.

For one moment, thanks to the sudden radiance of a lone lamp where the station's square ends, a grossly exaggerated shadow races beside the sleigh, climbs a billow of snow and is gone. . . . And let me not leave out the moon—for surely there must be a moon, the full, incredibly clear disc that goes so well with Russian lusty frosts. So there it comes . . . it glazes the runner tracks left on the road. . . . Very lovely, very lonesome. But what am I doing in this stereoscopic dreamland? How did I get here? Somehow, the two sleighs have slipped away, leaving behind a passportless spy, standing on the blue-white road in his New England snowboots and stormcoat. The vibration in my ears is no longer their receding bells, but only my old blood singing. All is still, spellbound, enthralled by the moon, fancy's rear-vision mirror. The snow is real, though, and as I bend to it and scoop up a handful, sixty years crumble to glittering frost-dust between my fingers. [*Speak, Memory*, pp. 99–100]

Unlike Humbert Humbert, whose life tapers to a neat, fictitious point, an achieved selfhood in which the fruits of the past have ripened (into solid remorse) and from which all alien elements have been winnowed out, Nabokov's own present and his correlative sense of self are as fluid, as ungeneralized and densely patterned as his past: "the evaporation of certain volatiles and the melting of certain metals are still going on in my coils and crucibles" (*Speak, Memory*, p. 14).

If the pattern of his life is found within his autobiography, it is not because Nabokov accepts the fiction of an a priori shape, an identity fixed forever by a process of religious conversion or historical necessity or even the "laws" of association. The discovery of pattern is a creative act, involving imagery and careful counterpoise to bring out the design which otherwise might be undetectable. "Neither in environment nor in heredity can I find the exact instrument that fashioned me, the anonymous roller that pressed upon my life a certain intricate watermark whose unique design becomes visible when the lamp of art is made to shine through life's foolscap" (*Speak, Memory*, p. 25).

Nabokov's individuality is nothing more or less than the "unique design" of certain recurrent themes of his past and present, thematic repetitions which become discernable only when the isolated and evanescent details of a lifetime are held fast for a moment—as they were not and cannot be in life—within a work of art. His present sense of self is merely the nucleus of the pattern, the central point defined by the continuum, shifting as the pattern itself appears to change.

In a sense, all poetry is positional: to try to express one's position in regard to the universe embraced by consciousness, is an immemorial urge. The arms of consciousness reach out and grope, and the longer they are the better. . . . Lost in thought, he taps his knee with his wandlike pencil, and at the same instant a car (New York license plate) passes along the road, a child bangs the screen door of a neighboring porch, an old man yawns in a misty Turkestan orchard, a granule of cinder-gray sand is rolled by the wind on Venus, a Doctor Jacques Hirsch in Grenoble puts on his reading glasses, and trillions of other such trifles occur—all forming an instantaneous and transparent organism of events, of which the poet (sitting in a lawn chair, at Ithaca, N.Y.) is the nucleus. [*Speak, Memory*, p. 218]

This organism of events does not exist without the "wandlike pencil" of the poet, but neither is the poet anything more substantial than a central point within the pattern he unifies within his consciousness. Memory is, of course, a mode of consciousness, and recollection is a way of expanding its purview. Nabokov therefore is materially changing his position as he writes his autobiography, embracing ever-wider contexts of time and place. Whatever the man Vladimir Nabokov "is," his identity cannot be separated from what he is making of himself by means of *Speak, Memory*.

Although I had been composing these chapters in the erratic sequence reflected by the dates of first publication given above, they had been neatly filling numbered gaps in my mind which followed the present order of chapters. That order had been established in 1936, at the placing of the cornerstone which already held in its hidden hollow various maps, timetables, a collection of matchboxes, a chip of ruby glass, and even—as I now realize—the view from my balcony of Geneva Lake, of its ripples and glades of light, black-dotted today, at teatime, with coots and tufted ducks. [*Speak, Memory*, pp. 10–11]

The act of composition appears to contain the self—the present moment, the very perceptions achieved in the act of writing, are only part of a thematic pattern implicit at the inception of the work, some thirty years before. Indeed, Nabokov ends by putting his own name in the index at the back of the book—an index which is a major addition to his "revisited" autobiography.

Nabokov, Valdimir Vladimirovich, 9–16, 19–310, *passim*. [*Speak, Memory*, p. 315]

The entry refers the reader to the introduction Nabokov has also added to his revised edition—pages 9–16—subordinating not only remembered experience but his experience as a writer to the overall design of *Speak, Memory*.

Thus, Humbert's pseudo-objectivity is here replaced by something like a true impersonality: "As far back as I remember myself (with interest, with amusement, seldom with admiration or disgust)" (*Speak, Memory*, p. 33). Although like Humbert Nabokov frequently discusses his actions in the third person, it is usually the indefinite third person, "one," a pronoun equally applicable to any individual undergoing such an experience or placed in such circumstances. "One would lag back and shuffle and slide a little on the smooth stone floor of the hall, causing the gentle hand at the small of one's back to propel one's reluctant frame by means of indulgent pushes" (*Speak, Memory*, p. 83). Nabokov treats himself as a transparency rather than an image, a means of access to experience rather than an actor.

I can easily refeel the exhilarating change from the thickly padded, knee-length *polushobok*, with the hot beaver collar, to the short navy-blue coat with its anchor-patterned brass buttons. In the open landau I am joined by the valley of a lap rug to the occupants of the more interesting back seat, majestic Mademoiselle, and triumphant, tear-bedabbled Sergey, with whom I have just had a row at home . . . as I look up I can see . . . great, tensely smooth, semi-transparent banners billowing . . . undoubtedly celebrating now in the city of memory, the essence of that spring day, the swish of mud, the beginning of mumps, the ruffled exotic bird with one bloodshot eye on Mademoiselle's hat. [*Speak, Memory*, p. 111]

It is the "essence of that spring day"—an essence composed equally of the excitement of the thaw and the personal discomfort of nascent disease—which is dominant in this passage. The figure of the boy gives way and we rush into the vaccuum created by his disappearance, taking his sensations for our own.

While Humbert pursues his shadows and delights in an impressionistic haziness more tractable to sexual mirage, Nabokov comments on the clarity of an act of recollection and pays as much attention to the mechansim of perception as to the object it perceives. "In looking at it from my present tower I see myself as a hundred different young men at once. . . . Not only is the experience in question, and the shadows of all those charming ladies useless to me now in recomposing my past, but it creates a bothersome defocalization, and no matter how I worry the screws of memory, I cannot recall the way Tamara and I parted" (*Speak, Memory*, p. 240). Nabokov does not limit himself to visual analogies, but employs the full manifold of consciousness—aural, tactile, and even olfactory awareness enters into his autobiographical act. It is significant, in this connection, that Humbert's moment of tragic recognition comes to him when he stands upon a cliff above a city filled with children whom he can hear at play but cannot see. This is the final experience he describes for us, and it is here that both his life and his manuscript end, since he cannot be an aural voyeur. For Humbert "seeing is believing," but for Nabokov it is only one of many available modes of perception, and all of them are part of the artistry of consciousness. In fact he stresses the "ars" of his "ars memoria" by using verbs such as "reconstruct" and "remember" interchangeably. His performatives are often deliberately fantastic; he uses a language drawn from magic—"conjure," "flying carpet"—from theater, and even from gymnastics—"setting," "puppet show," "bicycle act." The act of writing assumes a life of its own, so dense with images does it become. "A large, alabaster-based kerosene lamp is steered into the gloaming. Gently it floats and comes down; the hand of memory, now in a footman's glove, places it in the center of a round table. The flame is nicely adjusted, and a rosy, silk-flounced lamp shade, with inset glimpses of rococo winter sports, crowns the readjusted (cotton wool in Casimir's ear) light. Revealed: a bright, stylish ("Russian Empire") drawing room" (*Speak, Memory*, p. 100).

At another point, the process of reconstruction is likened to the creation of a classic nineteenth-century Russian novel: " 'And what about Yaremich?' I asked M. V. Dobushinski, one summer afternoon in the nineteen forties, as we strolled through a beech forest in Vermont. 'Is he remembered?' 'Indeed, he is,' replied Matislav Valerianovich" (*Speak, Memory*, p. 94). This is a novelistic dialogue, with a characteristic alternation of last names and first names with patronymic, and it is, moreover, wholly imaginary—which can be ascertained by recalling the description, several pages earlier, of Nabokov's childhood dream of plunging through the picture frame and entering the "enchanted beechwood" of a drawing hanging on his bedroom wall. The conversation with his former drawing teacher never took place, but any way of rendering the "consequences" of the past simplifies them, fictionalizes them; and to this extent autobiography and novel are alike. "When I learned of these later developments, I experienced a queer shock; it was as if life had impinged upon my creative rights by wriggling on beyond the subjective limits so elegantly and economically set by childhood memories that I thought I had signed and sealed" (*Speak, Memory*, p. 93).

The "truth" of autobiography comes only with the recognition that "things past" are never captured in their original form: "One is moved to speak more eloquently about these things, about many things that one always hopes might survive captivity in the zoo of words—but the ancient limes crowding close to the house down Mnemosyne's monologue with their creaking and heaving in the restless night" (*Speak, Memory*, p. 233). The autobiographical act is inevitably creative, its realities ineluctably unreal. But if one observes the disparities, if one calls attention to the responsibilities undertaken and the temptations which accompany the act, then and only then will a new, no longer naive autobiographical fact emerge. "Have I really salvaged her from fiction? Just before the rhythm I hear falters and fades, I catch myself wondering whether, during the years I knew her, I had not kept utterly missing something" (*Speak, Memory*, p. 117).

Humbert Humbert engages in an act which is the inverse of Nabokov's, although he sometimes expresses a queasy doubt of his procedure. "The beastly and beautiful merged at one point, and it is that borderline I would like to fix, and I feel I fail to do so utterly. Why?" (*Lolita*, p. 137). Humbert has no answer for his question, but his attentive reader can easily see the inevitability of failure in a writer who confesses "in order to enjoy my phantasms in peace I firmly decided to ignore what I could not help perceiving" (p. 285). His crabbed and frantic pursuit of proof and self-approval leaves him neither opportunity nor inclination to examine his evidence critically. Thus he misses even as he transmits the truth of his condition. Wherever there is an order which is not his own, Humbert sees only chance or the deliberate machinations of a personal emeny. The excerpts and random lists which he mindlessly includes for the sake of verisimilitude—the catalog of the prison library and the class list of Lolita's school, the tour books which have miraculously survived his travels and arrest and a passage from *Who's Who in the Limelight*—are not as haphazard as he might suppose; they actually contain the ciphers of his own destiny. "Like *Who's Who in the Limelight* (pp. 33–4) and the 'cryptogrammic paper chase' (pp. 252–3), the 'poetic' class list serves as a kind of magical mirror. The list is printed on the back of an unfinished map of the U.S., drawn by Lolita, suggesting the scale of the gameboard on which the action is played. The image of the map secreted in the *Young People's Encyclopedia* prefigures their journeys (on which H. H. will 'finish' the map by showing Lolita the country), just as the class list prefigures and mirrors an extraordinary number of other things."[17]

The pattern extends beyond Humbert's death, touching his manuscript in unexpected ways. Humbert had never planned on an editor, or on his curt prefatory remarks: "For the benefit of old-fashioned readers who wish to follow the destinies of the 'real' people beyond the 'true' story, a few details may be given. . . . Mrs. 'Richard F. Schiller' died in childbed, giving birth to a stillborn girl, on Christmas Day 1952" (*Lolita*, p. 6). This information coming from beyond the autobiographer's ken or control guards the approach to Humbert's manuscript. The revelation of Lolita's marriage is already stale when Humbert announces it and his attempt to resolve his autobiography with the heroic gesture of a romantic visionary and prophet is rendered empty, a glaring deceit, however sincere in its intention: "Dolly Schiller will probably survive me by many years. . . . I hope you will love your baby. I hope it will be a boy. . . . I am thinking of aurochs and angels, the secret of durable pigments, prophetic sonnets, the refuge of art" (*Lolita*, p. 311). Humbert's highest rhetorical and emotional achievements become low comedy for an audience which knows the twists and turns of fate long before reading a single one of Humbert's words.

The privacy of Humbert's vision is his ruin, both as an autobiographer and as a hero. All the while he is writing, his materials (and certain unknowns in himself) are in revolt against him, forming connections that he does not, in his madness or his cowardice, seem to recognize. The foreword gives the icily succinct account of Lolita's death, listing it among the indifferent destinies of other characters major and minor. But within Humbert's own manuscript there is a curious foreshadowing of editor John Ray's death notice: " 'And *you* know where her grave is,' I said controlling myself, whereupon I named the cemetery—just outside Ramsdale, between the railway tracks and Lakeview Hill. 'Moreover,' I added, 'the tragedy of such an accident is somewhat cheapened by the epithet you saw fit to apply to it. If you really wish to triumph in your mind over the idea of death—' 'Ray,' said Lo for hurray, and languidly left the room" (*Lolita*, p. 288). Humbert misconstrues what he has reported, but in giving Lolita's own words, he has naively included yet another thread from the pattern of a fate which surrounds and has always surrounded him. His offer to make Lolita "triumph" over death—an offer he repeats in the concluding apostrophe to his book—is exploded by the subtle interpolation of a painful "actuality" which withstands the power of his fantasies.

Humbert's grim insistence on his *verbatim* record, exactly reproducing conversations long since past (often without aid of notes or memoranda), is itself dubious and is made more so by his own carelessness. " 'Lo,' I said, 'you got it all wrong. I want you to leave your incidental Dick, and this awful hole, and come to live with me and die with me, and everything with me' (words to that effect)" (*Lolita*, p. 280). *Speak, Memory*, in contrast, shuns the pretense of direct quotation, rendering instead the mental silence of memory, broken only by a few habitual mannerisms of speech, a few ofttimes repeated, favorite expressions which made themselves memorable. His own diffused character never speaks directly in Nabokov's autobiography, unlike Humbert Humbert's verbose mannequin.

But more important is the way this realistic speech betrays its author, making it possible to construct alternative interpretations and allowing Lolita a place to demonstrate her own vulgar humanity free from Humbert's solipsistic version of her. "My Lolita remarked: 'You know, what's so dreadful about dying is that you are completely on your own'; and it struck me . . . that I simply did not know a thing about my darling's mind and that quite possibly, behind the awful juvenile clichés, there was in her a garden and a twilight, and a palace gate—dim and adorable regions which happened to be lucidly and absolutely forbidden to me" (*Lolita*, p. 286). Here, for a moment, the captive transcends her jealous captor, and Dolores Haze emerges as the heroine of the book.

But none of the devices of documentary realism conspire against Humbert as completely and as successfully as his representation of time and space. It is the absence of naturalistic sequence and contiguity which prevents Humbert from seeing any order or meaning in the lists and catalogs he includes. Traveler and would-be escape artist that he is,

Humbert's landscapes show a tendency to flatten out, to shrink from three dimensions to two-dimensional illusions. "Parody of a hotel corridor. . . . There was a double bed, a mirror, a double bed in the mirror, a closet door with a mirror, a bathroom door ditto, a blue-dark window, a reflected bed there, the same in the closet mirror" (*Lolita*, p. 121). It is in this maze of mirrors, a hotel room in Briceland, that Humbert finally possesses his nymphet, only to discover that he can never possess her fully. As he lies on this bed, a breathless inch from the fulfillment of his most exuberant fantasies, space suddenly warps and the familiar volume of an inhabitable world turns into a floor plan, a map of the hotel: "The clatter of the elevator's gate—some twenty yards northeast of my head but as clearly perceived as if it were inside my left temple . . . immediately east of my left ear (always assuming I lay on my back, not daring to direct my viler side toward the nebulous haunch of my bedmate), the corridor would brim. . . . When *that* stopped a toilet immediately north of my cerebellum took over. . . . Then someone in a southern direction was extravagantly sick . . . the avenue under the window of my insomnia, to the west of my wake . . . degenerated into the despicable haunt of gigantic trucks" (*Lolita*, pp. 131–32).

Humbert not only tolerates this strange, collapsible world, he actually depends upon its being so. His favorite vista is the distinct plane of a window—"thus isolated, thus removed, the vision acquired an especially keen charm" (p. 22). He needs the reductive and dehumanizing quality of the second dimension to make the universe a screen for his own projected lusts. Looking at American geography, he sees a "crazy quilt," a melange of private associations, literary allusions, fairy settlements—in much the same way that he sees the form of Clare Quilty in the scraps of his frustrated and miserable experience.[18] The memoirist is even capable of seeing the implications of such a warped perspective, while failing utterly to see that it is the same viewpoint behind his own memoirs. "The stark, stiff, lurid rhymes correspond very exactly to certain perspectiveless and terrible landscapes and figures, and magnified parts of landscapes and figures, as drawn by psychopaths" (*Lolita*, p. 259).

And yet, though Humbert claims he has "safely solipsized" Lolita and bends all his physical and narrative efforts to confining her to the private kingdom of his dreams, it is clear, as the book progresses, that Humberland itself is circumscribed, as it increasingly becomes an object in alien phenomenal fields.[19] "She had entered my world, umber and black Humberland, with rash curiosity; she surveyed it with a shrug of amused distaste, and it seemed to me now that she was ready to turn away from it with something akin to plain repulsion" (*Lolita*, p. 168). From the spider who weaves his strategems around his victim, Humbert declines into the helpless postulant who pleads with Lolita "in the most abject manner for clarification, no matter how meretricious of the slow awfulness enveloping me" (p. 238). In the second half of the story, it is Lolita and not Humbert who is the center of orientation, the pole for measuring how all movement "comes" and "goes." When Humbert finally realizes, dimly, transiently, his true situation within a larger destiny, he gives the culminating expression to this hidden force magnetizing his text: "I stood listening to that musical vibration from my lofty slope, to those flashes of separate cries with a kind of demure murmur for background, and then I knew that the hopelessly poignant thing was not Lolita's absence from my side, but the absence of her voice from that concord" (*Lolita*, p. 310).

Humbert cannot perceive this gradual reorientation because of his ignorance and evasion of another variable. Time. A world without time is necessarily two-dimensional, since there is no continuum, nothing to connect isolated points in space. As a professional of his perversion, Humbert is at war with mutability and writing to sustain his own never-never land of ageless children.

"In fact, I would have the reader see 'nine' and 'fourteen' as the boundaries—the mirrory beaches and rosy rocks—of an enchanted island haunted by those nymphets of mine ... insidious charm ... separates the nymphet from such coevals of hers as are incomparably more dependent on the spatial world of synchronous phenomena than on that intangible island of entranced time where Lolita plays with her likes" (*Lolita*, pp. 18–19). But what the memoirist would have is decidedly not what he gets. His recorded adventures are continuously foiled by disguised appearances of time. For example, lured on by the promise of a visit to "Our Glass Lake"—what beaches could be more "mirrory"? what better chance for a solitary idyll with little Lo?— Humbert finds himself instead suddenly entangled in the matrimonial schemes of Lolita's decaying mother. When he ultimately visits the lake in Mrs. Haze's amorous company, Humbert discovers it to be not an exemplar of wonderland and solipsism, but the domain of time itself, "Hour Glass Lake."[20] It is the memory of this lake which returns to haunt him at the climax of the book, when Lolita reveals to him the long-sought name of his rival. Although there are several reasons why Humbert might associate the name of Quilty with an earlier lakeside conversation concerning Quilty's uncle, it is significant that the word which springs to Humbert's mind—"waterproof"—was originally a reference to his wristwatch, a timepiece which could not be stopped even by the enchanted waters of "Our Glass Lake."[21]

Fighting to suppress every trace of time, even avoiding terms like "remember," Humbert is more easily taken by surprise when its passage overtakes him while he writes his manuscript. "When I started, fifty-six days ago, to write *Lolita*. . . . I thought I would use these notes in toto at my trial. . . . In mid-composition, however, I realized that I could not parade the living Lolita. I still may use parts of this memoir in hermetic sessions, but publication is to be deferred" (*Lolita*, p. 310). The tenseless opening of his text (which is also situated at the zero-point of space, within Humbert's very body) is a collection of lyric ejaculations and verbless sentence fragments, a grammar meant to leave him free of a commitment to time: "Lolita, light of my life, fire of my loins. My sin, my soul. Lo-lee-ta: the tip of the tongue taking a trip of three steps down the palate to tap, at three, on the teeth. Lo. Lee. Ta" (*Lolita*, p. 11). Yet it is a grammar he cannot long sustain, and most of his manuscript is in the imperfect past. Only at the very end does Humbert reach out to touch Lolita and his past, to bridge the temporal distance which like spatial distance is required to preserve the purity of anticipation, the "great rose-gray never-to-be-had" which is the perfection of desire. "Furthermore, since the idea of time plays such a magic part in the matter, the student should not be surprised to learn that there must be a gap of several years . . . between maiden and man to enable the latter to come under a nymphet's spell . . . a certain distance that the inner eye thrills to surmount" (*Lolita*, p. 19). In his memoirs, Humbert simply reverses his position, looking backward at his illusions instead of looking forward, but the angle of his lust remains unchanged. Time is coterminous with his very consciousness. It accompanies him even as he hopelessly strives to flee it, in his ceaseless travels with a captive whose nymphet days are mortally numbered, in the remorseful writing of his tale. Time creates and time destroys the phenomena of memory and nympholepsy—and time is the basis of that pattern in which Humbert is too enmeshed to see his own entrapment.

The whole of Humberland collapses if his readers catch a slight calendrical clue. According to the preface, Humbert Humbert died in his cell on 16 November 1952. Humbert himself mentions that his work on his memoirs has taken him fifty-six days, dating the first day of composition no later than 21 September 1952. Yet the fateful letter from Lolita, the letter which reunites them after her disappearance and allows Humbert to learn the name of his fiend-rival (and eventually to gain his murderous revenge) is said to have arrived on 22 September 1952. One could take Humbert's remark about the time of composition as an error or a rough estimate, or there might be a mistake in the date he has assigned to his receipt of Lolita's letter. It is also possible that his editor is wrong about the date of Humbert's death. But it seems more likely that this series of random errors is yet another instance of the contrapuntal pattern undercutting the autobiography. A supernatural explanation is still possible; the composition of *Lolita* may somehow be the feat of Humbert's afterlife. Certainly the enigmatic words near the conclusion of his tale could bear out this interpretation: "And do not pity C. Q. One had to choose between him and H. H. and one wanted H. H. to exist at least a couple of months longer, so as to have him make you live in the minds of later generations" (*Lolita*, p. 311). But even if Humbert Humbert is the phoenix of his confrontation with Clare Quilty, he does not thereby gain any greater insight into the difference between delusion and reality, for, as he tells Quilty during the murder scene: "The hereafter for all we know may be an eternal state of excruciating insanity" (p. 299).

The alternative conclusion we may draw is that Humbert Humbert does indeed compose his memoirs between the dates of 21 September and 16 November, and that all the incidents reported as occurring after the twenty-first—receiving Lolita's letter, recovering and ultimately losing her, and killing off Clare Quilty—are therefore purely fictitious. Perhaps the writing of *Lolita* is itself the surrogate for the final parting scene, Humbert's only opportunity to assert his sense of love and loss, to communicate his guilt and his remorse to Lolita, and to provide for her future as he tries to do when he gives her money in the Coalmont meeting. The murder of Quilty may also take place only within and by means of Humbert's autobiography. In the hindsight of his manuscript, he does succeed in piecing together the grotesque character of a foe whose menacing presence constantly attended him, interfering with the fulfillment of his desires and intruding upon his private paradise. The analogy between the corpse of his murdered rival and his own manuscript is implicitly acknowledged by the memoirist.

I could not bring myself to touch him in order to make sure he was really dead. He looked it: a quarter of his face gone, and two flies beside themselves with a dawning sense of unbelievable luck. [*Lolita*, p. 306]

This then is my story. I have reread it. It has bits of marrow sticking to it, and blood, and beautiful bright-green flies. [*Lolita*, p. 310]

In grappling with the nature of his enemy, seeking in prose if not in action for the fiend whose machinations have despoiled and poisoned all his dreams of bliss, Humbert actually does commit a murder. But the man he succeeds in destroying is himself, by torturing himself with memories of his own guilt and failure. In the process of writing, and ever more prominently in book II, Humbert's probings into the past are turned into the spasms of his diseased heart. If he cannot bear to do it consciously, he has at least subliminally sought and found the source of his defeat and the monster who destroyed Lolita's youth; he has revenged himself upon that monster in himself.

The "eternality of art," Humbert's final hope of refuge, turns out to be just one more in the series of his hopeless illusions, for composing his book has taken time, and time has aged and killed him. The temporal distance between him and his beloved only grows greater as he writes. Although he is symbolically joined to her in his final declaration of love, the process of time goes on, moving within his words. "I am thinking of aurochs and angels"—the progressive aspect mocks his claim to have discovered the "secret of durable pigments." One cannot take literal refuge within art as Humbert strives to do. As a result, the world of appearances, the temporal universe of "becoming"—the only life or even afterlife that Humbert will accept—is never left behind.

Humbert refuses to engage in conscious recollection or take the responsibility of art, autobiographical flaws which are overcome in *Speak, Memory*. Nabokov is the most conscious and the most responsible of autobiographical artists, carefully exposing the unnatural qualities of his re-created creatures and countrysides. "We shall go still further back, to a morning in May 1934, and plot with respect to this fixed point the graph of a section of Berlin" (*Speak, Memory*, p. 295). This void and abstraction is far removed from the comfortable and decidedly corporal immortality Humbert imagines he can create. Humbert is trapped within a world of time and space because he is unwilling to surrender his mundane perception of himself and his nymphet love; his need to know carnally and possess physically wars against his desire for another, timeless mode of being.[22] *Speak, Memory*, achieves this place outside of time, but only while showing how irrevocably both the pleasures and the pains of the third dimension must be left behind. In the sixth chapter of the autobiography, Nabokov takes the reader on a butterfly hunt which begins in the Russian countryside of 1910 and gradually, wordlessly, changes until—we realize with a start—it is now 1943, in the American Rockies. The author ends this metamorphosis by stating: "I confess I do not believe in time. I like to fold my magic carpet, after use, in such a way as to superimpose one part of the pattern on another. Let visitors trip. And the highest enjoyment of timelessness—in a landscape selected at random—is when I stand among rare butterflies and their food plants. This is ecstasy. . . . It is like a momentary vacuum into which rushes all that I love" (*Speak, Memory*, p. 139). Ecstasy it may be, but it is an acquired taste, one far beyond the emotional and imaginative capacities of Humbert Humbert, who, natural man that he is, abhors a vacuum.[23]

Speak, Memory looks down from above on Nabokov's life as it has been lived in the third dimension, manipulating time and space at will. Temporal order is only one of many possible orders, and the least interesting one at that. It has therefore little of the trite suspense Humbert Humbert gives his memoirs. (For all his horror of time, Humbert cannot break the habit of linear plots in which incident follows incident in a neat progression toward the inevitable climax—which climax is usually frustrated, however, as events again conspire against him as they did in his interrupted coitus with little Annabel. The multi-murder of Clare Quilty, who refuses to die dramatically and must be shot again and again, is a case in point.) While each chapter of Nabokov's autobiography begins at a successively later date in his life, exposition within the chapter wanders crazily from place to place and from history into the present moment of composition. The book is constructed according to superimposed patterns, arbitrary coincidences of detail are given the same weight as "real" coordinates of time and space. Recognizing the conventionality of all measurements allows one to treat any moment as if it were the present and all places—even the far-off shores of Russia—as if they were here: "our ground-floor telephone, the number of which was 24–43. . . . I wonder by the way, what would happen if I put in a long-distance call from my desk right now? No answer? No such number? No such country? Or the voice of Ustin saying "*moyo pochtenietse!*" (the ingratiating diminutive of "my respects")? There exist, after all, well-publicized Slavs and Kurds who are well over one hundred and fifty" (*Speak, Memory*, p. 235).

The coalescing patterns allow Nabokov to move in two dimensions at once, creating what he himself calls, in a masked appraisal of his style, "the mirrorlike angles of his clear but weirdly misleading sentences" (p. 288). "I reread that passage in the course of correcting the proofs of the various editions, until finally I made a great effort, and the arbitrary spectacles (which Mnemosyne must have needed more than anybody else) were metamorphosed into a clearly recalled oyster-shell-shaped cigarette case, gleaming in the wet grass at the foot of an aspen on the Chemin du Pendu, where I found on that June day in 1907 a hawkmoth rarely met with so far west, and where a quarter of a century earlier, my father had netted a Peacock butterfly very scarce in our northern woodlands" (*Speak, Memory*, p. 12). The autobiographical act, with its spectacles and metamorphses, overlaps with the objects recollected and represented in the wet grass, and at the same time, another pattern suggests itself, as two generations of Nabokov lepidopterists coincide around that spot at the foot of the aspen.

Since the pattern is all one weave, an unbroken thread (despite ornamental detours and circumstantial differences in time and setting) which is still being woven into the present moment of writing, there is a continuity of tense in Nabokov's own autobiography that is lacking in his parody. Humbert believes—deludes himself into believing—that he has escaped his past and that what he now does and now is as an autobiographer is a wholly different matter. Nabokov treats his present and his past as equally proximate and equally distant from the point of view of the pattern as a whole. "As far back as I remember myself . . . I have been subject to mild hallucinations. Some are aural, others are optical, and by none have I profited much" (*Speak, Memory*, p. 33).

Nabokov characteristically begins and ends his chapters in the present tense, often arriving back in the present through a series of dizzying last-minute shifts in tense and aspect:

Thrice, to the mighty heave-ho of his invisible tossers, he would fly up in this fashion, and the second time he would go higher than the first and then there he would be, on his last and loftiest flight, reclining, as if for good, against the cobalt blue of the summer noon, like one of those paradisiac personages who comfortably soar, with such a wealth of folds in their garments, on the vaulted ceiling of a church, while below, one by one, the wax tapers in mortal hands light up to make a swarm of minute flames in the mist of incense, and the priest chants of eternal repose, and funeral lilies conceal the face of whoever lies there, among the swimming lights, in the open coffin. [*Speak, Memory*, pp. 31–32]

This passage, in which his father is tossed up into the air by a blanket held by some grateful peasants, also contains the premonition of his father's death—the two are simultaneous, superimposed as the iterative past merges with the habitual present in the timeless architecture of the text. Unlike Humbert Humbert's linear, ongoing process of writing, Nabokov's own act is most often suspended, still, perfective. Each moment connects to all other moments, each is a creative and created nucleus from which the spiraling design of all space and time spreads out, freed from linear necessity. "I have to have all space and all time participate in my emotion, in my mortal love, so that the edge of its mortality is taken off, thus helping me to fight the utter degradation, ridicule, and horror of having developed an infinity of sensation and thought within a finite existence" (*Speak, Memory*, p. 297).

A "global perspective"[24] on one's life can be achieved only by abandoning the illusion of reality for the reality of illusion. One cannot see the true pattern without simultaneously attending to one's own point of vantage. Late in his autobiography, Nabokov attacks positivism for its superstitious idolatry of naked fact, its failure to see the medium and mechanisms of knowledge which go along with the objects of knowledge: "the outside of the inside, the whereabouts of the curvature; for every dimension presupposes a medium within which it can act, and if, in the spiral unwinding of things, space warps into something akin to time, and time, in its turn, warps into something akin to thought, then, surely, another dimension follows—a special Space maybe, not the old one, we trust, unless spirals become vicious circles again" (*Speak, Memory*, p. 301). Getting out of the vicious circle, Humbert's circle of obsession, is the goal of *Speak, Memory*, and it is also the story it tells. With its fifteen chapters clustering into groups of five, the autobiography becomes an enactment of the spiraling "triadic series" Nabokov so frequently invokes. The overall design of the work seems to reduplicate precisely the progressive movement from space to time to thought, and so on to the fourth dimension.

The first five chapters, beginning not with Nabokov's birth but with the first moment of his self-awareness, cover themes connected with ancestry and infancy. Nabokov plays with primeval allusions and heraldic metaphor in these early sections of his book. "To fix correctly, in terms of time, some of my childhood recollections, I have to go by comets and eclipses, as historians do when they tackle the fragments of a saga" (*Speak, Memory*, p. 25). The focus of these chapters is on the estates and servants, the life-style into which Nabokov was born. The individuals who cared for him and who gave him his earliest instructions are depicted, and although the history of these persons—his mother, his uncle, his Swiss governess—is given in entirety, it is still the primary association that is stressed. Each chapter ends upon a note of childish defenselessness and innocent trust. "I see again my school room in Vyra, the blue roses of the wallpaper, the open window. Its reflection fills the oval mirror above the leathern couch where my uncle sits, gloating over a tattered book. A sense of security, of well-being, of summer warmth pervades my memory. That robust reality makes a ghost of the present. The mirror brims with brightness; a bumblebee has entered the room and bumps against the ceiling. Everything is as it should be, nothing will ever change, nobody will ever die" (*Speak, Memory*, pp. 76–77).

A natural termination of this opening section seems to be reached with the departure, in chapter five, of the last of his governesses, whom he and his entire family have outgrown. In chapter six there begins a series of adventures—butterfly hunting, "puppy love," school encounters, and the first serious pangs of sexual unrest—which show Nabokov as a young man rather than a protected infant. It is in this setting that Nabokov places his portrait of his father, as though to stress his new relationship with his family, one no longer based on dependence and maternal care. There is also a change in the manner in which inevitable fatalities are brought into focus at the close of a chapter. "Ten years were to pass before a certain night in 1922, at a public lecture in Berlin, when my father shielded the lecturer (his old friend Milyukov) from the bullets of two Russian Fascists and, while vigorously knocking down one of the assassins, was fatally shot by the other. But no shadow was cast by that future event upon the bright stars of our St. Petersburg house; the large, cool hand resting on my head did not quaver, and several lines of play in a difficult chess composition were not blended yet on the board" (*Speak, Memory*, p. 193). This moment of temporary security (created by the discovery that his father would not be forced to fight a threatened duel) cannot be extricated from the increasingly complex patterns of life which open up around the adolescent. This period of expectancy and frustration is brought to its poetic closure in chapter ten: "There it lay in wait, a family of serene clouds in miniature, an accumulation of brilliant convolutions, anachronistic in their creaminess and extremely remote; remote but perfect in every detail; fantastically reduced but faultlessly shaped; my marvelous tomorrow ready to be delivered to me" (*Speak, Memory*, p. 213).

Into the five chapters which follow, the last chapters of the book, are crowded all the events of Nabokov's maturity before his emigration to the United States. Beginning with the composition of his first poem and the seduction of his first love (whose pseudonym, "Tamara," is perhaps a pun on the dream of a "marvelous tomorrow" which ended the previous chapter), this section is dominated by Nabokov's life in exile. He at first adopts an elegaic stance toward his lost youth, his lost country, his lost first love—but this is only a preliminary, "antithetic" response to the experience of exile. Nabokov quickly modulates nostalgia into something more sophisticated:

Tamara, Russia, the wildwood grading into old gardens, my northern birches and firs, the sight of my mother getting down on her hands and knees to kiss the earth every time we came back to the country from town for the summer . . . these are the things that fate one day bundled up pell-mell and tossed into the sea, completely severing me from my boyhood. I wonder, however, whether there is really much to be said for more anesthetic destinies, for, let us say, a smooth, safe, small-town continuity of time, with its primitive absence of perspective. . . . The break in my own destiny affords me in retrospect a syncopal kick that I would not have missed for worlds. . . . What it would be actually to see again my former surroundings, I can hardly imagine. Sometimes I fancy myself revisiting them with a false passport, under an assumed name. It could be done.

But I do not think I shall ever do it. I have been dreaming of it too idly and too long. [*Speak, Memory*, pp. 249–50]

The separation between what can be dreamed in the fourth dimension and what can be physically sought and held in the first three becomes explicit in this passage. Loss is transcended by a simultaneous gain in insight and even the pattern of a painful destiny can be appreciated aesthetically, for its "perspective" and "syncopation." The last five chapters of *Speak, Memory* are at once the story of Nabokov's departure from all that he had ever known and valued and of his achievement of a new kind of knowledge and a new way of evaluating his world through the twin processes of creation and procreation. The autobiography ends with the birth of his son, in whose nascent experience he is able to see something of his own past, but in a form unavailable to him then. This is a dialectical return and not a mere repetition; it follows the pattern of "Hegel's triadic series" as Nabokov himself has described it. "Three stages may be distinguished . . . corresponding to those of the triad: We can call "thetic" the small curve or arc that initiates the convolution centrally; "antithetic" the larger arc that faces the first in the process of continuing it; and "synthetic" the still ampler arc that continues the second while following the first along the outer side" (*Speak, Memory*, p. 275).

Elegy, nostalgia, the remorseful and wishful thinking of Humbert

Humbert, are merely antithetic extensions of the past. In attempting to wrestle with his fate, Humbert is unconsciously "continuing" the destiny he tries to overcome. But by perceiving the perceptions of his own "creation"—his son—Nabokov steps outside his own condition and achieves a level of awareness impossible for Humbert. The primordial allusions which appeared in the first chapter of the autobiography reappear in the last, and the birth of consciousness, the genesis of a world, with which *Speak, Memory* began occurs again: "an infant's first journey into the next dimension, the newly established nexus between eye and reachable object, which the career boys in biometrics or in the rat-maze racket think they can explain. It occurs to me that the closest reproduction of the mind's birth obtainable is the stab of wonder that accompanies the precise moment when, gazing at a tangle of twigs and leaves, one suddenly realizes that what had seemed a natural com-ponent of that tangle is a marvelously disguised insect or bird" (*Speak, Memory*, p. 298). Consciousness constitutes and then transforms the world, creating new patterns with every stage of awareness. Conscious-ness thus transforms the past, as a new level of perception makes a new configuration accessible. Even at its most remedial level, it is a kind of art, constructing a universe around itself out of whatever relationships it registers. The final words of the autobiography catch consciousness in the act, performing one of its amazing transformations as it penetrates to the "marvelously disguised" ship which is to take Nabokov to America. "There, in front of us . . . where the eye encountered all sorts of strategems, such as pale-blue and pink underwear cakewalking on a clothesline, or a lady's bicycle and a striped cat oddly sharing a rudimentary balcony of cast iron, it was most satisfying to make out among the jumbled angles of roofs and walls, a splended ship's funnel, showing from behind the clothesline as something in a scrambled picture—Find What the Sailor Has Hidden—that the finder cannot unsee once it has been seen" (*Speak, Memory*, pp. 309–10). That ship's funnel is as buried in the sentence pattern which holds it as its original could ever have been buried in balconies and clotheslines. The "stab of wonder" which accompanies our recognition of it here is indeed the "closest reproduction of the mind's birth obtainable." But it is obtain-able only through art.

There follows this passage, in the revised edition, an index which redistributes all the various themes and preoccupations of the autobiog-raphy into various categories. One can see how themes are in fact recirculated through chapter after chapter, through the listing and cross-listing Nabokov here provides. In *Lolita* lists and catalogs provide ironic counterpoint to Humbert's own slavishly sequential plot, but the final rendering of themes at the end of *Speak, Memory*, following as it does immediately upon the passage cited above, appears to be the culmination of Nabokov's autobiographical method. Here we have the gestalt design, hidden and scattered through the pages of the text, gathered together in a final configuration which cannot be "unseen." One is told at the outset, in the foreward to the revised autobiography, that "Through the window of that index/Climbs a rose. . ." (p. 16), and one is thus alerted for the clues to the text's overall design which are to be found there. Three interlocking terms reveal themselves: "pavilion," "stained glass," and "jewels." There is a naturalistic explanation for this cross-indexing, since the pavilion Nabokov writes about does have stained-glass windows, windows where "the sun breaks into geometrical gems." But if one examines the description of this pavilion more closely, one uncovers the following additional bit of evidence: "the pavilion rising midway like a coagulated rainbow, was as slippery as if it had been coated with some dark and in a sense magic ointment. Etymologically, "pavilion" and "papilio" are closely related" (*Speak, Memory*, p. 216).

This etymological remark is dropped rather obtrusively into the middle of a paragraph with which it apparently has nothing to do. But in conjunction with the index, and in view of the secondary association between the magical, slippery covering of the pavilion and the silken cocoon in which the butterfly accomplishes its metamorphosis a hidden pattern does begin to emerge. Especially if one matches Nabokov's etymological clue with further dictionary research: "*pavilion*. n. (OF *paveillon*, fr. L *papilio* a butterfly . . .) . . . 3. The lower faceted part of a brilliant . . . 5. *Arch*. A light, ornamented building in a park, garden, or the like."[25] Thus the relationship the index suggests between "pavilion," "jewels," and (faceted) "stained glass" is firmly established, and the connecting link is the artful transformation of the butterfly. When we turn back to the text with the full configuration in mind, its architecture comes clearly into view and the crucial balance points in the spiral of consciousness are revealed. In the opening chapter, for example, we find a jewel associated with the birth of consciousness: "a certain beautiful, delightfully solid, garnet-dark crystal egg. . . . I used to chew a corner of the bedsheet until it was thoroughly soaked and then wrap the egg in it tightly, so as to admire and re-lick, the warm, ruddy glitter of the snugly enveloped facets that came seeping through with a miraculous completeness of glow and color. But that was not yet the closest I got to feeding upon beauty" (*Speak, Memory*, p. 24).

The jewel-egg is linked with the most primitive form of infant consciousness, the tactile awareness of a "reachable object" which, as Nabokov later informs us on the basis of his observations of his own infant son, is "an infant's first journey into the next dimension." Then in chapter six, initiating the next stage of the autobiography, we encounter Nabokov's first concentrated awareness and pursuit of butterflies. Once again there is an implied reaching out of consciousness, as Nabokov's pursuit of lepidopteral beauty takes him out of space and into time. "My Swallowtail, with a mighty rustle, flew into her face, then made for the open window, and presently was but a golden fleck dipping and dodging eastward, where it lost a tail . . . across Alaska to Dawson, and southward along the Rocky Mountains—to be finally overtaken and captured after a forty-year race, on an immigrant dandelion under an endemic aspen near Boulder" (*Speak, Memory*, p. 120).

In chapter eleven, another and final section of the autobiography opens on a view of the pavilion and on Nabokov's first experience of the "numb fury of verse-making." The quest for beauty now turns from pursuit and possession to creation, the effort of a mind to make "that whereby it rejoices." Although his first attempts at poetry are dismal failures, they open for him at least a dim awareness of another dimension of being. "The instant it all took to happen seemed to me not so much a fraction of time as a fissure in it, a missed heartbeat . . . the shock of wonder I had experienced when for a moment heart and leaf had been one" (*Speak, Memory*, p. 217). Time and space, the separation between subject and object, "heart and leaf,"—all are obliterated in this instant. Consciousness becomes conscious of itself: "I was richly, serenely aware of my own manifold awareness" (p. 219). Art thus provides the medium, the "special Space" within which thought and memory may act and simultaneously see themselves acting.

The index of Nabokov's autobiography is itself an aesthetic object as well as an aid for recognizing the artwork of the text. In describing the significance of his pavilion, he seems to be describing the principles behind all of *Speak, Memory*, down to its most trivial detail: "I dream of my pavilion at least twice a year. As a rule, it appears in my dreams quite independently of their subject matter, which, of course, may be anything, from abduction to zoolatry. It hangs around, so to speak, with the unobtrusiveness of an artist's signature. I find it clinging to a corner of the dream canvas or cunningly worked into some ornamental part of the picture" (*Speak, Memory*, p. 215). Even a simple index turns out to be complex, with the pavilion "cunningly worked into" it, the artist's signature concealed beneath the artless alphabet.

Of course, Humbert Humbert has also left his signature—one might almost say his fingerprints—on the pages of his memoirs, but it is hardly the signature of an artist. Despite the way he constantly calls attention to his own "bon mot" and pauses to congratulate himself on his triumphs as an author, his position is clearly false. "I gently grade my story" he remarks, ostensibly displaying his control, only to have his story take a sudden, grotesque hop or stumble into anticlimax. He shows himself possessed instead of self-possessed, as he "lingers gratefully in that gauze-gray room of memory" reenacting rather than analyzing his obsessions. He has no control over the magic of his tale; he is the enchanted instead of the enchanter, "lured on" by his need "to fix once and for all the perilous magic of nymphets" (p. 136). Traces of his thralldom are everywhere. He writes under a mysterious obligation: "I have to tread carefully. I have to speak in a whisper" (*Lolita*, p. 136). His autobiography, like his captive, seems to have escaped him, to act out its own designs, to seek its own protagonist and punish its own villain. "And I have still other smothered memories, now unfolding themselves into limbless monsters of pain" (*Lolita*, p. 286). Humbert's claims to omniscience and omnipotence as an author only exacerbate the incongruity, an incongruity that remains even in the final words he writes—"And this is the only immortality you and I may share, my Lolita"—the tentative quality of which, the expressed need for permission, give the lie to their prophetic finery. Moreover, in this final paragraph, Humbert abandons (or is abandoned by) the egomaniacal first person; the narrator is no longer "I" but "one": "one wanted H. H. to exist at least a couple of months longer, so as to have him make you live" (p. 311).

Here at least one sees the naked expression of Humbert's authorial role. Up until the final passage of his manuscript, Humbert has maintained a variety of postures—"sensualist," "reporter," "poet"—which in spite of their disparity at least share the common implication that Humbert is the source and not the instrument of his text. His vacillation between various titles for himself does do great damage to his proposed defense: "But I am no poet. I am only a very conscientious recorder" (*Lolita*, p. 74). "Emphatically, no killers are we. Poets never kill" (*Lolita*, p. 90). But whether he chooses one or many of these titles, he must have his incarnation, his book must be the extension of his failing heart and his hot breath: "Only in the tritest terms . . . can I describe Lo's features . . . oh, that I were a lady writer who could have her pose naked in a naked light!" (*Lolita*, p. 46).

Humbert's final noble gesture, in which he abandons himself to his fate and asks only to be an eternal artifact, a canonized exemplar of romantic love, is ostensibly an act of contrition, even of courage. But it is really only another of his characteristic ploys for the evasion of responsibility, one more failure or refusal to come to terms with the complexity of his situation. "At this or that twist of it I feel my slippery self eluding me, gliding into deeper and darker waters than I care to probe" (*Lolita*, p. 310). Humbert continues to accept a simplification of his condition, invoking it with his dying breath. He is always a character in his own eyes, whether as the hero of his own story or the author of his own autobiography. Rather than abandon his sense of personal identity, he surrenders his role as an autobiographer and fictionalizes himself.

Humbert is a carnal travesty, an inversion of the autobiographical performance Nabokov gives us in his own work. While it is true that Nabokov emphasizes his capacity as a narrator, what he "can" or "could" do, it is an emergent capacity which could not exist without the aid of art. "And now a delightful thing happens. The process of recreating that penholder and the microcosm in its eyelet stimulates my memory to a last effort. I try again to recall the name of Colette's dog—and triumphantly, along those remote beaches, over the glossy evening sands of the past, where each footprint slowly fills up with sunset water, here it comes, here it comes, echoing and vibrating: Floss, Floss, Floss!" (*Speak, Memory*, pp. 151–52). This is a peculiarly impersonal achievement. Creation is a new form of consciousness, transcending the limits of individual experience and personal memory even as it uses them.[26] Nabokov describes the way notions of self shattered in the composition of his first poem: "Looking into my own eyes, I had the shocking sensation of finding the mere dregs of my usual self, odds and ends of an evaporated identity which it took my reason quite an effort to gather again in the glass" (*Speak, Memory*, p. 117).

As he becomes the narrator of his autobiography, the same process of evaporation seems to occur. "Peasant girls . . . stark naked in shallow water, romped and yelled, heeding me as little as if I were the discarnate carrier of my present reminiscences" (*Speak, Memory*, pp. 137–38). The most common words for his narrative identity are spectral—"ghost," "invisible spy." There are also anagrams which rearrange the elements of his worldly identity and leave behind only the mask of a speaker or viewer totally subordinated to his immediate task: "Vivian Bloodmark, a philosophical friend of mine, in later years, used to say that while the scientist sees everything that happens in one point of space, the poet feels everything that happens in one point of time" (*Speak, Memory*, p. 218). "Vivian Bloodmark" is of course Vladimir Nabokov—the same anagrammatic signature worked into the canvas of *Lolita*—but it is equally a transformation of Nabokov into an impersonation and an impersonalization. In fact, Nabokov's authorial first person is exchanged freely for the impersonal pronoun: "Mnemosyne, one must admit, has shown herself a very careless girl." "I" is frequently only a position in a pattern. "I still seem to be holding that wisp of iridescence, not knowing exactly where to fit it, while she runs with her hoop ever faster around me and finally dissolves among the slender shadows cast on the graveled path by the interlaced arches of its low looped fence" (*Speak, Memory*, p. 152). Just as frequently, there is no actor named at all: "Certain tight parentheses have been opened and allowed to spill their still active contents" (*Speak, Memory*, pp. 11–12).

The agent, in figurative terms, behind the autobiographical act is memory, the force of inspiration summoned by the title. "I find the pattern curiously clear, and the images of those tutors appear within memory's luminous disc as so many magic-lantern projections" (*Speak, Memory*, p. 154). The narrator does not form the pattern but "finds" it already implicit in memory, playing the same role of "finder" which appears so prominently at the conclusion of the book. The autobiographical act, then, is a transaction between memory and the perception of that memory. At least two levels of awareness are necessary to escape Humbert Humbert's circular obsession with the past; perception must be perceived and memory must be understood. In order to achieve this trick of "manifold awareness," there must be a perfect fit between the material of the text and the act of the autobiographer. Nabokov's creative contribution is not something he claims, like Humbert, to control but rather something he experiences. "The hush of pure memory that (except, perhaps for some chance tinnitus due to the pressure of my own tired blood) I have left undisturbed, and humbly listened to, from the beginning" (*Speak, Memory*, p. 309). By constantly and consciously exposing the quality of this, his autobiographical experience, its emotional and perceptual flavor, Nabokov effects a merger between the original moment of cognition and its present recognition. By seeing what he does rather than searching for who he is—an image which could only be his own creation, after all—he establishes a purely epistemological and aesthetic continuity, a coincidence of pattern which is the only version of "recaptured time" he will allow.

As a memoirist, Humbert attempts to reify what Nabokov struggles to evaporate. One of his chief devices for this is the manipulation of his audience. Even if he himself cannot fully believe in his dreamy characterizations of his "movie star handsome" self, perhaps others can be gulled into accepting them and their gullibility in turn will shore up his failing confidence. The style of his interaction with his readers, however, would undo him even if nothing else in his manuscript did. The glance with which he fixes his readers, the alternate accusations and supplications which reach out to us from his pages, are unhealthy, symptomatic of everything he would deny about himself. For example, there is the way he confuses his audience with his own hallucinations. "Humbert Humbert, sweating in the fierce white light, and howled at, and trodden upon by sweating policemen, is now ready to make a further 'statement' (quel mot!)" (*Lolita*, p. 72).

Like hallucinations, Humbert's audience is subject to sudden and irrational transformations, from plural to singular, from distant to intimate, from vindictive to disinterested: "Mid-twentieth century ideas concerning child-parent relationship have been considerably tainted by the scholastic rigamarole and standardized symbols of the psychoanalytic racket, but I hope I am addressing myself to unbiased readers" (*Lolita*, p. 287). But the intermittent indications of control on Humbert's part are no less disquieting when one observes that it is tyranny rather than self-control that is his aim. When Humbert describes his audience, rationally and realistically, providing them with facial features, occupations, and preoccupations, he is in fact trying to treat them as characters he has created. ". . . my learned reader (whose eyebrows, I suspect, have by now traveled all the way to the back of his bald head) . . ." (*Lolita*, p. 50). Whether he calls to the "winged seraphs of Heaven"—seeing himself surrounded by the envious angels in "Annabel Lee"—or more discretely addresses his prospective mortal jury, Humbert is still engaged in "solipsizing" whomever he encounters. The reader who accepts these titles and fictional characterizations of himself becomes just another lifeless mirage, subject to Humbert's usual treatment of mirages—murder and seduction. We can see Humbert trying to win over the female members of his jury with the same "fatal charm" he has used on all the other women in his life: "Gentlewomen of the jury! Bear with me! Allow me to take just a tiny bit of your precious time!" (*Lolita*, p. 125). When, on the other hand, he addresses his masculine readers as "Bruder," we are reminded less of Baudelaire than of Clare Quilty, Humbert's double and his murder victim, whom he also addresses with this term.

Thus, despite the stunning change in Humbert's relation to Lolita, when he ceases writing about her and begins writing to her toward the close of his manuscript we are not—or should not be—convinced.

And I looked and looked at her, and knew as clearly as I know I am to die, that I loved her more than anything I had ever seen or imagined on earth, or hope for anywhere else. She was only the faint violet whiff and dead leaf echo of the nymphet I had rolled myself upon . . . but thank God it was not that echo alone that I worshipped . . . even if those eyes of hers would fade to myopic fish, and her nipples swell and crack, and her lovely young velvety delicate delta be tainted and torn—even then I would go mad with tenderness at the mere sight of your dear wan face, at the mere sound of your raucous young voice, my Lolita. [*Lolita*, pp. 279–80]

Certainly there is more humanity in this address than in all his stylized apostrophes to Lolita elsewhere in the book. But this evocation and the endearments it arouses are connected with the Coalmont scene—a scene which, as I have suggested above, may not have occurred. Moreover, in the pages following this tender exchange with his beloved, Humbert also tries to stage a conversation with his car: "I was soon to be taken out of the car (Hi, Melmoth, thanks a lot, old fellow)" (*Lolita*, p. 309). All of Humbert's proposed readers are imaginary, fantasies with whom he can communicate in ways otherwise impossible for him. His address to Lolita is an attempt to make her live, to make her share with him a love she could not participate in as the inert object of his lust; but she remains his projection to the last. "But while the blood still throbs through my writing hand, you are still as much a part of blessed matter as I am, and I can still talk to you from here to Alaska" (*Lolita*, p. 311).

Humbert's machinations are defeated by his editor, who quickly countermands all of Humbert's patient and impatient instructions for the reading of his tale.

Please, reader: no matter your exasperation with the tender-hearted, morbidly sensitive, infinitely circumspect hero of my book, do not skip these essential pages! Imagine me; I shall not exist if you do not imagine me; try to discern the doe in me, trembling in the forest of my own iniquity; let's even smile a little. [*Lolita*, p. 131]

In this poignant personal study there lurks a general lesson; the wayward child, the egotistic mother, the panting maniac—these are not only vivid characters in a unique story: they warn us of dangerous trends. [*Lolita*, p. 7]

Humbert's labor of love is lost upon Ray's "serious readers" who despise aesthetics and imaginative details, who search out the "ethical impact the book should have" and skim for the "general lesson" alone. Humbert Humbert will not be imagined and he will therefore cease to exist.

But perhaps Ray and other serious readers have fallen into Humbert's trap, after all. He had pleaded at the start of his manuscript: "Ah, leave me alone in my pubescent park, in my mossy garden. Let them play around me forever. Never grow up" (*Lolita*, p. 23). Observers like editor John Ray are not unfamiliar in Humbert's world; he has learned how to fulfill their expectations while simultaneously pursuing his own ends. "I discovered there was an endless source of robust enjoyment in trifling with psychiatrists: cunningly leading them on; never letting them see that you know all the tricks of the trade, inventing for them elaborate dreams, pure classics in style . . . and never allowing them the slightest glimpse of one's real sexual predicament" (*Lolita*, p. 36). Thus when Humbert claims that he has found "the secret of durable pigments," one is reminded of his earlier allusion to pigments: "what twists of lust you might see from your impeccable highways if Kumfy Kabins were suddenly drained of their pigments" (p. 119). His paints are meant to obscure rather than communicate his vision, and his "refuge of art" is simply a visionary asylum, a metaphysical repetition of all those psychiatric retreats which give him the privacy he needs for perfecting his delusions rather than being cured of them.

But if Humbert has managed to wall any intruders out of Humberland, he remains uneasy and insecure with his solitude. As the process of his writing goes on, his attempt to put questions into his readers' mouths gives way to his own anxious need to question. Humbert is forced to inquire of his audience, whose will and perception he has earlier attempted to destroy, what his own failing memory can no longer tell him. "Did I ever mention that her bare arm bore the 8 of vaccination? That I loved her hopelessly? That she was only fourteen?" (*Lolita*, p. 236). There are over a hundred instances in Humbert's manuscript in which he calls out hysterically to the reader, to the God he does not believe in, to his dead love, and over fifty occasions when he begs for the solution to his dilemma from the very alien intelligences he had hoped to dupe. In the end, he ceases to "prove" anything to his jury, and wistfully dreams that they will save him from the consequences of his own ineluctable ratiocination: "Unless it can be proven to me—to me as I am now, today, with my heart and my beard, and my putrefaction—that in the infinite run it does not matter a jot that a North American girl-child named Dolores Haze had been deprived of her childhood by a maniac, unless this can be proven (and if it can, then life is a joke), I see nothing for the treatment of my misery" (*Lolita*, p. 285). Once again Humbert has come to believe in his own fantasies; the audience which he began by creating must now sustain him. But such an audience cannot outlive its creator and must perish, like Lolita, when the book has ended, bringing down Humbert's visionary world and his dream of immortality through art.

Nabokov rejects the notion of a private art. For art there must be two stages, first the fabrication and then the recognition of what has been made—two distinct but intertwined dimensions of awareness. There must therefore be an autonomous audience in whose perception the pattern is recreated and authenticated. The art of autobiography lies not in vain attempts to repossess the past or to secure a miserly hold upon one's own experience, but in freely "turning over" one's life to another: "I did not know then (as I know perfectly well now) what to do with such things—how to get rid of them, how to transform them into something that can be turned over to the reader in printed characters to have *him* cope with the blessed shiver" (*Speak, Memory*, p. 212). Only interaction perfects vision and makes seeing and remembering into "what has been seen." There is thus a division of labor between the text of *Speak, Memory* and its ultimate audience, repeating on another level the converging efforts of narrator and memory. Appreciation must transcend what it recognizes—Nabokov therefore does not make characters of his readers. Indeed, the only persons represented in the book are dead or seen in guises they have now outgrown (the infancy of his son, for example). Nabokov's wife, Vera, is not a character at all but the principal addressee of the text, the "you" with whom the revelations of memory are so often shared. Unlike Lolita, Nabokov's love is never reduced to an object, something to be written about. Her presence is marked only by a pronoun, each occurrence of which is credited to her in the autobiography's index. But the reading public stands at a further remove. They do not share in his experiences or relish his preoccupations uncritically. Their dispassionate view in fact receives his wry encouragement: "I had found last spring a dark aberration of Siever's Carmelite (just another gray moth to the reader). In the ditch, under the bridgelet, a bright-yellow Silvius Skipper hobnobbed with a dragonfly (just a blue libellula to me)" (*Speak, Memory*, p. 132).

Nabokov does not allow this audience immediate participant status. There are no attempts to call on them directly, and only rarely does he use the first-person plural in its inclusive sense. Rather than Humbert's commandments, his badgering or mocking questions, the reader of *Speak, Memory* is given only oblique clues, disguised directions which he must decode for himself. "Let visitors trip." Whereas Humbert rises to tyrannize his readers, making them the objects or the victims of his autobiographical act, Nabokov makes beneficiaries out of each member of his variegated public. "The following passage is not for the general reader, but for the particular idiot who, because he lost a fortune in some crash, thinks he understands me" (*Speak, Memory*, p. 73). Even his disdain is treated as something acted out for the benefit of his reader, and not something he inflicts upon him.

The magical space between artificer and audience also means that Nabokov cannot predict, as Humbert belives he can, the actions of his audience or prescribe their responses as John Ray, Jr., might. Only vulgar readers have predictable responses. "To avoid hurting the living or distressing the dead, certain proper names have been changed. These are set off by quotation marks in the index. Its main purpose is to list for my convenience some of the people and themes connected with my past years. Its presence will annoy the vulgar but may please the discerning" (*Speak, Memory*, p. 16). The index, of course, does contain keys to understanding the formal pattern of his text, but these are keys to be discovered and not thrust rudely into unwilling hands.

Since the transactional nature of the autobiographical act requires that Nabokov himself take up the role of an observer and an auditor, a member of memory's audience, many of the infrequent imperatives and questions which appear in the text are directed by the autobiographer to himself, or to the source of his own inspiration. "And let me not leave out the moon—for surely there must be a moon" (*Speak, Memory*, p. 99). "How readily Mr. Cummings would sit down on a stool, part behind with both hands his—what? was he wearing a frock coat? I see only the gesture—and proceed to open the black tin paintbox" (*Speak, Memory*, pp. 92—93). Most of the remaining questions, orders, exclamations, are in fact chameleons, requests for information which turn magically into acts of creation, effecting the very thing they purport to doubt. "There our child kneeled motionless to be photographed . . . against the scintillation of the sea . . . silvery blue, with great patches of purple-blue farther out, caused by warm currents in collaboration with and corroboration of (hear the pebbles rolled by the withdrawing wave?) eloquent old poets and their smiling similes" (*Speak, Memory*, p. 308). Proclamations turn inward on themselves before they ever reach the reader: "The curse of battle and toil leads man back to the boar, to the grunting beast's crazy obsession with the search for food. . . . Toilers of the world, disband! Old books are wrong. The world was made on a Sunday" (*Speak, Memory*, p. 298).

It is only by means of such disguise that the role of the audience can become a pure potentiality, a part which may be taken up by any willing imagination, including the autobiographer's. Nabokov imposes no limitations on who may play his game; the act of discovery may take place for anyone, at any time or place. Any reader of *Speak, Memory* may become a "finder," and in doing so achieve a position that is the intellectual and aesthetic equivalent of Nabokov's own. There can be no condescension, no giving away of secrets, if the reader is to have what alone derives from an autonomous act of creation—"the stab of wonder that accompanies the precise moment" when one penetrates "a marvelous disguise." This alone will turn life into a pattern, impervious to time and transcending personal identity, something to be found again by each and every attentive reader of the autobiography. "Now and then, shed by a blossoming tree, a petal would come down, down, down, and with the odd feeling of seeing something neither worshipper nor casual spectator ought to see, one would manage to glimpse its reflection which swiftly—more swiftly than the petal fell—rose to meet it; and for the fraction of a second, one feared that the trick would not work . . . but every time the delicate union did take place, with the magic precision of a poet's word meeting halfway his, or a reader's recollection" (*Speak, Memory*, pp. 270–71).

CHAPTER SIX

===

CONCLUSION

===

> Everything is related to everything else. There are therefore
> collective desires, obsessions, anxieties, which have their own
> dynamic, their own dialectic. I take these collective desires, these
> collective obsessions, these collective anxieties and give them a
> system of relations, a dynamism, a dialectic, a pattern, a structure
> that is mine alone. . . .
>   I am determined. At the same time, I also determine. I make a
> choice, I change or I do not change things, and the fact that I do
> not change things causes them to change all the same.
>
>   Eugène Ionesco

To write or to read any piece of literature is to engage in action. The excitement and the potential aesthetic ambiguity of autobiography stem
from how closely the literary act borders on the literal, how immediately the decisions of the autobiographer and his reader reflect traits
and habits of an intellectual and social life beyond the pages of the
text. Yet autobiography, or rather the people who read and write it, has
tenaciously maintained its status as literature while many other genres
similarly dependent on pragmatic immediacy—history, sermon, and
lecture, for example—have lost their literary associations and become
science, scholarship, even advertising. Perhaps this is because autobiography has so frequently anticipated or coincided with the movements
of the English literary system as a whole, first toward individualism and
representational realism, psychological density, and sociological particularity, and then toward expressionistic form. Just at the point when
these claims would seem to have been exhausted, the skeptical aesthetics of modernist and postmodernist art, with its radical testing of
traditional techniques and its challenge to conceptions about the essential properties of literature, music, and the plastic arts, has made
autobiography once again problematic and provocative.

As a culture, we have not yet lost our appetite for seeing how
individuals go about constructing their experiences from the inside,
what resources they bring to the task, and what we might appropriate
from them or learn by their example to avoid. To this degree autobiography has retained the exemplary values it possessed for Bunyan and his
peers. Indeed, with so much of life and even identity beyond our
personal control, we perhaps cling all the more fiercely to an institution

which offers us at least one remaining area of symbolic power over our destiny as individuals. For despite attacks upon the notion of individuality, it is still at the center of the way we organize and imagine life in our society and in our literature. As a principal in the attack on individualism, Claude Lévi-Strauss, puts it in his own reluctant autobiography: "Not merely is the first person singular detestable: there is no room for it between "ourselves" and "nothing." And if, in the end, I opt for "ourselves," although it is not more than an appearance, it is because unless I destroy myself—an act which would wipe out the conditions of the decision I have to make—there is really only one choice to be made: between that appearance and nothing. But no sooner have I chosen than, by that very choice, I take on myself, unreservedly, my condition as a man"[1]

Autobiography has contributed to the way we frame our experience, and it has also sharpened our awareness of the endless possibilities of complication "between 'ourselves' and 'nothing' "—alerting us to our need for further information. In many ways, autobiography is the best argument for autobiography.

Yet the needs the genre has served and continues to serve are far from uniform. One can see easily enough how partial the agreement is between those few autobiographies I have treated in the preceding chapters—as well as how gradually and almost erratically agreement has come about. There are certain common tendencies, however. A leaning toward discontinuous structures, for instance, with disrupted narrative sequences and competing foci of attention. The "story" the autobiography tells is never seamless, and often it is not a story at all but a string of meditations and vignettes—fractional events that may be painful or joyous in their partial disinterment, irrepressible or simply casual in their transient spontaneity. Never, except in cases of deliberate iconoclasm such as Nabokov's (and even in his case, only with the additional apparatus of foreward and index), can one speak of an autonomous and self-sustaining textual pattern. The order, the meaning or rhythm of the composition, becomes clear only when we look for the person and the personality which holds it all together, whether by means of publicly ascertainable religious convictions or by a private, implicit set of values and associations. This is not a failed coherence but a different kind of coherence, arising from the responsibilities peculiar to the autobiographical act. Because of the nature of his subject matter, there must always be something which is just outside the autobiographer's immediate field of vision, something he can reach only by turning his text back upon itself to examine the vantage point rather than the view. Thus an autobiography typically calls attention to its own devices, to the progress it is making in unfolding its tale, to its successes and even more often its failures to capture and communicate its subject. But what is palpable is less the mechanics of a text than the consciousness of an author who finds himself implicated in his every word. The fullness of his *mise en scène*, the deftness of his phrase and figure, becomes a personal rather than a theoretical achievement. Indeed, the only way of overcoming a paralyzing self-consciousness or an infinite autobiographical regress may be to surrender one's person entirely—to God, to fame, or to art.

Despite their disparities then, the autobiographies of Bunyan and Boswell, De Quincey and Nabokov are alike in their almost-exclusive orientation around the individual who is writing—although Nabokov recognizes this and takes steps to prevent the personal space and the egocentric time of his private world from ultimately enclosing him. It may be that the conditions of the autobiographical act actually exacerbate idiosyncratic perspectives. As the autobiographer struggles to describe and at the same time penetrate the meaning of his own description, his attention is easily distracted from his audience, and his work may become hermetic. The perspective of audience and autobiographer, the amount and kind of information each brings to their encounter, is necessarily different at the start or there would be no point in either writing or reading. But with autobiography, there is the added risk that the readers' perspective will recede even further as the writer progresses, their notions of him come to seem a poor tangle of distortions and vulgar simplifications.

These technical and strategic concomitants of the autobiographical act, its problems but also the source of its peculiar pleasures, seem to have been there from the start. Yet paradoxically, they were not there until time, other writers, and other readers, made potential effects actual, turning accidents into intentions and making alien structures familiar enough for both problems and achievements to emerge clearly. If we take the four autobiographies studied above as points along a (highly schematic) historical continuum, the progressive ability of each author to communicate his intention with greater economy, to manipulate his effects with more assurance or even with more skepticism, is readily apparent. Time allows for repetition and recognition, for the diffusion of activities to a broader population, thereby taking off the edge of idiosyncrasy and innocence. Neither De Quincey nor Nabokov need spend a quarter of the space Boswell and Bunyan must give to justifying the act in which they are engaged, searching out exemplars and providing suitable rationalizations. Both of the later authors have a far clearer sense of their own goals and the means available for effecting them, whereas the two earlier writers are more conscious of a perilous adventure and thus more hesitant and, in Bunyan's case, defensively derivative. Nabokov and De Quincey write for a general public, although each does so in his separate way, while Bunyan and Boswell have no assurance of a broad or extensive readership, however longingly Boswell gazes toward an invisible future. One can also gauge the relative legitimacy of autobiography from the way each writer treats a comparable endeavor. Bunyan and Nabokov, for example, treat autobiography as the equal, in terms of familiarity, of their fictional works, whereas Boswell's journal is almost as experimental as De Quincey's *Sketches* are hackneyed.

Thus each autobiographer responds to what precedes and surrounds him, if only to the fact that he has a precedent and is or is not writing in isolation or against the common grain. But each new autobiography is also a further exploration and articulation of the possibilities and limits of the genre, defining what has gone before it and shaping what will survive it. The question of which forms, for example, are appropriate to autobiography may be opened afresh by any autobiographer. The experiments conducted by Boswell and others like him were tests of the reliance of autobiography on borrowed forms such as hagiography and family genealogy. Boswell's performance is also a graphic demonstration of how easily the power of earlier sectarian autobiographies survives translation into nonreligious terms and how little of the genre's power depends on heroic or exemplary experiences. Bunyan himself had recognized the need for demonstrations of piety and imaginative restraint when writing in his own person, but Boswell makes this nearly accidental narrative responsibility a central feature of the act; autobiography must thereafter embody as well as record evidence of its author's character and sensibility. Yet in answering one question, an autobiographer may simultaneously provoke others. Boswell's commitment to subjective truth as crucial to autobiography—a commitment which was difficult enough for him—is even more complex for his posterity. De Quincey pursues this subjectivity to the point where any personal identification is numbed and verification becomes meaningless. Although his autobiographical record is not false, it cannot be as absolute in its claims to truth as Boswell's had been. De Quincey may believe what he writes and even accept the posture and the voice he adopts as in some measure his own, but he is also aware that he is not speaking all of his beliefs and is admitting few of his doubts, and he is therefore far less hopeful than Boswell that autobiography can aspire to unqualified truth. Finally, the mirror inversions of Nabokov's twin texts, his autobiography and his autobiographical parody, together serve to illustrate the instability of De Quincey's compromises and the glibness of his prefabricated identity. The contradictions implicit in self-conscious sincerity are made explicit in Nabokov's mockery of Humbert Humbert. No one who has read Nabokov can afterward retreat from the prospect of autobiographical bad faith which has been opened to him. Goals once sought naively may continue to be sought by post-Nabokovian autobiographers, but naiveté itself will no longer be possible. Of course his is not the last word. There will be those who reject Nabokov's irony as evasion rather than solution, who will uncover implications in his work he had not foreseen or return to his predecessors from a new angle, with new interests and new sympathies—who will by their own witting and unwitting departures make us aware of what always was there but had not yet been seen.

So one must speak cautiously of the "same" autobiographical act, and be prepared to recognize subtle differences in emphasis, associations, and purpose even in the midst of undeniable continuity. Does a tamed and familiar activity have quite the same meaning as one that is startling and unpredictable? At what point does a change in ambience transform the essence of a genre? For example, Bunyan, Boswell, and De Quincey share to some extent the attempt to expose private experience to public scrutiny. But for Bunyan this act of exposure has the flavor and the significance of martyrdom, whereas for Boswell it is alternately shamefully indecorous and empirically stimulating, and De Quincey finds "confidentiality" admirable rather than objectionable, an ability which is far rarer than the negative capacity for discretion. Changes in the context and the alignment of the autobiographical act—changes which are the product of time, but also of social, regional, and individual differences—can thus alter the value and meaning of the act. A contemporary autobiographer not only has no need to argue his exemplary credentials or his precedents but would look odd, eccentric, or even suspicious if he were to do so. It would be extremely difficult, on the other hand, to write a didactic autobiography like Bunyan's for an audience which does not associate the genre with sermons, controversial pamphlets, and religious allegory. Had Bunyan himself attempted to define his act in terms of its departure from biography, the distinction would have been lost on his own audience, while if Nabokov were to do the same, his discriminations would either be banal or take on the appearance of subterfuge.

Autobiographies sanctioned in different ways take on different colorings, alterations which include the scope and the interests of the intended audience, the shape of the autobiographer's own role and assumed identity, and the style and structure of his composition. De Quincey, for example, has a perspective on his life which is just as teleological as Bunyan's; yet naturalistic growth requires a different narrative frame than spiritual development. The *Sketches* are rooted in chronology and pay far more attention to the transitions and epochs of infancy and childhood than *Grace Abounding*, where such wholly mundane and physical discriminations are irrelevant and where the chief concern is sin and doctrine, the problems of a fully conscious, fully culpable adult. Since De Quincey is writing the autobiography of a writer, however, his story ends when he has reached sufficient intellectual and rhetorical facility, and other changes in his adult life—marriage, fatherhood—are ignored. Since it is the capacity and not the content of his mind which interests him and his audience, further stages of belief such as those detailed by Bunyan are not distinguished. Both men write of transcendental modes of being, but only Bunyan finds autobiography an adequate and appropriate vehicle for this kind of writing. The curiosity of the multitude, not God or the promise of salvation, stands behind De Quincey's autobiographical performance.

Of course, an autobiographer may reject or modify whatever franchise he receives, as Nabokov does when he artfully and not a little haughtily refuses to pander to public inquisitiveness about his wife, his lost wealth, and the gory political details of his father's assassination— or as Boswell does, secretly stretching the limited sanction Johnsonian culture gives him for his journalizing. Neither autobiography is written to meet a localized, extrinsic need, and neither therefore must accept an imposed point of textual closure or confine itself to an established identity or a conventional process for determining identity. Without a predetermined end, a convergence of past and present, potentiality and actuality, which must be reached, the autobiographer's tale need not be teleological. Boswell is far more disconcerted than Nabokov with his inability to fix himself or his story into the mold of a progressive development, as one can see from his agonies of surprise and his attempts to explain to himself the unexpected outcome of his autobiographical method. Unlike Nabokov, Boswell lacks both the support of an external authority and the security of a certain acceptance and recognition for his work in the absence of such authority; he must come to rely more and more upon his own peculiarity, his personal uniqueness for the motive and the meaning of his effort. Although Nabokov also emphasizes the peculiar pattern which is the foundation and the purpose of his autobiographical record, he is without Boswell's sense that individuality of this sort need be unusual or exotic. Boswell distinguishes between himself and the faceless mass of ordinary men, but Nabokov distinguishes himself from other selves, other lives which are potentially as richly patterned as his own. It is De Quincey rather than Nabokov who more closely resembles Boswell in his autobiographic idiosyncrasy, but it is an idiosyncrasy which has been thrust upon him. Both men abandon this posture when they write in other genres, but whereas Boswell diminishes himself to take on the "normal" sensibility of the narrator of the *Life of Johnson* and turns his quicksilver character into the caricature of a buffoon, De Quincey finds greater imaginative freedom when he is no longer hampered by the peripheral accumulations of his individuality. For Bunyan, purely idiosyncratic experience would be primordial, godless chaos; he must master and reduce his peculiarity, find its typological parallels in doctrine and biblical tradition, before he can make any sense out of his evidence and before his writing will have any meaning or purposiveness in his own eyes.

Autobiography necessarily isolates and individuates its author; yet the value of this singularity varies with changes of environment and differences in the use to which it is being put. An autobiographer may speak of it willingly or unwillingly, be minute or superficial in his treatment of it. Boswell's idiosyncrasies are discovered as he writes, Nabokov's are created, De Quincey's merely reproduced, and Bunyan's eliminated even as they are revealed. The genre allows each autobiographer to make his own adjustments in the nature and the breadth of the material he will consider, according to what he feels to be his duty or merely his desire. Each author is also free to create a different hierarchy of identity, a different separation between the noumena and phenomena of self. Bunyan's case is the clearest and most rigid in this regard of those autobiographies I have considered. His whole activity is designed to strip himself of the alien demons which accuse and weaken him and to reach a stainless, spiritual center from which he never need depart. Bunyan is fierce and absolute in his rejection of any portion of his experience that will not conform; he is his own wrathful diety, damning any sinful impulse utterly. De Quincey's weapons are condescension and irony, but he is without Bunyan's overwhelming personal need. His essential stature is unchallenged, and it is not even an identity he has sought or wishes deeply to maintain. Boswell wants to establish his identity as desperately as does Bunyan, although he is not as single-minded in his quest for a particular identity, as long as he finds one that is attractive and workable. But Boswell finds the act of uniting his experiences baffling; there seems to be no end to it if he pursues it honestly. He finds parts of himself curious and unaccountable, recalcitrant and even badly flawed, but he has no principle for isolating "Boswell" from this mass of contradictory experience, and so his journal sprawls and swells, embracing, eventually, an entire lifetime. Nabokov has no such commitment to brute honesty, although he shares Boswell's inability to divide his experience, the entire range of what he has seen and done, into essential and inessential categories. The essence of Nabokov is identical with the crossing and recrossing of thematic elements which Mnemosyne suddenly reveals, nor is there any other incarnation of this identity than that which is achieved within the act of writing. Nabokov therefore sees himself aesthetically, since for him there is no other way of seeing self that is not rife with delusion.

Convention as well as personal preference or existential commitment may be résponsible for determining what will be central to an autobiographer's identity and how much tolerance there will be for marginal features. Communities and epochs vary in the amount of weight they give to originality, in autobiographical identity as well as in technique and style. Bunyan and his sectarian contemporaries, for example, have scant use for deliberate inventiveness in either the person or the devices of the autobiographer. But there are also individual differences with regard to the sources of information and standards of evaluation that will be acceptable. De Quincey employs a standard that is not his own, but has difficulty accepting the identity that results as entirely authentic. Boswell is also ambivalent, unable to reject the appearance he assumes in the eyes of others and at the same time unable to ignore his own often radically divergent impressions of himself. Nabokov does not attack what others might make of him, but does insist that autobiographical art provides the most adequate and perspicuous method for constructing an identity. All this is complicated by the fact that autobiography is an act of communication, and that the readers who look on as the autobiographer explains himself have their own explanations and impressions of the writer. Anthony Wilden has studied the implications of this autobiographical paradox in the essays of Montaigne: "As the locus of a subject in an ongoing system of communication, the subject-who-says-I-in-the-*Essays* felt that he had lost himself, that he was being stolen from himself, that the vanity of the world was smothering his authentic self in its inauthenticity. . . . He writes "for himself"—but then he publishes his writings for others."[2] Every autobiographer must face the possibility that he is tacitly in competition with his audience, although he may not confront the problem directly or might assume that there is perfect agreement and sympathy. Perhaps he even tries to establish agreement by voluntarily assuming the perspective of his own reader. Yet there is no certainty that his willed disinterest will coincide with the genuine interests of his audience, as Nabokov makes clear in the grotesque errors and visible contortions that are the result of Humbert Humbert's solipsistic calculations. Since an autobiographer like Bunyan actually profits from the hostile reactions he foresees, experiencing as he withstands them an even more intense evidence of his own heroism, there is obviously a broad range of workable relationships between autobiographer, audience, and overlapping versions of identity—from Nabokov's distant and indirect cooperation to Boswell's intimate yet imperialistic plea for ratification and approval.

By virtue of culture, time, tradition, and individual temperament, autobiographers are far from uniform; the four I have chosen only hint at their diversity. For some, autobiography effects a personal transformation; yet for others this is precisely what it does not and must not do. Other autobiographers in Bunyan's situation might have attempted to widen the circle of their admirers, to convert rather than confound their enemies. But Bunyan relies too heavily on his autobiography as a private memorial to concern himself with his success as an apologist. He needs it to sharpen his mental control over certain details of his experience and to reawaken his sense of horror and gratitude. The alterations of his condition brought about by the act of writing are ostensibly changes only in degree, similar to what has already taken place in his conversion and his ministry. The man John Bunyan and the facts of his existence antedate the autobiography, although Bunyan does remind himself of their true weight and meaning in the transcendental lesson he abstracts from them. No fundamental changes are recognized, however, despite the fact that Bunyan is released from his victimization at the moment when he gives it voice. His experience as a writer is unclouded by hallucinations; it is literal, solid, an absolute product of rationality and will. However great his empathy for the man he once was, however painful his former afflictions remain, Bunyan is no longer passive or bewildered when he narrates *Grace Abounding*. As in his preaching, Bunyan takes on the symbolic power of an instrument of God when he writes, but with the additional advantage that in writing he may be simultaneously instructor and instructed, the judge of his own testimony and the beneficiary of his own martyrdom.

Boswell begins his journalizing with the intention of maintaining scrupulous accuracy and thus gaining undistorted self-knowledge, but he also half believes, half wishes, that he can use autobiography reflexively to influence the shape of his subject matter, improving his character and the conduct of his life. Some of his initial expectations are shattered as it becomes increasingly clear that the act of writing simply extends without resolving the wayward and ungovernable nature of his experience. The direct expression of self, unmediated by ulterior purposes and as proximate to the page as he can render it, is what ultimately engages Boswell's finer efforts. The journal is equipment in an experiment, the means for making gratifying or disheartening discoveries. But though he may be able to still it with a retrospective glance, his immediate experience is of a process of authorship; his journal is a thing in motion as he moves and is alive with his own life. Since it is impossible to separate the content of his record from his recording of it, Boswell is able to indulge himself in speculation and fantasy—the more so because he owes allegiance to nothing beyond each passing moment. In fact the more absorbed he can become in these indulgences, the more likely is his journal to catch its subject off guard and expose him utterly. He must forestall reflection and direct communication, or at least prepare himself to accept the latent irony of evaluations yet to come and the potential absurdity of his sagest gestures.

De Quincey is more arch, although equally conspicuous, about his presence in his *Autobiographical Sketches*. However his is not a performance which will provide the basis for discovery, since it carefully reveals nothing with which he and his public are not already acquainted. He knows as well as Boswell that his act is an immediate reflection of himself, but he chafes at the unnatural constraints of autobiography and consciously refrains from confidential behavior where it is neither warranted nor appreciated. De Quincey does not fully trust his situation; he lacks Boswell's faith in the adequacy of conscientious records and the profundity of self-consciousness. Yet he will not admit to any material alterations. All he adds to his life is a patina, the professional polish of intelligibility which comes from his expertise as a writer. He takes pride in demonstrating his control over his tools, but his cleverness does not give him a symbolic power over his life as Bunyan's autobiography had done, and the effects he achieves as an author have grown too familiar with long use.

Nabokov is at once the most disillusioned of these four autobiographers and the most absolute in his claims for the autobiographical act. His life would fall to pieces without the aid of art; yet what it is and what he is are little more than finely wrought optical illusions. He is more skeptical about the possibilities of communication but also far less inclined to believe that there is anything which is not, unconsciously, the product of a fabrication. His autobiography is therefore truthful in exposing its own lies and expressive in its silences and deliberate euphemism. He is the creator of his own experience, and at the same time admits that he can do no more than experience the act of creation. But for Nabokov, experience remains responsible, a manifold autobiographical awareness.

The varying significance of the autobiographical act, then, is not a matter of familiarity alone. The conditioning factor of other available genres must be considered: the way the possibilities of lyrical expression make autobiography appear artificial and shabby in De Quincey's eyes, for example, or the threat of mockery which is never far from Nabokov's sight. Literature and even language are subject to crises in confidence, some vestigial traces of which appear in the nominalism of *Speak, Memory*. But common conditions provide the basis for recognizing and appreciating independent departures, giving the richness and significance of individuality to each autobiography. An autobiographer establishes his particularity by extending or upsetting expectations, or simply by combining what is expected of him in his own way. These may be only small variations on a common theme, but they open the way to reformulations of the genre, to the emergence of new genres and the obviating of old—a restlessness which separates the quick of living literature from moribund predictions and prescriptions.

===

NOTES

===

INTRODUCTION

The epigraph is quoted in Quentin Bell, *Virginia Woolf: A Biography* (New York: Harcourt Brace Jovanovich, 1972), p. 173 n.

1. Alastair Fowler, "The Life and Death of Literary Forms," *New Literary History* (Winter 1971):201.

2. Translated by Rex Warner (New York: New American Library, 1963), pp. 24–25.

3. Roy Pascal, *Design and Truth in Autobiography* (Cambridge, Mass.: Harvard University Press, 1960), pp. 148, 158, and 160.

4. Interview by Simona Morini, "Nabokov Talks about His Travels," *Vogue*, 15 April 1972, p. 77.

5. Vladimir Nabokov, *Speak, Memory: An Autobiography Revisited* (New York: G. P. Putnam's Sons, 1967), pp. 101–2.

6. Ibid., p. 58.

7. *Glory*, trans. Dimitri Nabokov in collaboration with the author (New York: McGraw-Hill, 1971), p. 3.

8. John Addington Symonds, Introduction, to *The Life of Benvenuto Cellini, Written by Himself*, ed. and trans. Symonds (New York: Brentano's, 1906), p. 44.

9. Syntactic categories are also functional, of course. The physical marks on a page or the sounds in the atmosphere must be assigned a syntactic value by the speakers of the language; acoustic or literal form does not determine, or even reflect, in any precise, one-to-one manner the value it is assigned within the linguistic system, as linguists ever since Saussure have recognized. Syntax exists inasmuch as there is a set of rules or shared criteria for evaluating a certain form as an instance of a certain morpheme or a particular "deep structure." The many/one relationship of form and function is the basis for the generative-transformational model of language which recognizes the syntactic synonymy of disparate "surface structures."

10. Cf. J. L. Austin, *How to Do Things with Words* (New York: Oxford University Press, 1968); P. F. Strawson, "Intention and Convention in Speech Acts," *Philosophical Review* 73 (October 1964): 439–60, and idem, "Phrase et Acte de Parole," trans. Paul Gochet, *Langages* 17 (March 1970): 19–33; J. R. Searle, *Speech Acts: An Essay in the Philosophy of Language* (Cambridge: Cambridge University Press, 1969).

11. Literature itself may be a superordinate type of illocutionary action, and thus one among the types making up "ordinary language." For an interesting discussion of the emergence of "literature" as a category and the various functions that have since been associated with it, see Henryk Markiewicz, "The Limits of Literature," *New Literary History* 4 (Autumn 1972): 5–14.

12. Searle, p. 66.

13. Maurice Merleau-Ponty, "Institution in Personal and Public History," in *Themes from the Lectures at the Collège de France, 1952–1960*, trans. John O'Neill (Evanston, Ill.: Northwestern University Press, 1970), p. 40.

14. Searle, pp. 51–52.

15. Günther Bornkamm has a discussion of the rhetorical devices of antique history in his treatment of New Testament history in *Paul*, trans. D. M. G. Stalker (New York: Harper and Row, 1971), p. xx. See also Robin Lakoff's treatment of these conventions in "Tense and Its Relation to Participants," *Language* 46, no. 4 (1970):846–47.

16. *The Oxford Annotated Bible: Revised Standard Version*, ed. Herbert G. May and Bruce M. Metzger (New York: Oxford University Press, 1962), p. 656. Also on this topic, see Georg Misch, *A History of Autobiography in Antiquity*, trans. with E. W. Dickes (London: Routledge and Kegan Paul, 1950), vol. 1.

17. Misch, 1:16–17, mentions the influence of the Athenian trials upon sophistic and Platonic "autobiographies," particularly that of Isocrates.

18. Maurice Merleau-Ponty, *Signs*, trans. Richard C. McCleary (Evanston, Ill.: Northwestern University Press, 1964), p. 42.

19. Misch, 1:5–8.

20. Margaret Bottrall, *Every Man a Phoenix: Studies in Seventeenth Century Biography* (London: John Murray, 1958), p. 161.

21. Jurij Tynjanov, "On Literary Evolution," trans. C. A. Luplow, in *Readings in Russian Poetics: Formalist and Structuralist Views*, ed. Ladislav Matejka and Krystyna Pomorska (Cambridge, Mass.: MIT Press, 1971), p. 69.

22. Ibid., pp. 68 and 70.

23. As Tynjanov states it, "The differentiation of one interrelated type leads to or better, is connected with, the differentiation of another interrelated type" (p. 71).

24. Ibid., p. 69.

25. Fowler has made much the same point in his study of literary forms, although he reserves the term "genre" for only the early stages of development and prefers to rename the later stages "modes." For his instructive three-phase model see pp. 212–14 especially.

26. L. D. Lerner, "Puritanism and the Spiritual Autobiography," *Hibbert Journal* 55, no. 4 (1957):373–86.

27. I have loosely adapted Searle's system of speech act rules for the use of ordinary language, pp. 54–71 and pp. 66–67.

28. Irving's unsuccessful attempt received a great deal of publicity in the American press, particularly in *Time*, "Fabulous Hoax of Clifford Irving," 21 February 1972, pp. 12 and 17.

29. Hans Robert Jauss, "Literary History as a Challenge to Literary Theory," *New Literary History* 2, no. 1 (1970):7–38, cites G. Buck's *Lernen und Erfahrung* (Stuttgart, 1967), p. 56, in this connection: "previous knowledge ... is an element of experience itself and ... makes it possible that anything new we come across may be read, as it were, in some context of experience." Jauss's treatment of reception as a factor in literary history and literary theory raises many challenging questions about the relationship between the "previous horizon of expectations" and the later adjustments of the reader.

30. There have been several recent, interesting studies of this aspect of autobiography, including Francis Hart's "Notes for an Anatomy of Modern Autobiography," *New Literary History* 1, no. 3 (1970):485–511; William L. Howarth's "Some Principles of Autobiography," *New Literary History* 5, no. 2 (1974):363–82. and James Olney's *Metaphors of Self: The Meaning of Autobiography* (Princeton: Princeton University Press, 1972).

31. Alfred Schutz extends Husserl's concept of "typicality," or the "horizon of typical familiarity and preacquaintanceship," in several of his papers collected by Maurice Natanson under the title *The Problem of Social Reality* (Collected Papers I) (The Hague: Martinus Nijhoff, 1962). See particularly "Common-Sense and Scientific Interpretation of Human Action," pp. 7–10, and "Concept and Theory Formation in the Social Sciences," pp. 59–60.

32. Nelson Goodman presents an analysis of the distinction between such sampling or "exemplificatory" relationships as distinguished from representation in *The Languages of Art* (Indianapolis: Bobbs-Merrill, 1968), pp. 52–53. Jean Starobinski develops such an approach to autobiography in his essay "The Style of Autobiography," in *Literary Style: A Symposium*, ed. Seymour Chatman, pp. 285–96 (London: Oxford University Press, 1971).

33. Laing, H. Phillipson, and A. R. Lee, *Interpersonal Perception* (London: Tavistock Publications, 1966), pp. 5–6.

34. Searle, p. 70.

35. Ludwig Wittgenstein, *Philosophical Investigations*, trans. G. E. M. Anscombe (Oxford: Basil Blackwell, 1967), p. 11.

36. Robert Weimann, "French Structuralism and Literary History: Some Critiques and Reconsiderations," *New Literary History* 4, no. 3 (1973):63.

37. Maurice Merleau-Ponty, "Materials for a Theory of History," *Themes from the Lectures*, pp. 29–30.

38. See *Signs*, p. 59 for further discussion of the "field of investigation," and Merleau-Ponty's characterization of history as search in "Institution in History," *Themes*, p. 41.

39. Weimann, p. 63.

40. Jauss, pp. 18–19.

CHAPTER 1

The epigraph is from *The Geographical History of America* (New York: Vintage Books, 1973), p. 235.

1. John Gumperz, "The Speech Community," *International Encyclopedia of the Social Sciences* (New York: Macmillan, 1968), 381–86, reprinted in Pier Paolo Giglioli, ed., *Language and Social Context* (Harmondsworth, Middlesex: Penguin Books, 1972), p. 220. For a fuller treatment of these issues see William Labov's "The Study of Language in Its Social Context," *Studium Generale* 23 (1970):66–84, and Dell Hymes's *Foundations in Sociolinguistics: An*

Ethnographic Approach (Philadelphia: University of Pennsylvania Press, 1974), both of which stress that linguistic phenomena cannot be understood without ethnographic information.

2. See Hymes, pp. 45–66, and Roman Jakobson, to whom Hymes acknowledges his debt, "Concluding Statement: Linguistics and Poetics," in *Style in Language*, ed. T. Sebeok pp. 350–73 (Cambridge, Mass.: MIT Press, 1960).

3. (New York: Rinehart, 1948), p. 91.

4. (Boston: Houghton Mifflin, 1918), p. 504.

5. Roger Brown and Marguerite Ford, "Address in American English," in *Language in Culture and Society*, ed. D. Hymes (New York: Harper and Row, 1964), 235–44; and Roger Brown and Albert Gilman, "The Pronouns of Power and Solidarity," in *Style in Language*, ed. T. Sebeok, pp. 253–76 (Cambridge, Mass.: MIT Press, 1960).

6. Frank L. Huntley, ed. (New York: Appleton-Century-Crofts, 1965), pp. 1 and 2.

7. *Selected Poetry and Prose*, ed. Robert D. Thornton (Boston: Houghton Mifflin, 1966), p. 190.

8. See E. A. Schegloff, "Notes on a Conversational Practice: Formulating Place," *Language and Social Context*, pp. 110 and 130.

9. (New York: Berkley Medallion Books, 1963), p. 9.

10. (Boston: Anti-Slavery Office, 1845: reprinted Garden City: Doubleday, 1963), p. 1.

11. Geoffrey N. Leech, *Towards a Semantic Description of English* (Bloomington: Indiana University Press, 1969), p. 306.

12. Charles J. Fillmore, "Deictic Categories in the Semantics of 'Come,' " *Foundations of Language* 2 (1966):219–27.

13. John Lyons, *Introduction to Theoretical Linguistics* (Cambridge: Cambridge University Press, 1969), p. 306.

14. James D. McCawley, "Tense and Time Reference in English," in *Studies in Linguistic Semantics*, ed. Charles J. Fillmore and D. Terrence Langendoen, pp. 103, 111–12 (New York: Holt, Rinehart, and Winston, 1971), states that tense should be regarded as a pronominalization of such temporal adverbs.

15. Ibid., pp. 104–5, and also Robin Lakoff, "Tense and Its Relation to Participants," *Language* 46, no. 4 (1970); 844. My discussion of tense and aspect owes much to these sources, as well as to Lyons.

16. Lakoff, p. 841.

17. *The Autobiography of Bertrand Russell* (New York: Little, Brown 1967; New York: Bantam Books, 1968) 1:4.

18. M. A. K. Halliday, "Functional Diversity in Language," *Foundations of Language* 6 (1970); 325, and 342.

19. *The Aleph and Other Stories: 1933–1969*, ed. and trans. Norman Thomas Di Giovanni in collaboration with the author (New York: E. P. Dutton, 1970; reprinted New York: Bantam Books, 1971), p. 135. Further citations are to this edition.

20. Sherman Paul, ed. (Boston: Houghton Mifflin, 1957), p. 1.

21. *The Genius of John Ruskin*, ed. John D. Rosenberg (Boston: Houghton Mifflin, 1963), p. 496.

22. Labov, pp. 79–82, and J. R. Searle, *Speech Acts: An Essay in the Philosophy of Language* (Cambridge: Cambridge University Press, 1969), pp. 66–68.

23. *Selected Writings and Designs*, ed. Asa Briggs (Harmondsworth, Middlesex: Penguin Books, 1962), p. 36.

24. This is the formulation given to Grice's "cooperative principle" in David Gordon and George Lakoff, "Conversational Postulates," in *Papers from the Seventh Regional Meeting: Chicago Linguistic Society* (April 1971), p. 68.

25. John Addington Symonds, Introduction to *The Life of Benvenuto Cellini, Written by Himself*, ed. and trans. Symonds (New York: Brentano's, 1906), p. 71.

26. J. M. Cohen, trans. (Harmondsworth, Middlesex: Penguin Books, 1954), p. 17.

27. (New York: Playboy Press, 1971), pp. 10–11.

28. According to Searle, "the illocutionary force indicating device operates on a neutral predicate expression to determine a certain mode in which the question of the truth of the predicate is raised vis-à-vis the object referred to by the subject expression" (p. 122).

29. V. N. Vološinov, "Reported Speech," trans. Ladislva Matejka and I. R. Titunik, in *Readings in Russian Poetics* (Cambridge: MIT Press, 1971), p. 172. I am indebted to Vološinov's seminal work throughout my discussion of quotation.

30. *Quite Early One Morning*, (New York: New Directions, 1954), p. 34.

31. "The author's message, in incorporating the other message, brings into play syntactic, stylistic, and compositional norms for its partial assimilation," according to Vološinov, pp. 149.

32. *Quite Early One Morning*, p. 34.

33. Book One, in Carlos Baker, ed., *The Prelude: Selected Poems and Sonnets* (New York: Holt, Rinehart, and Winston, 1966), p. 208.

34. (New York: Macmillan, 1916; reprinted 1965), p. 1.

35. Here and throughout my treatment of the subject I have relied on the theory of "case grammar" developed by Charles Fillmore, in particular his "Subjects, Speakers, and Roles," *Working Papers in Linguistics: Ohio State University*, no. 4 (1970), pp. 31–63.

36. (New York: Charles Scribner's Sons, 1913; reprinted 1941), p. 2.

37. Leon Edel, ed. (New York: Dodd, Mead, 1934; reprinted 1964), p. 232.

38. Halliday, "Functional Diversity," along with another essay, "Language Structure and Language Function," in *New Horizons in Linguistics*, ed. John Lyons, pp. 162–64 (Harmondsworth, Middlesex: Penguin Books, 1970).

39. Halliday, "Functional Diversity," and Ruquaiya Hasan, "Grammatical Cohesion in Spoken and Written English: Part One," *Programme in Linguistics and English Teaching*, paper no. 7 (London: Communications Research Centre, University College, London, and Longmans, Green, 1968), describe the "textual function" in language.

40. Tzvetan Todorov discusses the "enchainment of a text" in these terms in "Poétique," in *Qu'est-ce que le structuralisme?*, ed. François Wahl (Paris: Edition de Seuil, 1968), pp. 97–166.

41. (New York: G. P. Putnam's Sons, 1959; reprinted 1966), p. v.

CHAPTER 2

The epigraph is from *Grace Abounding to the Chief of Sinners*, ed. Roger Sharrock (Oxford: Clarendon Press, 1962), pp. 3–4. All further citations are to this edition.

1. Paul Delaney *British Autobiography in the Seventeenth Century* (London: Routledge and Kegan Paul, 1969), p. 57.

2. Ibid., p. 9.

3. L. D. Lerner's quotation from Baxter appears in "Puritanism and the Spiritual Autobiography," *Hibbert Journal* 55, no. 4 (1957): p. 380.

4. Delaney, p. 88.

5. *The Oxford Annotated Bible, Revised Standard Version*, ed. Herbert G. May and Bruce M. Metzger (New York: Oxford University Press, 1962), p. 1412. Several persons have commented on Bunyan's use of the Pauline model, but I here rely particularly on Roger Sharrock's introduction and annotations to *Grace Abounding*, passim.

6. Lerner, passim. Sharrock's notes to the autobiography also discuss the conventional nature of this pattern, p. xxxix.

7. Delaney, p. 78.

8. John Bunyan, *The Pilgrim's Progress*, ed. Roger Sharrock (Baltimore: Penguin Books, 1965), p. 159. All further citations are to this edition.

9. Sharrock, notes to *Grace Abounding*, pp. 145–46.

10. See William L. Howarth's discussion of autobiography as "oratory," in "Some Principles of Autobiography," *New Literary History* 5, no. (1974): 369–71. Bunyan's is one of the oratorical autobiographies described by Howarth as achieving their effect by the authority of their doctrine and their rhetorical power. The oratory is representative, according to Howarth, of "self control."

11. Delaney quotes Calvin's Institutes (II, v, 19), p. 35. U. Milo Kaufman, *The Pilgrim's Progress and the Tradition in Puritan Meditation* (New Haven: Yale University Press, 1966), has an interesting treatment of Bunyan's rebellion against the Puritan ban on the free exercise of imagination in his novel.

12. Sharrock, introduction to *Grace Abounding*, p. xxvi.

13. Howarth, p. 368.

14. Kaufman, pp. 25–60 passim illustrates how the common practice of interpreting the Old Testament typologically was extended by seventeenth-century English Puritans to the typological interpretation of everyday life.

15. Ibid., p. 108, describes how the narrative appears to unfold what is simultaneous and eternally present in the mind of God; Roy Pascal, "The Present Tense in *The Pilgrim's Progress*," *Modern Language Review* 60 (1965): 13–16, also considers this aspect of the novel.

16. William James has the classic discussion of Bunyan's "verbal automisms" in *The Varieties of Religious Experience* (1902; reprinted New York: New American Library, 1958), pp. 133–39.

17. Sharrock, notes to *Grace Abounding*, p. 151, mentions the reappearance of the passage, without, however, associating it with the Bedford vision.

18. Ibid., pp. 138–39.

19. Ibid., pp. 144 and 150.

20. Roger Sharrock, "Spiritual Autobiography in *The Pilgrim's Progress*," *Review of English Studies* 24, no. 94 (1948), passim, develops the resemblance between conversion narratives and the pattern of the novel.

21. Sharrock, notes to *Grace Abounding*, pp. 155–56. In discussing slanders occurring after his release from prison, Bunyan in fact comes close to falsifying chronology, suggesting that the actual sequence was slander/imprisonment: "Now as Sathan laboured by reproaches and slanders to make me vile . . . so there was added hereto a long and tedious Imprisonment" (p. 95).

22. Quoted by Kaufman, p. 153.

23. G. R. Owst, *Literature and Pulpit in Medieval England* (Cambridge: Cambridge University Press, 1933), describes the influence of Ramus on older sermon forms; see also Norman Nelson, *Peter Ramus and The Confusion of Logic, Rhetoric, and Poetry* (Ann Arbor: University of Michigan Press, 1947).

24. Kaufman cites the "memorability" criterion for Puritan sermons, pp. 25–60 passim.

25. Henri Talon, *John Bunyan: The Man and His Works*, trans. Barbara Wall (London: Rockliff, 1951), p. 197, compares Bunyan's own internal demons with those found in the *Progress*.

26. Ibid., pp. 198–99.

CHAPTER 3

The epigraph is quoted from Boswell's collected journals by P. A. W. Collins, *James Boswell*, Writers and Their Works, no. 77 (London: Longman's, Green, 1956), p. 19.

1. *Boswell's London Journal, 1762–1763*, ed. Frederick A. Pottle (New York: McGraw-Hill, 1950), p. 102. Citations here and throughout are to this edition.

2. Donald A Stauffer, *The Art of Biography in the Eighteenth Century* (Princeton: Princeton University Press, 1941), p. 81, treats the role of realistic fiction in reversing the process as well as advancing representational realism in biography.

3. *Life of Johnson*, R. W. Chapman, ed., corrected by J. D. Fleeman, 3d ed. (1953; reprinted London: Oxford University Press, 1970), p. 22. Hereafter referred to as *Life*, all citations will be to this edition.

4. John Butt, *Biography in the Hands of Walton, Johnson, and Boswell* (Los Angeles: University of California Press, 1966), is among the contemporary writers treating Boswell's journals as rough drafts intended to "enable the future autobiographer to catch, as it were, a view of himself, or an interpretation of himself that could be presented as an independent work" (p. 34).

5. *The Correspondence of James Boswell and John Johnston of Grange*, ed. Ralph S. Walker, The Yale Edition of the Private Papers of James Boswell, Correspondence vol. 1 (New York: McGraw-Hill, 1966), p. 54.

6. Frederick A. Pottle discusses Boswell's clashes with his father over various publication schemes in *James Boswell: The Earlier Years, 1740–1769* (New York: McGraw-Hill, 1966), passim. Boswell had very nearly been disinherited for publishing a collection of the letters he had exchanged with Andrew Erskine. This all took place during the period in which he wrote his *London Journal*, which like the letters, he had stored with John Johnston—suggesting that Boswell might have planned to publish his autobiography as well, but for his father's rage over the letters. The peculiar circumstances surrounding the *London Journal* therefore make it the most likely candidate for extended literary analysis.

7. Frederick A. Pottle, "James Boswell: Journalist," in *The Age of Johnson: Essays Presented to Chauncey Brewster Tinker*, ed. Frederick W. Hilles (New Haven: Yale University Press, 1949), p. 17.

8. John Morris, *Versions of the Self* (New York: Basic Books, 1966), pp. 187–88.

9. Ibid., p. 181.

10. Bertrand Bronson, *Johnson and Boswell: Three Essays*, University of California Publications in English, vol. 3, no. 9 (Berkeley: University of California Press, 1944), pp. 403–4.

11. Stauffer, p. 338, illustrates the movement away from the "ruling passion" theory in later eighteenth-century biography.

12. Ralph W. Rader, "Literary Form in Factual Narrative: The Example of Boswell's *Johnson*," in *Essays in Eighteenth Century Biography*, ed. Philip B. Daghlian (Bloomington: Indiana University Press, 1968), p. 6, argues in much the same terms. He also contends that the *Life* should be treated as literature rather than biography and that Boswell has made Johnson an "empathetic character"—contentions with which I cannot agree.

13. *Selections from "The Tatler" and "The Spectator,"* ed. Robert J. Allen, 2d ed. (1957; reprinted New York: Holt, Rinehart, and Winston, 1967), p. 209.

14. Bronson, pp. 404–5. See also William L. Howarth's treatment of "dramatic" autobiography in "Some Principles of Autobiography," *New Literary History* 5, no. 2:372–75.

15. Ian A. Gordon, *The Movement of English Prose,* English Language Series (London: Longman's, Green, 1966), pp. 144–45, describes the characteristic Johnsonian style.

16. Pottle's notes to the *London Journal,* p. 293 n, point out the parallels in these two passages.

17. Boswell expresses the wish in his biography that his readers "endeavour to keep in mind" the texture of Johnson's speech, and alludes to the "ingenious method of Mr. Steele" for transmitting the rhetorical quality and tone of remarkable speakers by means of a musical score sheet (*Life*, pp. 599–600). Rader, p. 7, discusses Boswell's treatment of Johnsonian speech.

18. Paul K. Alkon, "Boswell's Control of Aesthetic Distance," *University of Toronto Quarterly* 38 (1969); reprinted in *Twentieth Century Interpretations of Boswell's Life of Johnson,* ed. James L. Clifford, pp. 58–60 (Englewood Cliffs, N.J.: Prentice-Hall, 1970), first suggested this pattern to me.

19. Frederick A. Pottle, *Boswell in Holland, 1763–1764* (New York: McGraw-Hill, 1956), cites the essay, p. 375 n.

20. See Pottle's discussion of the memoranda in his notes to the *London Journal,* p. 45 n, and examples on p. 67 n.

21. Boswell was careful to suit his *Life of Johnson* to a wider British audience, providing rules for the pronunciation of unfamiliar Scottish names, for example.

22. Alkon, p. 61, discusses some of the aspects of reader-narrator relations in the *Life.*

CHAPTER 4

The epigraph is from "De Quincey's General Preface in 1853," *The Collected Writings of Thomas De Quincey,* ed. David Masson (London: A. C. Black, 1889), 1: 9–10.

1. Aileen Ward's foreword to *Confessions of an English Opium Eater and Other Writings,* Ward ed. (New York: New American Library, 1966), p. xiv.

2. Masson treats the history of the Collected Edition in his "General Preface by the Editor." See pp. xiii–xvi in particular.

3. Masson ed., 1:9.

4. "Style," *The Collected Writings,* Masson ed. (London: A. C. Black, 1890), 10:227.

5. Arguments about the meaning of De Quincey's term "impassioned prose" are many. Rene Wellek, "De Quincey's Status in the History of Ideas," in *Confrontations* (Princeton: Princeton University Press, 1965), is among those who link this designation with De Quincey's distinction between the "literature of power" and the "literature of science." There is no general agreement about the formal characteristics of "impassioned prose," however, in part because of critical disagreements about the source of prose rhythm. Lane Cooper, *The Prose Poetry of Thomas De Quincey* (Leipzig: Verlag von Dr. Sede, 1902), finds a greater frequency in the use of personal pronouns, voiced speech elements, and topics drawn from dreams, magic, flight, and pursuit in De Quincey's impassioned style than in his other styles; Oliver Elton, *A Survey of English Literature, 1780–1880,* (New York: Macmillan Co., 1920), 2:312–33, finds the distinctive quality of this prose to be the way a stem sentence breaks down into bifurcating clauses to create contrast and antiphonal balance.

6. "Style," p. 227.

7. Masson ed., 11:56, quoted in Frederick L. Burwick, "The Rhetoric and Aesthetic of Thomas De Quincey," Ph.D. diss., University of Wisconsin, 1955, pp. 162–63, along with a useful discussion of the problem.

8. Masson ed., 8:15, cited in J. Hillis Miller's *The Disappearance of God* (Cambridge: Harvard University Press, 1963), p. 27.

9. A note is necessary on my use of the term "lyric" for *Suspiria de Profundis.* It is, I realize, a term with a history even more complex than that of "autobiography" itself, a shifting constellation of values, defined now by metrical, now by thematic, now by functional criteria. As I use it here, it is a rough equivalent of De Quincey's more cumbersome "impassioned prose," but I also use it to emphasize the qualities of texture and design which link the prose *Suspiria* with English Romantic poetry. While it is by no means as brief as the conventional lyric poem, the *Suspiria* does aspire to the same instantaneous or atemporal totality, relying on the same implicit, subliminal patterns for its coherence (rather than on the logic of argument or narrative). Thus, because of its reiterated imagery and rhythmic phrasing, its spontaneously evolving form, and its concern for the nuances of intimate subjective experience and the

expressive play of a single, self-communing voice, there is ample justification for treating *Suspiria de Profundis* as a lyric (or at least a Romantic lyric) in prose.

10. My text of the *Autobiographical Sketches* is taken from Masson's edition, 1:28–416. Since there is no better edition in print, all citations will be to this volume. Masson is not a fully reliable editor of the *Sketches*, since he has added additional material and to some degree obscured the original shape of De Quincey's text. But he is at least scrupulous in recording any changes he has made, thus allowing one to reconstruct the original form of the work.

11. Miller, p. 20.

12. The most complete and reliable text of *Suspiria de Profundis* appears in Malcolm Elwin's *Confessions of an English Opium-Eater in Both the Revised and the Original Texts with Its Sequels Suspiria de Profundis and the English Mail Coach* (London: MacDonald, 1956), pp. 445–551.

13. Judson S. Lyon, *Thomas De Quincey*, Twayne's English Authors Series, no. 83 (New York: Twayne, 1969), p. 98.

14. The *Suspiria* was never given the fully expanded shape De Quincey had planned for it, but sketches for the completed project appear in De Quincey's footnotes to the text and in his *Posthumous Works*, ed. Alexander H. Japp (London: William Heinemann, 1891), 1:1–6. These indicate that De Quincey would have retained the pattern of his published version and provided additional examples for each stage of emotion.

15. Miller, p. 39, uses these words from Baudelaire's *Les Paradis Artificiels* in his treatment of De Quincey's process of infinite regress in the *Suspiria*, a process which he associates with De Quincey's search for transcendency.

16. Lyon provides a summary of these findings, pp. 163–65.

17. Burwick, pp. 282–85.

18. Elton, pp. 328–33.

19. Masson ed., 10:136, quoted by Hugh Sykes Davies, *Thomas De Quincey*, Writers and Their Works, no. 167 (London: Longmans, Green, 1964), p. 20.

20. Masson ed., 5:231–32, in Davies, p. 19.

21. Masson ed., 1:9.

22. "Impassioned Prose," *Times Literary Supplement*, 16 Sept. 1926, p. 602.

23. Masson ed., 1:14.

24. Charles I. Patterson, "De Quincey's Conception of the Novel as 'Literature of Power,' " *PMLA* 70, no. 3 (1955):777.

25. John E. Jordan, "Thomas De Quincey," in *English Romantic Poets and Essayists*, ed. Carolyn W. Houtchens and Lawrence H. Houtchens (1957; rev. ed. New York: New York University Press, 1966), discusses De Quincey's reputation as a humorist in the nineteenth century (p. 313).

CHAPTER 5

The epigraph is an excerpt from the eighth stanza of Nabokov's "The Paris Poem" (1943), reprinted in *Poems and Problems* (New York: McGraw-Hill, 1970), p. 123.

1. A. M. Taylor, *Imagination and the Growth of Science* (New York: Schocken Books, 1967), passim, but especially pp. 52–53.

2. Vladimir Nabokov, *Nikolai Gogol* (New York: New Directions, 1944), p. 119.

3. The phrase is used in Alfred Appel's preface to his edition, *The Annotated Lolita* (New York: McGraw-Hill, 1970); he also quotes from the autobiography in this connection, pp. xxxii–xxxiii.

4. There are also countless points of similarity between Humbert's pursuit of Lolita and Marcel's pursuit of Albertine and his "lost time" in Proust's massive *Bildungs-roman*. Several authors, including Appel (preface and notes) and Page Stegner, *Escape into Aesthetics: The Art of Vladimir Nabokov* (New York: William Morrow, 1966), p. 109, have alluded to Humbert's connections with the great French subjectivists Rousseau and Proust.

5. All citations will be to *The Annotated Lolita*, Appel ed. Here, p. 106.

6. Andrew Field, *Nabokov: His Life in Art* (Boston: Little, Brown, 1967), p. 330, among others, discusses the self-accusation which is so rife in Humbert's manuscript.

7. Appel's preface to *Lolita*, pp. xxi–xxii.

8. Nabokov's translation of *Speak, Memory* into Russian also influenced his second effort, according to his foreward to the revised work.

9. Carl R. Proffer, *Keys to Lolita* (Bloomington: Indiana University Press, 1968), pp. 31–32.

10. Appel discusses the "metamorphosis" of names and identities as one aspect of the fairy-tale transformations effected in the novel (preface and notes to *Lolita,* passim).

11. G. D. Josipovici, "Lolita: Parody and the Pursuit of Beauty," *Critical Quarterly* 6, no. 1 (1964): 44, makes several interesting points about Humbert's attempt to possess carnally what he can only possess imaginatively—Lolita and language.

12. Appel quotes Poe's poem, p. 331, in his notes to *Lolita.*

13. Appel, notes to *Lolita,* p. 356.

14. Field, pp. 34–36.

15. This citation, pp. 170–72, and all others will be to the revised edition of *Speak, Memory: An Autobiography Revisited* (1951; reprinted New York: G. P. Putnam's Sons, 1966).

16. Alfred Appel, "An Interview with Vladimir Nabokov," in *Nabokov: The Man and His Work*, ed. L. S. Dembo (Madison: University of Wisconsin Press, 1967), p. 32.

17. Appel, notes to *Lolita,* pp. 359–60; Proffer treats this aspect of the book as well.

18. According to Appel's preface, pp. lxvi–lxvii, "the ambiguities of human experience and identity are not to be reduced to mere 'dualities.' Instead of the successful integration of a neatly divisible self, we are left with 'Clare Obscure' and 'quilted Quilty,' the patchwork self. . . . *Lolita* locks Humbert within that prison of mirrors where the 'real self' and its masks blend into one another."

19. See, for example, D. J. Hughes's comments on Lolita's later "dismissal" of Humbert as a character when they meet again in the Coalmont scene, in "Reality and the Hero: *Lolita* and *Henderson the Rain King*," *Modern Fiction Studies* 6, no. 4 (1961–62):354. Quilty also treats Humbert as a "hallucination" (*Lolita,* p. 296).

20. Appel, notes to *Lolita,* pp. 368–69, mentions the change in name as part of Humbert's "Obsession with time."

21. Humbert actually describes only the appearance of Lolita's mouth rather than the word she pronounced. Her pucker could, of course, as easily produce "you" as the initial "Q" in Quilty's name. I am grateful for Carl Proffer's remarks on Nabokov's phonetic play, leading to this connection, in his seminar on Nabokov (University of Michigan, 1971).

22. Josipovici, p. 44.

23. As he says, attributing his own problems to Lolita: "I had to devise some expectation, some special point in space and time for her to look forward to. . . . Otherwise, deprived of a shaping and sustaining purpose, the skeleton of her day sagged and collapsed." (pp. 153–54).

24. The words are Nabokov's own, from his study *Nikolai Gogol,* p. 145.

25. *Webster's New Collegiate Dictionary* (Springfield, Mass.: G. & C. Merriam Co., 1961), p. 617.

26. Appel's preface to *Lolita* treats the theme of limited awareness as an important one in Nabokov's fictional characterizations, such limitation to be overcome only by the act of creating characters (pp. xxxii–xxxiii).

CHAPTER 6

The epigraph is from *Present Past: Past Present: A Personal Memoir*, trans. Helen R. Lane (New York: Grove Press, 1971), pp. 115 and 56.

1. *Tristes Tropiques*, trans. John Russell (New York: Atheneum, 1972), p. 398.

2. "Montaigne on the Paradoxes of Individualism," in *System and Structure: Essays in Communication and Exchange* (London: Tavistock Publications, 1972), p. 90.

INDEX

Adams, Henry (as autobiographer), 1, 21
Apology, 9, 12
Appel, Alfred, 131, 135, 141, 179 nn.3–4,
n.7, 180 n.10, nn.12–13, nn.16–18, n.20,
n.26
Augustine, Saint (as autobiographer), 1–2
Austin, J. L., 5, 29, 173 n.10
Autobiography: audience's role in, 10–16,
21–31, 167, 170; autobiographer's role in,
10–16, 21–31, 167; change and development of, 1–2, 7, 10, 14–18, 27, 33–34,
61–63, 93–95, 127–29, 163–72; common
features found in, 164–65; definitions
proposed for, 1–4, 6–7, 10–11, 14;
diacritical value of, 6–9, 15–18, 166–68,
172; formal features insufficient to define,
2–5, 10, 18; forms associated with, 166–67;
as illocutionary act, 4–17, 31, 163;
individual identity and, 163–64, 166–72;
and language, 19–31, 172; as literature, 7,
62–63, 93–94, 96, 163, 165–66;
obsolescence of, 15, 96, 129, 172;
originality in, 10, 170; prehistory of, 6–7,
34; rules for, general, 10–13, 169; rules for,
local, 14–17, 166–68, 170; sanctions for,
167–69; teleology not necessary for, 3,
167–68. *See also* Boswell, James; Bunyan,
John; De Quincey, Thomas; Genre;
Nabokov, Vladimir

Baxter, Richard, 34
Biography, 7, 62. *See also* Boswell, James
Borges, Jorge Luis (as autobiographer), 25
Boswell, James, 18, 61–93, 165–72; Addison,
Joseph (role in journal of), 69, 73, 75;
autobiographical audience vs. biographical
audience, in work of, 83–93; autobiographical narrator vs. biographical narrator, in
work of, 76–89; autobiographical
self-imaging vs. biographical characterization, in work of, 65, 67, 70–77, 80–81, 83,
88–92; autobiography as discovery vs.
biography as preservation, in work of,
83–85, 89–91; autobiography as subjective
truth vs. biography as objective truth, in
work of, 66, 71–72, 75–77, 80–81, 85,
88–91; Boswell, Alexander (father, role in
journal of), 63, 68–69; compared to other
autobiographers, 18, 61–63, 76, 165–72;
Hawkins, Sir John (rival biographer to), 87;
Johnson, Samuel (role in autobiography and
biography of), 62, 64–65, 67–73, 83–84,
93; Johnston, John (recipient of journal of),
63, 86–87, 177 n.6; language, in work of,
64–65, 71, 74, 76–79, 81, 86–90, 92; *Life
of Johnson*, 62, 64–67, 70–74, 78–81,
84–90; literary value of autobiography of,
62–63, 75, 93; *London Journal*, 62–70,
72–83, 85–87, 90–91; *London Journal* and
Life of Johnson, compared, 62–63, 67–68,
70–71; MacHeath (hero of Gay's *Beggar's
Opera*, role in journal of), 65, 69, 75;
modality (autobiographical vs. biographical), in work of, 66, 75, 83, 85, 87, 89–91;
Piozzi, Mrs. Hester (Mrs. Thrale, rival
biographer to), 87; realistic novel and
autobiography of, 62–63; Reynolds, Sir
Joshua (role in biography of), 71; Scotland
(role in journal of), 68–70; space
(autobiographical vs. biographical), in work
of, 84; the Sublime and characterization, in
work of, 72–73; textual coherence
(autobiographical vs. biographical), in work
of, 64–65, 67, 70, 78, 85, 90–91; time
(autobiographical vs. biographical), in work
of, 64–66, 71, 83–85
Bronson, Bertrand, 71, 75, 177 n.10,
178 n.14
Brown, Sir Thomas (as autobiographer), 22
Bunyan, John, 10, 17–18, 33–60, 165–72;
allegory, in work of, 40–41, 48–49;
autobiographical audience vs. fictional
audience, in work of, 34–35, 39, 46, 49, 51,
53–60; autobiographical narrator vs.
fictional narrator, in work of, 37–41,
46–47, 49–60; autobiographical self-
imaging vs. fictional characterization, in
work of, 42–44, 48, 50–60; autobiography
as fact vs. fiction, in work of, 37–39, 41,
45, 58, 60; autobiography as literal vs.
fiction as imaginative, in work of, 38–39,
48–49, 51; autobiography as logical vs.
fiction as chronological, in work of, 46–49;
Calvinist strictures on imagination and work
of, 38, 48; as controversialist, 36–37;
experience, in doctrine of, 42–44; *Grace
Abounding to the Chief of Sinners*, 33–37,
40–60; language, in work of, 40, 50–60;
memory, in doctrine of, 43, 45–49;
modality (autobiographical vs. fictional), in
work of, 51, 53, 57–60; Pauline Epistles
(role in work of), 34–36, 42–44, 48; *The
Pilgrim's Progress*, 36–37, 39–41, 44–46,
50–58; *The Pilgrim's Progress* and *Grace
Abounding* compared, 37–39, 40–45;
Ramistic interpretation and work of,

181

Library of Congress Cataloging in Publication Data

Bruss, Elizabeth W
  Autobiographical acts.

  Includes bibliographical references and index.
  1. Autobiography. 2. English prose literature—
History and criticism. 2. Nabokov, Vladimir Vladimiro-
vich, 1899—Conclusive evidence. I. Title.
PR756.A9B7   809   76-13460
ISBN 0-8018-1821-4